THE SCHOOL BOOK

FOR PEOPLE WHO WANT
TO KNOW WHAT ALL THE
HOLLERING IS ABOUT

THE SCHOOL BOOK

FOR PEOPLE WHO WANT
TO KNOW WHAT ALL THE
HOLLERING IS ABOUT

NEIL POSTMAN

CHARLES WEINGARTNER

DELACORTE PRESS / NEW YORK

Other books by Neil Postman and Charles Weingartner

LINGUISTICS

TEACHING AS A SUBVERSIVE ACTIVITY

THE SOFT REVOLUTION

LANGUAGE IN AMERICA

LIBRARY OF CONGRESS CATALOGING IN PUBLICATION DATA

POSTMAN, NEIL.
THE SCHOOL BOOK.

Bibliography: p.
1. Education—United States—1945–
I. Weingartner, Charles, joint author. II. Title.
LA210.P67   371'.00973   73–7556

TO MARC, ANDREW,
MADELINE,
AND JAN

ACKNOWLEDGMENTS

WE WISH to acknowledge the help given us by Connie Friedman and Jeanne Roiter, both of whom are indefatigable researchers; and Ruth Steinberg and Linda Steinberg, for their editorial assistance.

We also wish to acknowledge the help given us by our editor, Nancy E. Gross. This is the third book we have done under her guidance. In every case, both we and our work have been improved by her professionalism, empathetic criticism, and stronghearted friendship.

Finally, we wish to apologize to our women readers for our use, in this book, of a sexist grammatical convention. We were unable to find or invent a stylistically graceful substitute for the pronouns *he* and *him* in instances where we obviously mean to refer to both male and female.

N. P.
C. W.

CONTENTS

JUST WHO DO
WE THINK YOU ARE,
ANYWAY?

ON THE subject of education, there is a fearful amount of hollering. The hollering started in the late 1950s, when the Russians—who were then our enemies but are now (1973) our friends—launched *Sputnik I*. With each passing year since then, the hollering has increased. Time was when it was clear who the hollerers were, and who the hollerees. Now, everyone has gotten into the act, and it has become very difficult for an ordinary, reasonably attentive person to understand or even hear what is being said. This is a very serious—maybe even dangerous—situation because most of the hollering concerns the children of ordinary people. Every hollerer, it seems, has at least three different plans for making children smarter, or freer, or happier, or generally more fit, and some of the plans are not half bad. But that's not the point. The point is that the plans concern your children, and you have a right to know what those plans are, and whether or not they fit in with your own.

Which brings us to the question of who you are, and who we are. If we have done this book right, you are an ordinary citizen. By "ordinary," we mean someone who is not a professional educator and who does not spend most of his/her spare time thinking about education. You have children (or plan to have them) and they are (or will be) required to attend schools, for which you, in turn, are required to pay—plenty. Your interest in schools is lively *while* your children are there, but it is likely to diminish rapidly when the ordeal is over. In other words, you are not especially interested in revolutionizing the schools; you merely want your children to have what used to be called "a decent education." You may have tried, or have been tempted to try, an experimental program or school for your kids. You may have moved from one place to another because of "the schools." You may be among the reputed 65 percent of American parents who think the schools are not so bad, or among the 35 percent (reputed) who think they are somewhere between useless and terrible. The point is that if you read a book about schools, you do so only in the hope that you can discover what all the hollering is about and how it might affect your own children. In other words, you are an amateur whose most important possessions must be placed in the hands of professionals. This much is clear to you: you have more at stake than they do.

Now you know who you are, or who we think you are. Who are we?

Well, we are two of the hollerers, and professional ones, at that. That is, we used to be hollerers, and we may take it up again—if things get too quiet. But at this point, we have another goal in mind: to state, simply and clearly, the ideas of the professionals so that "ordinary" people can make informed choices about the education of their own children. That is the purpose of this book, and it occurs to us that our efforts might even be useful to teachers and administrators who have, themselves, been confused by some of their more vigorous colleagues. In any case, we know our effort is presumptuous, since we are assuming that we know what these confusing and even mystifying ideas are, and how to sort them out and explain them. We know, too, that the effort requires restraint. It is not easy for ex-hollerers to confine themselves to explaining rather than exhorting. However, we have been practicing for two years now, by addressing ourselves not to professionals but to ordinary citizens and sometimes puzzled teachers in various places throughout the country. We think we have learned from them what they want to know. And what we need to do.

If you are who we think you are, and if we have learned what we think we have, this book should help you to understand, without significant distortion, what the present school situation is like: what are its important ideas, and its dead ones; how its vocabulary works, or doesn't; who are its significant people, and why; what has happened in the past decade, or hasn't; and finally, what's going to happen, or should, or might. Some hollering has undoubtedly seeped in—if sarcasm or ridicule may be called hollering (which, of course, they are). But our basic intention is not to add to the noise. Rather, we want to modulate it so that ordinary people can decide whether or not to keep tuned.

The School Book is divided into two parts, each with a different purpose. Part I provides a perspective from which we think it reasonable to view the current school scene. Toward that end, it begins with a mini-history of school criticism during the past fifteen years. This is followed by a chapter which makes some important distinctions between education and school, and which tries to say what the structure of school really is. This is *not* a book about education. It is a book about school. A book about education would include a description of the resources available in a community. It would tell you where and when you can see things and hear things and come in contact with stimulating people, ideas, services, and products. *The Whole Earth Catalogue* is a book like that. So is the Yellow Pages, for that matter, and any good encyclopedia. A book about school, on the other hand, is about a highly specialized institution—an institution whose role in education is limited to those functions its structure permits. Part I includes, therefore, several chapters in which we discuss specific changes that school is undergoing, or can undergo, or perhaps should undergo. Some of these you may find desirable, some innocuous, some even hateful. That's up to you. What's up to us is to make sure that you understand what the changes are, and the basis for them. Then, if you want to become a hollerer, you're in the clear. In fact, we have included a chapter specifically designed to help you evaluate a school, and to holler effectively about a bad one. Part I concludes with a chapter in which we try to imagine what schools might be like, say, at the turn of the millennium (i.e., A.D. 2001).

The purpose of Part II is quite different. While we have worked hard to make everything in it readable (would you believe, fascinating?), it is intended as a reference section. For example, you will find there descriptions of seventy people who are important in one way or another to the school scene. The descriptions are slightly opinionated, mostly informational. You will also find a small dictionary of terms whose meanings are important to an understanding of school talk. Each term is explained in a narrative which, according to our editor, is a model of economy and eloquence. At least that's what she said we should aim for. No doubt our aim exceeded our grasp. Even so, we are hoping you find our explanations useful and agreeable to read. You will also find in Part II a description and explanation of some of the more important (and mostly recent) court decisions affecting the schools. And you will find as well an annotated list of books, periodicals, films, and other resources that will help increase your knowledge of schools should you wish to go beyond this book.

One final point: Because we want *The School Book* to be readable as well as informative, we have tried to avoid, as much as possible, the academic trappings of footnotes and cross-references. A few are included—but only those we felt absolutely necessary. If anything, we have erred on the side of exclusion. But our index is complete and reliable. We urge you to consult it whenever a name or term comes up—either in Part I or Part II—with which you are unfamiliar.

PART ONE

1

A HISTORY OF
THE HOLLERING

JOHN DEWEY was just beginning to get comfortable in his grave when the Russians, of all people, reached down and stuck a spear into his heart. It was 1957. Dewey had died five years earlier, secure in the knowledge that he was America's preeminent education philosopher. And then the Russians launched *Sputnik I*. As Walter Cronkite might say, this meant that we were behind in the race for space. A lot of Americans went into a grim panic. In those days, you may remember, whenever things went badly for us, the custom was to assume that one of our own had sold us out. On this occasion, Dewey was fingered.

The indictment went something like this: John Dewey was the father, and maybe the mother, of the Progressive Education movement. Progressive education was a kind of gooey, precious, romantic philosophy which stressed permissiveness and life adjustment. There was no place in it for rigorous thinking, discipline, or social responsibility. Moreover, progressive education was championed by know-nothing education professors and had taken over as the dominant philosophy of American schools. As a result, our country had been burdened with at least two generations of self-indulgent ignoramuses—specifically, kids who had no stomach or preparation for building rockets and other important things. And that's why we were losing to the Russians. *Life* magazine and the *New York Times* stressed these points pretty hard, but they were moderate in comparison with

Admiral Hyman Rickover, who, for a time, devoted most of his energies to attacking the schools and their Dewey-istic leanings. Rickover, the father (and maybe the mother) of the atomic submarine, was, among other things, under the impression that a child's school day was mostly absorbed by "frill" subjects such as basket weaving and free-form dancing. He ferociously denounced the waste of it all, urging that we return to what he called the basics. He was joined by many others who accused the schools of quackery and of not understanding the perilous position we occupied as leader of the free world.

A good history of those times does not exist, and we are not prepared to give one. But it is necessary for us to make these points: (1) the reaction immediately following the launching of *Sputnik I* represents the first phase of what might be called contemporary school criticism; (2) most of the complaints during that period were made by politicians, military men, and college professors, not by teachers, students, or parents; and (3) most of the criticisms were prodigiously misinformed. For example, it was *not* true that the philosophy of American schools was dominated by Dewey's "progressive" ideas. It probably *was* true that professors of education rated Dewey the foremost theoretician in their field, but this did not mean much in the day-to-day functioning of most schools. In other words, there did not exist then, nor does there now, a great confluence between theory and practice.

Neither was it true that students were spending an inordinate amount of time on "frill" subjects. The school curriculum was substantially the same in 1957 as it was in 1917. There were, of course, some silly courses that had not existed ten or fifteen years earlier, but the school curriculum in its modern version began to form in the 1880s, became more or less established in the 1920s, and remains intact, alas, in most schools to this day.

Finally, Dewey was badly misinterpreted by critics who had obviously not read him "personally." To the extent that teachers were being permissive, they were probably more influenced by their conceptions of Freud than of Dewey. If Dewey stands for anything, he stands for rigorous thinking, self-discipline, and social responsibility. (So does Freud—but that's another matter.) It is virtually impossible to read Dewey without coming to this conclusion, unless, of course, the reader is in a curiously mangled state of mind.*

But for all the misinformed ill will of post-*Sputnik* school criticism, there was at least one positive aspect to it. For the second time in this century (the "progressives" had done it first), the question was raised, What are schools for? Of course, for many critics, the question was rhetorical. Their purpose in raising it was to give a preformed answer: schools were an instrument of national foreign policy, a weapon in the cold war. It followed from this that the best thing schools could do was to produce inspired scientists and competent technicians, and fast. Thus, the first and shortest-lived phase of modern school criticism—let us call it Panic Phase 1—amounted to an attack on such "frill" courses as existed and a call for an increase in science and math programs. But the question, What is school for?, hovered about, and in a short time, a new group of critics was to grab hold of it and give it a very different set of answers.

But that did not come until the second phase of school criticism had ended. The second phase began roughly in 1960 and was concerned, as Jerome Bruner has put it, principally with the reconstruction of curriculum. What happened was that the professionals moved in. Not the "know-nothing educationists," who were still reeling from the blows aimed at them in Phase 1, but the "real" professionals: professors of mathematics and science. And then, a bit later, professors of history and English. As the professionals saw it, if the schools were to produce good scientists and engineers, then it was up to our best scientists and mathematicians to turn out the programs that would do the job

* Such as Rickover was. If you want to verify this statement, read Rickover's *Education and Freedom* (1959). Then read Dewey's *The Child and the Curriculum* (1902).

most efficiently. What they did, in effect, was to bypass the question, What is school for?, and go straight to the question, What is a subject for? In a now famous conference held at Woods Hole, Massachusetts, in 1959, the professionals—led by Jerrold Zacharias of MIT and Jerome Bruner of Harvard—mapped out their strategy. Some curious things followed. For one, as the scientists began to ask themselves, "What is physics for?" or, "What is chemistry for?" they found themselves turning back to John Dewey. As Bruner put it, "The ideal was clarity and self-direction of intellect in the use of modern knowledge" —an elegant way of saying that the scientists rejected the notion that a student's head needed to be filled with someone else's answers to someone else's questions—that is, a lot of facts. Instead, they embraced the idea that the purpose of studying a subject was to learn *how to think*, which is not only the title of one of Dewey's most famous books, but also a lifelong concern of his.

In *The Process of Education* (1960), a report on the Woods Hole Conference, Bruner introduced the phrase "the structure of a discipline." By that term he meant to convey that each subject has a unique way of asking questions and finding answers, and that this "structure" is what students ought to learn. Moreover, he recommended that the best way to learn it is by doing it. Which, of course, is what John Dewey had been saying for roughly forty years. Thus, in the early 1960s the phrase "inductive method" became popular, as the scientists tried to invent problems that would engage students in a process of inquiry, presumably to help them become self-directing, creative thinkers. At this point, Dewey started to rest comfortably again in his grave.

It came to pass, of course, that professors of history and English wanted to get into the act (there were lots of government grants available), and within two or three years—certainly by 1965—we had not only the New Math and the New Science, but the New English and New Social Studies as well.

Moreover, since the scientists and other university scholars learned fairly quickly that there is more to schooling than they had at first supposed, there developed a rapprochement between the scholars (who knew about subjects) and the educationists, including workaday teachers (who knew about students). Organizations like the National Council of Teachers of English and the National Council of Teachers of Social Studies invited the active and influential participation of prominent university specialists, who advised elementary and secondary school teachers on content. The teachers contributed their knowledge of children and the realities of school life. Together, they would solve the problem of the schools by teaching students to learn how to learn.

For a while, somewhere around 1964 or 1965, it seemed as if they could. One thing was sure: the United States was back in the lead in the race for space. No thanks to the schools, of course, but at least the schools had gotten back on the right track and were protected from the charge of quackery through their alliance with our best scholars. Everything looked rosy, except for a few minor details. One of them was the problem of the ghetto school. Everyone knew that in such schools, reading scores were low and dropout rates high, but amid the prevailing optimism, the belief was strong that these problems could be overcome by the application of proper techniques. The New Curricula could fix most of what was wrong, and if they couldn't, we would just work harder to fix the new curricula. At some point, we would know enough about language learning, reading difficulties, and the rest so that ghetto schools could benefit as much as any from the "revolutionary new approaches," as they were called.

Up to this point, the public had not had much to say, and the students nothing at all. True, laymen had been aroused to a state of concern by the early critics, but only for a short time before the professionals moved in. When that happened, everyone kept still in deference to the great American religion called

Expertise. There is an analogy to be drawn on this point between the school problem and the space problem. In the early 1960s, the technicians at Cape Kennedy, née Canaveral, were working on the problem of how to get to the moon by 1970. Since no one was asking whether or not we *should* go to the moon, and since laymen had no qualifications to discuss how to get there, silence was the only option. Similarly, in the early 60s, since no one was asking what a school is for, and since laymen believed they had no qualifications for discussing the reconstruction of curriculum, a comparable silence followed. But not for awfully long. The experts, as usual, had asked the wrong question, and this fact could not go unnoticed forever. Paul Goodman noticed it. And so did Edgar Friedenberg. And Jules Henry.

Goodman and Friedenberg were sociologists, Henry an anthropologist, and what they noticed, first of all, was that the dropout rates were going up among all social classes; that "psychic" dropout rates were astronomical; that in spite of the enthusiasm of many teachers and professional organizations for the new curricula, students were becoming increasingly alienated from learning and from almost anything else related to school. They also began to notice the ways in which school, as a social institution, functioned to support other institutions, some of which did not need or want people to be self-directing and creative. They explored the gap between the official rhetoric about the purposes of school (e.g., to widen the horizons of students) and the *real* purposes of school, and they found it enormous. In short, they discovered that the problem of the schools had not been seriously confronted. Rickover had only touched the subject. Zacharias and Bruner had avoided it altogether. The problem had to do with the question of what school is for in the first place, and had little to do with how to make instruction more efficient. As a matter of fact, from the point of view of Goodman, Friedenberg, and Henry, the schools were astonishingly efficient. According to them, schools trained the young remarkably well to be obedient, passive, and mechanical, and to accept alienation as a way of life.

Two things must be noted at this point. First, the insights of Goodman and the others were not really discoveries. Social scientists rarely discover anything new, in the sense that biologists do. For the most part, social scientists *re*discover. They call attention to things people once knew but have forgotten. There was nothing new in showing how schools serve the needs of corporations, government, advertisers, even demogogues, but the reminders were nonetheless astonishing and reopened philosophical (why) rather than technical (how) questions. Second, Goodman, Friedenberg, and Henry were slightly ahead of their time. Their publications came between 1956 and the early 1960s, when very few people were thinking seriously about the schools. Their work was, so to speak, only the gathering clouds. The first drops of rain came in 1964, in the form of John Holt's *How Children Fail* and Bel Kaufman's *Up the Down Staircase*. The books caught on almost immediately, to a large extent because they were written by teachers who could speak in concrete terms about what schools did to children. These were no abstract sociological analyses. Instead, they were an almost daily record of how fear of failure and obedience to rigid conventions destroyed the curiosity and natural love of learning of real children.

Soon after, the trickle became a deluge. From everywhere, and seemingly simultaneously, there appeared dozens of books, each one stronger than the other in its denunciation of a school system devoted not to the welfare of children, but to the service of a war-loving state and a dehumanizing economy. It was as if the question Admiral Rickover asked in the late 1950s was finally getting an answer. What are schools for? Well, not to help build atomic subs, baby. So answered the new wave of school critics, who, significantly, seemed to come from all walks of life. There were, of course, the practicing teachers, such as Jonathan Kozol, Herbert Kohl, and James Herndon. There were also journalists and writers, among them George Leonard, Nat

Hentoff, and George Dennison. And psychologists, men like Carl Rogers, William Glasser, and Jerome Bruner (who by now understood the error of his earlier ways). And sociologists David Rogers, Frank Riessman, and Marilyn Gittell. And parents, such as Ellen Lurie. And students, such as Donald Reeves. And even a couple of know-nothing education professors, Postman and Weingartner. Education magazines began to sprout all over the place, as did education conferences and antischool organizations. Inevitably, some people—feeling that the public schools were beyond reform, let alone redemption—began to start their own schools, thus beginning what is known as the Free School movement.

Between 1965 and 1970, there was more ferment over the schools than anyone had seen since the heyday of progressive education. And just to excite matters a little more, people in the ghettos became aroused, then militant. Although few school critics were black or Hispanic, the messages they were sending were not lost among the poor and disenfranchised.

What were those messages? The new indictment went something like this: Somehow, during the last thirty years, control of the American school had passed out of the hands of the people and into the hands of the bureaucrats. Perhaps the people didn't care enough, occupied as they were with an affluence achieved by the vice of a war economy. More likely, their indifference was the result of a pervasive cultural trend toward moving people farther and farther away from control over their own institutions. In any event, it was clear that school was not devoted to the interests of individual children, to helping them become autonomous, creative, inquiring people who have the will and intelligence to determine their own destiny. In fact, the new critics argued, the school functions to defeat such goals. Instead, it now functions as a service agency to the dominant bureaucracies of our society. Almost all the conventions of school—grading, grouping, labeling, record keeping, bell ringing, testing, etc.—are designed to make students accept the decisions of others, accept fear, accept alienation. Moreover, the argument went, it is no accident that children in the ghettos fail repeatedly. The conventions of school are so arranged as to guarantee that result. Our present economy still demands a large source of cheap labor, and the school is deeply implicated in a kind of conspiracy to keep the poor, poor. As for the curricula, even the newest of them, they are at best irrelevant, at worst, obsolete—all in all, a source of distraction that prevents students from thinking about the true nature of their situation.

So ran the indictment. The defendants, who in this case consisted mostly of beleaguered teachers and administrators, replied by denouncing the critics as romantic and, in some instances, paranoid. The trouble with such criticism, the defense argued, is that it comes from people who are not familiar with what really goes on in school, and who expect the schools to implement utopian schemes. To which the critics replied that they were only too familiar with the realities of school (which in some cases was not true) and that there was hardly anything utopian in their proposals (which in most cases *was* true). In fact, it should be stressed that in spite of the idealized images of school evoked by the "romantics," most of their complaints were against the conventions of the schooling process, not its basic structure. For example, the critics did not, for the most part, question whether or not the schools should exist, or even whether or not students should be compelled to attend them. What they wanted was an overhaul of the procedures governing the relationship among students, teachers, and administrators. They took for granted that schools *could* function humanely; they were angry about the fact that they didn't.

Somewhere around 1970, the Romantic Phase came to an end. Some of the critics were not educators to begin with, and so moved on to other things. Some became discouraged by the capacity of the system to resist change. And some simply became tiresome. Those who remained at their stations were soon overrun by a new wave of critics, who represented—as a sizable group still does—a stage of almost total disillusionment with the schools. In a way, this is Panic Phase 2—the Second Coming of the idea that our schools are a betrayal and an abomination. Only this time, the attack comes from the Left, not the Right. Its leading figure is Ivan Illich, whose book *De-Schooling Society* (1971) presents the case for eliminating schools altogether and replacing them with an informal, noncompulsory network of educational resources. In Illich's view, the conventions of schooling are trivial and hardly worth changing. The trouble with school, he contends, is in its basic structure. Schools compel. Schools judge. Schools mandate. Schools discriminate. Schools certify. Schools punish. Therefore, why try to make them better? The school, according to Illich and many of his followers, is our latter-day medieval church, through which all must pass who wish to achieve any status in our society. The school is essentially a political institution, not an educational one. Europe eventually dechurched itself. Why shouldn't America (and other similarly "schooled" countries) deschool itself? If it did, we would have a more humane and democratic society, one which values pragmatic performance and which provides many and diverse avenues to education, to success, to a decent life.

Illich's critique of the schools is not essentially different from Goodman's or Friedenberg's. What is different is that Illich has abandoned any hope that schools can be reformed, and has tried to offer a comprehensive alternative to them. Those who have criticized Illich's views have tended to reply that what he is saying about the function of schools has already been said, and that for all of its truth or even half-truth, there is no possibility that schools will be eliminated in America. Therefore, his arguments are irrelevant. Among those who have found his views appealing, there are some who believe it is not necessary to eliminate schools but only to rebuild their basic structure—for example, through such means as the voucher system. There are also a number of deschoolers who are engaged in developing free learning systems as a kind of transitional stage between a schooled society and a nonschooled one.

There you have a fifteen-minute history of the past fifteen years of school criticism. Naturally, a number of important details are omitted, but we believe the narrative contains no serious deformities, as far as it goes. As you may have noticed, we have *not* alluded to a number of issues that, over the years, have appeared on the front pages of newspapers as "school problems," e.g., busing, violence, drugs. Some of these matters are dealt with in Part II (under busing, neighborhood schools, community control, etc.). Still others are treated in Chapter 5, in the section on Present and Future Issues. We have excluded them here because they have not been the focal point of any serious attempt to achieve *school reform*. Most of these "crises" are symptoms of large social and political problems, and while they clearly affect (and infect) the schools, they are not susceptible to solution by the schools themselves. For example, the issue of busing arises not out of any deficiency in schools but simply because in America black and white people do not live in the same neighborhoods. And not even Ivan Illich has offered a solution to that. To take another example: Without question, problems in the schools are linked in several ways to the problem of technology, the problem of decaying cities, the problem of large demographic shifts, and certainly to the problem which Professor Martin Hamburger calls "surplus people." According to Hamburger, the social milieu in which young people grow gives distinctive clues as to how much they are needed in their society. The milieu is the message, he says, and in countries like Japan and Israel children are eager learners, not because their schools are delightful or even interesting but rather because they know that their society needs them, most especially as workers. In America, for a variety of reasons, the economy does not presently need all its people. Our government now stipulates that 5 percent of the population may be "acceptably unemployed." (And this 5 percent does not include any of the 12 percent on welfare.) Moreover, it is fairly clear by now that all those television commercials urging the young to stay in school for economic gain are misleading: the majority of youngsters who stay in school don't do much better economically than those who drop out. Thus, the message of our milieu is that, in some respects, it doesn't matter if you are a diligent learner in school.

The point we are making here is that these considerations are important to a general understanding of how schools are affected by other social systems. And, as we said, we have included discussions of these matters in other parts of the book. But we have not included them here because we have been talking about the development of a body of criticism about how *schools* operate, not other social systems.

Assuming, then, within this limitation, that our narrative of the recent history of school criticism is accurate, what does it all mean?

Well, in the first place, school critics, like other critics, tend to overestimate the influence of their ideas. The fact is that many schools in the country have not been touched by any of this. For example, there are no doubt teachers and administrators in every city in America who are just getting around to reading Admiral Rickover. Moreover, there are many teachers and administrators who have heard the hollering but have been outraged rather than changed by it. Large numbers of school people have heard the hollering, however, and have made some effort to modify the schooling process. In Chapter 3 we will talk about specific changes that are being made, and why. Here, it is necessary to say that although we have compartmentalized school criticism into phases, with beginnings and endings, the reality of the situation is much more complex and fluid. This is due largely to the fact that the critics we have discussed really asked different questions. To Rickover and his group, the critical question was, How can school best serve the national interest? (Rickover would be stunned to know it, but John Dewey, George Counts, and some other progressives were also absorbed by the very same question, but with "national interest" more broadly defined.) To Zacharias, Bruner, and other curriculum builders, the key question was, How can a subject best be taught? To the romantics, the question was, What is school for? And to abolitionists like Illich, the real question is, How can we best get an education?

Each of these questions has infused the school scene with interest and vitality, and together they have led inexorably to the most important question of all: What role can school realistically play in the education of our youth?

In the next two chapters we will deal with that question. Whether they like it or not, the schools will be dealing with it for the next twenty-five years.

2

WHAT IS SCHOOL?

UNDERSTANDING something usually means being able to make distinctions. In this chapter we want to offer several distinctions—none more important, for our purposes, than the one between education and school. It is an obvious enough one, although many people talk and act as if it isn't. Simply, education is a lifelong process of learning how to negotiate with the world. For "negotiate with" read: understand, accept, cope with, manipulate, triumph over, enjoy, be-one-with, or whatever is your fancy. For the moment, the important part is that it is lifelong—which means it begins before you enter school, and ends when you do.

Of course, it is entirely possible for someone to *mis*educate himself—that is, not learn how to negotiate with the world very well; or at least, not learn how to negotiate with important parts of his world. And it hardly needs stressing that one's education requires the presence, attention, and support of other people, preferably people who have learned how to conduct their own affairs with some degree of satisfaction. But education is a do-it-yourself job, whether done badly or well. As someone once said of Mussolini, he was a self-taught man who was a bad student, and who had an even worse teacher. Perhaps that can be said of most of us. In any case, education is not an institutional responsibility and never can be. Each person will educate himself in a unique way, using as much of a community's resources as he has the will and intelligence to appropriate.

Now, school is another matter. It is true enough that in theory the most important purpose of school is to give an individual some assistance in educating himself, which means that ultimately the quality of a school may be judged by its capacity to achieve that purpose. But like any complex institution, school can easily get sidetracked by political, social, and economic considerations, and this fact has sent many a school critic in search of some other line of work. It is best to acknowledge, at the outset, that school serves many masters, yields to many constraints, has many items on its agenda, and therefore cannot always concentrate its resources on assisting an individual in educating himself. Thus, "to be schooled" is not the same thing as "to be educated."

If you are a parent, one of the obvious implications of this distinction is that it would be foolhardy to leave your child's education up to the schools—for example, to expect the schools to teach a love of art or music or literature, or a respect for good manners, or a distrust of drugs, or a healthy attitude toward sex. And it doesn't make any difference whether they are "good schools" or "bad schools." The effect that even the best school has on the total education of a child is vastly overrated and, in comparison with the home (not to mention friends, relatives, and television), relatively small. If you are a student, you will be deceiving yourself if you blame any deficiencies in your education on schools. And, as we said, if you are an education critic, you will be constantly disappointed if you expect school to assume an all-encompassing role in the education of the young. (That is why John Holt, one of this decade's most eloquent education critics, has announced that he is no longer interested in schools.)

Now, what we are saying should not be construed as either an apology for or an attack on schools. We mean simply to point out that there are important differences between a personal goal and a social institution, and that to ignore these differences is fatal to an understanding of either. The distinction between education and school is similar in this respect to the distinction between love and marriage. The song to the contrary, love and marriage do not necessarily go together, and only a fool expects the institution of marriage—all by itself—to transform him into a loved and loving human being. To say this is not an accusation against marriage—any more than it is an attack on the courts to point out that the institution of law is not the same as the personal quest for justice, or an attack on the church to say that participation in a religious institution is not the same as leading a religious life. Quite the contrary. By pointing out the limitations of an institution, we do away with the need to defend it against unreasonable demands, and we clear the way for a realistic appraisal of what it *can* do—and might do better.

What we are talking about, then, are the limitations of the schooling process: education and school are *not* synonymous and the failure to keep this difference clearly in mind can lead to grievous and expensive errors.

So much for what school is not. What, then, *is* it? As we said earlier, school is an institution. This means that, like the church or marriage or the law, it has a history, a specialized vocabulary, a population of bureaucratic functionaries, and a complex set of rules and procedures all its own. It assigns different roles, rights, and responsibilities to the various people involved in it. It structures authority in a particular way. And it is surrounded by a network of support systems which ensure its survival. But for all their significance, these features are peripheral, not central, to the definition of school. *What defines school as an institution is the specific set of essential functions it serves in our society.* Everything else about school—its language, its rules and procedures, its authority structure, its support systems—is simply a set of instruments for carrying out those functions.

This distinction—between the essential functions of school and the conventional ways in which it carries them out—is critical to an understanding of how schools can be changed, or can't be. Perhaps an analogy or two will help to illustrate our point. Suppose you were in a position to make significant changes in our prison system. What are the possibilities? Well, you could improve the quality of food and medical care. You could provide prisoners with more meaningful work to do, and pay them more for it. You could introduce more serious efforts at rehabilitation (whatever that means). There are many things you could do, but there are just as many that you could not, *and still have a prison.* You could not, for example, decide that there should be no guards (although you could have better-trained guards). You could not decide that prisoners will determine the length of their stay (although you could improve the parole procedures). You could not decide to permit prisoners to live in their own homes (although you could allow more frequent visits by friends and relatives). It is among the *essential functions* of prison to supervise prisoners carefully, to detain them for periods of time established by law, and to isolate them from the rest of society for the duration of those periods. These functions, along with a handful of others, *define* the prison as an institution. To change them does not reform the institution; it abolishes it.

The specific procedures by which prison accomplishes its functions, on the other hand, are conventions—and therefore subject to change. You do not need steel bars and thick walls, for example, to isolate prisoners from the rest of society. The same function can be achieved, and has been, by confining prisoners to an island surrounded by hostile waters or, for that matter, to a fairly comfortable farm. Either way, you still have a prison.

Let's take one more analogy. In our culture, it is an essential function of criminal law to inform a defendant of the crime of which he is accused; another is to define what shall and shall not constitute admissible evidence at a trial; and still another is to provide a jury to consider the evidence and reach a decision about it. You might make significant reforms in the law by changing the time, place, and language in which the defendant is informed of the charges against him; or by changing the rules regarding evidence (e.g., to admit wiretap information); or by altering the procedures for selecting jurors. You might even decide to reduce the number of jurors from twelve to nine, or to seven, or to five. To do so would change the conventions of law, but leave the basic functions of the institution intact. But you could not decide to do away with the jury altogether, or abolish all rules of evidence, or leave the defendant wondering about the nature of the charges against him. That would change the essential functions which *define* law as an institution—and it would thereupon cease to exist.

The point of these analogies is not that the law and prisons and schools are alike in their social and political roles (although that case *has* been argued), but that their existence implies certain basic functions that cannot be altered without "disappearing" the institution altogether. It may be a good idea to have prisons, or it may not; but if you have them, you cannot pretend that they are convalescent homes. It may be a good idea to have schools, or it may not; but if you have them, you cannot pretend that they are resort hotels.

All of which brings us to the central question of this chapter: What are the essential functions of school as an institution, and what are simply conventions for carrying out those functions?

To begin with, and to avoid pointless, abstract philosophical objections, we must say something about our use of the word essential. We do *not* mean it in the Platonic sense of an essence. We mean simply this: When you look carefully at all those places that are called schools, you find that no matter how much they may differ, they share some common functions. These functions derive their authority from tradition and law, as well as from the conceptions (and misconceptions) a society holds about human development. Among those who do systems analysis, such functions are called invariants. They are the scaffolding that gives the institution its particular shape. Exactly how the scaffolding originated and evolves is a subject for the historian. Suffice it to say that these structural invariants are supposed to ensure the fulfillment of the main purposes of the institution. When they do not, you are left with a pointless design, which needs to be torn down and replaced by something else. It has been argued that such is the case of the institution known as school. But we do not think most people believe that such a point has been reached. It is entirely possible that in the years ahead, the essential functions we are about to specify will completely disappear, replaced by ones manifestly more suitable to social conditions and beliefs. But as things stand now—for us, in this time and place—the institution known as school, for all of its irritating, even preposterous defects, does not appear to be in jeopardy of crumbling. *We are not saying that this is either good or bad, but only that it is so.* As a consequence (as we shall try to show in the next chapter), the most realistic hope of improving school lies in modifying its conventions, not its essential functions.

One other point. We want to call attention to the level of abstraction we will be working at. For example, in addressing the question, What is school?, one may give answers such as these: School is an institution for keeping people in line, for keeping poor people poor, for regulating the economy, for promoting sexual inhibition, etc. These answers may be true or not, but in all cases, they are highly debatable and, most important, exceedingly abstract. As you will see in a moment, we have settled, for the most part, on a lower level of abstraction because it seems to us that at this level one can best see—if you are a parent (or teacher or student)—why schools operate the way they do. If you are a parent who wishes to understand or change some procedure in a school, it would be ludicrous to approach an administrator or teacher with the idea that he is serving the military-industrial complex, or trying to keep children off the labor market. To the extent that such statements might be true, they have little to do with him, or you, or your child. Therefore, we have directed our aim at a level of discourse that can provide the basis for practical discussions about what is happening in school.

And so, to the question, What are the essential functions of school, and what are its conventions?

Perhaps the most obvious institutional essential of school is its time-structuring function. Just about every school that ever was has assumed the responsibility of organizing, in some fashion, the way its students occupy their time—and, not incidentally, the way their parents occupy *their* time. This is as true of the most "progressive" free school as it is of the most "reactionary" traditional school. In each of them, there is a time when something called school starts, and a time when it stops. There is also a time when certain activities take place, and a different time for others. Without that, you have no school. On the other hand, the particular way in which a school slices up time is conventional. The 10-month school year, the five-day week, the six-hour day, the forty-five-minute period—these are all conventions. You don't need that particular set of conventions to have a school, any more than you need bad food to have a prison, or twelve jurors to have a court of law. But you do need some way to serve the time-structuring function. That's essential.

Another essential function of school concerns what students *do* during the time structure provided. That is, every school structures, in one way or another, the activities in which students are to engage. This means that, by definition, there is no such thing as an unstructured school. There are only schools that use different conventions to structure activities. The major difference between a "free" school and a "traditional" one is that the former includes as one of its activities the student's *choosing* what he will do next. And his choice is structured, obviously, by the options the school provides. Whether a school provides twenty activity options or none, and whether choosing is considered a legitimate student activity or not, is a matter of convention. What's essential is the activity-structuring function itself.

The way in which schools carry out their time structuring and activity structuring depends on the way they exercise another essential function: the defining of "intelligence," "intellectual ability," "achievement," and "good behavior." Without some standard (implicit or explicit) of what constitutes *intelligent* behavior, *important* knowledge, *necessary* skills, and *good* deportment, you don't have a school. Here, the *content* of those definitions is conventional, and will vary from one school to another, and even from one age to another. The traditional school may define intelligence as reading skill; the progressive school may define it as question-asking ability; the free school may define it as self-knowledge. Good behavior may mean uninhibited self-expression in one school, cooperation in a second, obedience in a third. (Needless to say, the content of a school's definitions will determine the way it structures activities and time.) But the important point is that, no matter what conventions they use to do it, every school is compelled to provide such basic definitions.

Out of that institutional essential grows another: evaluation, or more plainly, judging. All schools exist, in part, to judge some aspect of a child's behavior—usually, the skills and attitudes the school has defined as essential to its conception of intelligence or good behavior. What those skills and attitudes are, we have already noted, is a matter of convention. Time was when most schools evaluated a student's knowledge of Latin. Nowadays, such knowledge is usually not thought worthy of evaluation. For some curious reason, schools presently want to evaluate such things as map-reading skills. But that's how conventions are. They change. Not quickly, not easily, not even for the better, but change they do. As, for example, the procedures used to evaluate students. Standardized tests, grading systems (A, B, C, or whatever), report cards—these are all conventions, which means that they can be, and have been, replaced by other procedures. But whatever procedures schools use, they must evaluate *something* if they are to remain schools.

The school's responsibility for evaluation leads to still another essential function: to differentiate between those who are evaluated and those who do the evaluating. In other words, schools always create a separation between the roles of teachers and students, between the judges and the judged. In a progressive school, the role of the teacher may be quite different from the role of a teacher in a traditional school. Even their titles may be different. But whether they are called "masters" or "facilitators" or "resource persons," *in all schools* teachers have one role—whatever it may be—and students another. That's essential. What is conventional is whether the teacher is authoritarian or democratic, progressive or traditional, certified or not. There are schools today that are even using students as teachers, which we think is a splendid new convention. The point is that you still know who are the teachers and who the students in any given situation. If not, you may have a "dynamic learning environment," or an "ongoing education happening," or a "total life experience"—but you don't have a school.

One characteristic of what we are calling institutional essentials is that they are most clearly observable in the breach. That is, the essential functions of school are often more visible when they are *not* being served than when they are. This is especially true of the school's supervisory function. Very few teachers would list "to supervise and control the young" among the important functions of school. But you have only to imagine the consequences of failure in this function to see at once that supervision is essential. So essential, in fact, that it is one of the few requirements *every* state government specifies in its definition of school. The procedures used to provide supervision are, of course, conventional. Consequently, the legal definition of what constitutes adequate supervision will vary from state to state. But in the eyes of the law, and most everyone else, an institution must provide *some* form of supervision of the young, if it is to qualify as a school.

The responsibility of the school to supervise reflects a broader function: to serve the economic, social, and political interests of the group that nominally pays to support it. Whether a given school is fulfilling that function well or badly is often a topic of heated, even vicious, public debate. But in the end, through one set of conventions or another (e.g., school board elections, PTAs, community control), the school is held accountable to its constituents. The form such accountability might take is now one of the most disturbing issues in public education (see the acountability issue, p. 70).

Accountability is not confined to the *existing* needs of the community. It includes a responsibility to the future as well. Every school has, as one of its essential functions, to prepare students in some way for the economic and social realities they will encounter as adults. More specifically, school functions as both a training ground for and an entry point into higher education, the professions, other social institutions, and jobs. Most schools exercise this function through the convention known as a curriculum. The content of the curriculum is determined, in theory at least, by the requirements of college and industry—or, to be more accurate, by the school's *perception* of those requirements. Whether any given curriculum does, in fact, prepare students for the future is an open question. What is not so open is the fact that, through one set of conventions or another, every school attempts to meet that responsibility.

The function of school we have just described—to prepare students for the social and economic realities they will encounter as adults—helps us to stress a point we may not have made clear enough in the preceding pages. It is that every essential function of school we have identified is integrally related to every other function. We have said that *school functions theoretically to prepare students for their future*. To fulfill that function, it must identify the knowledge, skills, and attitudes young people will need to survive. In doing so, *school defines intelligence, intellectual ability, and good behavior.* To determine how well or poorly the student's performance matches up with those definitions, *school evaluates behavior.* To serve its evaluating function, *school differentiates between the roles of teacher and student.* On the basis of its evaluation, *school structures time* and *structures activities* in an attempt to modify or control the student's behavior. By structuring time and activities, *school ensures supervision of the young.* In providing supervision, as in its other functions, *school is accountable to those who pay for it.* And as part of its accountability, *school aims at preparing students for the economic and social realities they will encounter as adults.*

So there you have a capsule definition of school: it's an institution which serves that particular set of functions. We do not claim that this is the only way to define a school. We *do* claim that this distinction—between essential functions and conventions—is important to keep clearly in mind, especially for any parent who wants to evaluate criticism of the schools, or who wants to play a role in helping to change a school, or even to start one. There have been several school critics, as we have already pointed out, who have attacked with great eloquence the foundations on which the idea of a school rests—what we are calling institutional essentials. They have, in effect, called for the elimination of such functions as time structuring, evaluation, and role differentiation. In all cases of which we are aware, such critics have ultimately become discouraged and have either dropped out altogether or have turned away from schools toward larger educational issues. In either instance, they are no longer a force for school reform and will have very little practical effect on the lives of our children. Criticism of the institutional essentials makes interesting reading, quick reputations, and, sometimes, first-rate sociology. But it does not get you very far in generating practical changes in schools. Practical changes come about through the re-creation of conventions. And this is true in all social systems, especially the school. Of course, to some (e.g., radical critics), practical change is a synonym for insignificant change. But this is the case only when those trying to make change are timid or lack imagination. In the next chapter we will discuss thirty-five specific changes that the schools are presently moving toward—all of them practical; none, in our opinion, insignificant.

3

WHAT IS A GOOD SCHOOL?

WHAT IS school? The question was answered in the last chapter: school is a place that performs the functions we outlined, and is held accountable for their performance. Can such a place help one to get an education? Well, as we said, only partly. You may have noticed that in the last chapter, we did not list *educating* as an essential function of school. This was not a snide omission. In theory, educational experiences are supposed to be the *consequences* of all the essential functions and carefully developed conventions of the schooling process; and once in a while, in practice, it may actually work out that way. Quite often it does not—which is why Ivan Illich has attracted a wide following of "deschoolers."

If school cannot always provide educational experiences, should we have such an institution? As we have implied, this is a nonproductive question. We have it, and it is not going to go away. At least not all at once and not in the near future. There are at present 48 million children attending public schools, another 6 million in private schools. That means, among other things, that school is one of America's largest industries, the total elementary and secondary school budget coming close to $50 billion annually. Anything less than a cataclysm on the order of the melting of the glacial ice caps will leave school intact, insofar as its essential functions are concerned.

Well then, can schools be made better by changing their conventions? This is an extraordinarily difficult question. To begin with, we have the problem of what "better" means. To Admiral Rickover it would mean one thing, to Jerrold Zacharias another, to Jonathan Kozol still another. To Ivan Illich the question is analogous to asking, Can we improve cancer? Obviously, there are positions in this matter which cannot be reconciled. Nonetheless, from the perspective of many school people and school critics, as well as parents and students, the answer is yes, schools can be made better. But that's just the beginning of an answer. To most people (although they would hardly put it this way), a school is good when its conventions serve all the essential functions of the institution, without *preventing* children from having educational experiences. A school is *very* good when its conventions actually promote educationally valuable experiences. But what are educationally valuable experiences? And how are they promoted? Here is where the problem gets sticky. For example, it is an essential function of school to supervise the behavior of children. One of the many conventions invented to serve that function is the requirement that elementary school children line up before entering their classrooms. (This is so in many schools, not all.) Is there anything educationally valuable about that? Some say yes. It teaches children to be orderly and disciplined. Some say no. It has nothing to do with orderliness and discipline. It is strictly a convenience for teachers. Supervision, they say, does not require immobility. And immobility is neither natural nor valuable for children.

Here's another example: It is a convention of most schools that children with similar reading or IQ test scores be grouped together. This is a means of achieving a more efficient structuring of student activities which, in turn, is supposed to facilitate learning. Does it really? Some say yes. Children learn more when they are all doing the same thing at the same time. Therefore, there should not be great ability differences among them when they start out. Some say no. Children can learn just as efficiently, if not more so, when they are with others of a wide range of ability. Moreover, grouping according to test scores creates a caste system, and makes many children believe they are dumb—permanently.

A final example: Schools must evaluate. In order to do that, most schools have a highly competitive grading system. Is this convention educationally valuable? Those who say yes believe that real life is competitive and that children need to learn early that their success will always come through someone else's failure. The grading system, therefore, reflects the way things really are and prepares students to face reality in the future. Those who say no believe that this is a false concept of success and failure, and that, in any case, there is time and opportunity enough for children to learn about competition. Schools should help everyone grow in confidence, and therefore no one should fail.

You can see, then, that in developing a concept of a good school or an improved school, there are two questions that have to be resolved. First, what are educationally valuable experiences? Second, what conventions will best promote them?

These questions, in point of fact, have been more or less resolved by many active school people and school critics. All of the hollering over the past fifteen years has not been for nothing. It has resulted in a pattern of consensus as to how to proceed in making a school better. You may not agree with these conclusions. You may even feel that what has been defined as better is your definition of worse. Nonetheless, what we are about to describe is, in fact, *the direction in which most school change is presently moving.* Here goes:

TIME STRUCTURING

A school is good . . .

⊬ when its daily time sequences are not arbitrary (45 minutes for this, 45 minutes for that, etc.) but are related to

what the students are doing. If something takes 20 min-
untes to do, why drag it out? If something takes an hour
and 20 minutes to do, why cut it short?

✛ when children are not expected to do the same thing in
the same amount of time. This amounts to a recognition
of the fact that there is a difference between expecting a
student to learn something and expecting him to learn
something at a predetermined pace. Learning rates vary,
and a good school is one that does not penalize or reward
such variation but accepts it as natural. It also accepts the
fact that the rate at which something is learned is related
to the interest of the learner more than anything else. In
bad schools, a "slow" learner is often being punished simply
because of lack of compliance, not ability.

✛ when students are not required merely to serve time in
courses, like in a jail sentence. In a bad school, there is a
preoccupation with "taking" courses, such as English 6,
Social Studies 8, and Science 7. A good school is more concerned with the achievement of competence than it is with
time serving. Thus, in a good school, the question is not,
"Have you taken . . . ," but "Have you learned . . . ?"

✛ when it allows students, at least to some extent, to organize
their own time—i.e., decide how they will use it. In educating oneself, one must make that decision continuously.
The idea here is to help children learn to organize and use
time by giving them that experience in school.

ACTIVITY STRUCTURING

A school is good . . .

✛ when the activities it requires are not arbitrary (e.g., "We've
always done that") or based on discredited claims (e.g.,
"The study of grammar strengthens the mind"). A school

is good when it can assert on some empirical and rational basis that its activities have relevance to the lives of children. This does not necessarily mean, "You can use this later in the afternoon." It does mean, "There is some demonstrable evidence that many students have, at some time or other, found these activities useful in the pursuit of an education." Of course, if you can learn something in the morning that you *can* use later in the afternoon, it does wonders for your morale.

✛ when it does not require all students to engage in the same activities, but gives them considerable latitude in choosing from among many options. Since educating oneself involves making decisions about one's activities as well as one's time, it is a good idea for a school to give students a chance to learn how to choose among activities. This does not necessarily mean there should be no requirements. A good school may or may not have them, but it will always allow for individual variations and for considerable student participation in identifying and suggesting worthwhile activities.

✛ when it recognizes that no matter how logical its activity structuring may be, the process is next to worthless if students are alienated from their activities. In other words, the *psycho*-logic of activities is more important than their logical structure. For example, it may seem logical to require *Julius Caesar* in tenth grade, *Hamlet* in eleventh, and *Macbeth* in twelfth. Or it may seem even more logical to start with geometry, then move to algebra, then to trigonometry. But if these or any other sequences are turning students off, what good are they?

✛ when its activities are *student* activities. That may seem obvious, since it can't be much of an activity if the students aren't doing it. But the fact is that in many schools, subjects like English, history, and science are mostly teacher activities, in that teachers do most of the reading, writing, talking, and thinking. Students take notes, which is a hell of an activity for training stenographers but not much good for anything else. A school is good when its activities require students to do the heavy work. Moreover, student work should have some relationship to what scholars in a particular field actually do. The more correspondence between student intellectual activity and scholarly intellectual activity, the better.

✢ when its activities are not confined to a single building but include the resources of the whole community. Activities that put students in touch with real people and problems outside the school walls have an enormous educating potential, because they are real, they are unusually dynamic, and they have variety.

✢ when its activities bring together students of great diversity in background and ability. There is, in fact, no evidence that "bright" children learn less when they are with "slow" children than when they are with other "bright" children. There *is* evidence that when children are labeled "slow," they tend to develop a bad—sometimes incurable—case of low self-esteem.

DEFINING INTELLIGENCE, WORTHWHILE KNOWLEDGE, GOOD BEHAVIOR

A school is good . . .

✢ when it moves away from valuing memorization and ventriloquizing and moves toward valuing question asking, problem solving, and research. This does not mean a good school forgoes all information giving—for example, through lectures and text assignments. It does mean that a good school wants students to do as much inquiring, generalizing, and verifying as possible.

✦ when it rejects passive acceptance and encourages involvement and independence. Thus, what in the past may have been considered impertinent or disobedient may now be considered healthy, aggressive skepticism, and much to be valued.

✦ when it moves away from valuing knowledge "for knowledge's sake" and moves toward valuing the use of knowledge in daily life. In other words, a good school comes very close to saying that if you don't *act* as if you know something, then you don't know it.

✦ when reading ability is considered only one of several possible ways through which students can express intellectual competence and interest. This does not mean that a good school is not interested in reading skill. It does mean that a good school also values talking, film making, audiotaping, photography, videotaping, and other communication skills. "Valuing" means here that students can earn brownie points with their teachers by demonstrating competence in these skills. In the past, the high priority given to reading and writing has been justified by their importance in the culture; that is, the culture defined them as important, and the schools reflected that definition. Today, the culture is requiring a broader definition of literacy, and the better schools are now reflecting that fact. (We discuss this matter in considerable detail in Chapter 6.)

✦ when it accepts as legitimate many of the new subjects invented, say, during the past 75 years or so—e.g., anthropology, sociology, cinematography, ecology, cybernetics, linguistics, meteorology, marine biology, musicology, futuristics, urbanology, etc. The curriculum makers of a good school are not so sure as curriculum makers used to be about what are basic subjects. As a consequence, students are offered the widest possible range of subjects from which to choose. In other words, a good school recognizes the knowledge explosion that is taking place, and tries to reflect its consequences in its definition of worthwhile knowledge.

⊷ when it includes as part of its definition of worthwhile knowledge, *self*-knowledge—that is, knowledge of what is going on inside one's skin. In a good school, a student's *feelings* are not considered an intrusion upon his pursuit of knowledge, but a subject of inquiry themselves. This does not mean that a good school must become a psychiatric hospital. It does mean that a systematic effort is made to help a student understand himself, get in touch with his own feelings, monitor his own behavior, and so on.

EVALUATION

A school is good . . .

⊷ when it moves away from aversive responses and toward reinforcing ones. No matter what one's opinion may be of B. F. Skinner, it is well established that acceptance and approval are far more effective than rejection and punishment as a means of controlling behavior. In a good school, students are rewarded for acceptable behavior, but not necessarily punished for unacceptable behavior. If the rewards are worthwhile (to the student) and consistently given, the procedure usually works. (It even works in rehabilitating prisoners.) In several good schools, a revised grading system has been introduced, in which a student is given credit for doing "passing" work, but does not get an F for unsatisfactory work. He simply gets no credit. Thus, to some extent, failure is deinstitutionalized; only success is recorded. There is an analogy here with a driver's license. If you pass the driving test, you get your license. If you fail it, you do not get a "nondriver's license." And no one notes your failure on a permanent-record card, either. By eliminating the stigma of failure, you eliminate a great deal of fear and anxiety, neither of which contributes to enthusiastic learning.

✢ when it moves away from factorylike processing procedures and toward more humanistic, individualized judgments. In the best schools this means a relatively nonpunitive grading system, no homogeneous grouping, a minimum of labeling ("good student," "slow student," etc.), and no permanent record-keeping. In a few good schools, respect for the privacy of an individual has led to a policy of revealing the teacher's appraisal of any learning experience to no one except the student and his parents (not even to next year's teachers). In an increasing number of schools, students are playing a role in evaluating their own performance. (They usually turn out to be tougher on themselves than any teacher.) The idea here is to make evaluation a learning experience, which, in theory, all schools recommend but which, in practice, few accomplish.

✢ when its priorities are broadly conceived, rather than narrowly hierarchical. For example, in many schools a student may be judged slow solely on the basis of reading and mathematical ability. The same student may be an excellent musician, actor, or even group leader, but will receive very little formal recognition for these skills. This is patently unjust, and in good schools the evaluation system has been adjusted to deal with this problem. In a few good schools, students are even allowed to work out (with the guidance of their teachers) their own priorities for learning. In this way, students can utilize and capitalize on things they do well and are interested in.

✢ when it makes as explicit as possible what kinds of behaviors it wants, assuming that such behaviors are reasonable.

In many courses, students are uncertain about how they will be judged because it is not clear to them what they are expected to learn, or how they are supposed to demonstrate competence. Granted, it is not always possible or even desirable to provide students, at the outset of every learning opportunity, with a detailed set of specifications for the goals they are expected to achieve. Nonetheless, there are many instances when it is. One of the best ways to do this is to give the students their final exam at the beginning of the year. If the exam is trustworthy, it will reveal explicitly what students ought to know, or what they ought to be able to do, by the end of the year. This raises another important point about evaluation: it is highly desirable to make quite certain that you actually evaluate what you say you want to, not something else. For example, in some schools, a subject like literature is taught with the aim of increasing the student's interest in reading. But the test the student is asked to pass is about his knowledge of particular literary works. There is nothing wrong with such a test if communicating the content of those works was your aim in teaching the subject. But if your stated goal was something else, then either the test or the goal was dishonestly conceived.

✚ when it does not use standardized tests, or uses them only with extreme caution and skepticism. Standardized tests have a way of tyrannizing schools into teaching for the test. In effect, the curriculum degenerates into coaching for the test. In some cases, this would no doubt represent an improvement over what presently exists, but in most cases it does not. The makers of standardized tests are businessmen, who have their own motives for creating their tests, and certainly have no interest in the particular needs of particular children. Testing should grow from what is taught. And what is taught should grow from who is taught. If a test fits, then it might be useful. Otherwise, the tail is wagging the dog.

✛ when there are constructive, nonpunitive procedures for the evaluation of teachers and administrators, as well as students. In many recent cases, attempts to evaluate teachers and principals have failed because the evaluation was done by angry students or parents in crisis situations. But when evaluation procedures are set up in a rational, cooperative, nonemergency context, they usually work, and they contribute to an increase in school spirit and teaching effectiveness.

SUPERVISION

A school is good . . .

✛ when it moves away from adversary relationships between teacher and student and toward collaborative effort. It is difficult to institutionalize such a change; everything really depends on the willingness and ability of teachers to forgo an authoritarian role. Teachers can be encouraged to do this, however, by eliminating such supervisory conventions as getting everyone in size places, alphabetical order, and permanent seats. Depriving students of autonomy in controlling their own bodily movements is the best way of making them feel like victims and prisoners. In good schools, teachers try to keep such control to an absolute minimum.

✛ when students are given opportunities to supervise themselves. For example, some schools ask students to handle discipline problems, to serve as crossing guards, to administer tests, to help keep the building in repair, and so on. The idea, of course, is to give students a sense of control in the functioning of the school. There may be no more effective way to teach the need for order and discipline.

⊬ when it is small enough so that supervision (and just about everything else) can be a personal—i.e., human—problem, not a logistics problem. It is practically impossible for collaborative and meaningful associations to occur in a building with 5,000 students, or 3,000. No one really knows what the maximum size of a humanized school is, but in various experiments around the country, the figure that keeps coming up is somewhere around 250.

ROLE DIFFERENTIATION

A school is good . . .

⊬ when teachers forgo their role as sole authority figures, view themselves as learners, and try to develop the idea of a learning community in which the teacher functions more as a coordinator or facilitator of activities than a dictator. Such a role is particularly suitable to junior and senior high schools, although it is being widely accepted in elementary schools on the basis of its success in the British Infant Schools.

⊬ when it places in a teaching role the greatest variety of people—for example, paraprofessionals, interested laymen, and even students. Incidentally, the best research we have on teaching effectiveness suggests that (1) students learn more when they are taught by other students than when they are taught by teachers, and (2) students who function as teachers learn more than when they are functioning as students. That's a parlay that only the foolish would neglect, and in the best schools ample use is made of students as teachers. Selective use is also being made of knowledgeable, talented laymen (e.g., bankers, artists, carpenters, dancers) who are interested in working with children. The big problem with using students and laymen as teachers is over the question of professionalism. How professional are "professional" teachers? The most realistic answer now being given goes something like this: Although teachers are professionals in many legitimate meanings of the word, they are not professionals in one sense. They do not have command of a complex body of knowledge or generally accepted, replicable procedures which ensure that they will obtain better results than people who have not been certified as teachers. This means that there is a considerable difference between an amateur teacher and, say, an amateur neurosurgeon. We may reasonably assume that there is a considerable knowledge gap between an amateur and a professional in the field of neurosurgery. *There is no such gap between an amateur and a professional in teaching.* This does not mean that teachers don't know anything. It does not mean that there are no extraordinary teachers. And it does not mean that anyone could become, overnight, an adequate teacher. It does mean that much of the knowledge a good teacher uses is of a practical, nonspecialized nature, available to almost anyone with eyes and ears open. For example, a parent who is raising a child or two has as much opportunity to learn about child development, motivation, reinforcement, evaluation, structuring experiences, and the like, as any good teacher is likely to know and use. Any specialized technical knowledge teachers have is minimal and, in any case, is easily communicated to anyone—with or without a degree—who wants to know it.

ᴴwhen it is so organized that it can capitalize on what its teachers do best and know most about. (See differentiated staffing and team teaching.) Too often, teachers are assumed to be knowledgeable about everything included within a subject, when in fact they might be strong in some aspects of it but quite weak in others. In a good school, teachers need not try to conceal this fact. Working in conjunction with other teachers, they can exploit their strengths and receive help with their weaknesses.

✤ when students are not objects to which things happen, but are encouraged to be active shapers of their own school experiences. In many good schools, for example, students play a role in designing the curriculum, in evaluating themselves, and in forming general school policy. In a few places, student government is actually a viable medium through which students are a potent political force in school. This is considered a good idea, not for political reasons, but for educational ones. If students are given a chance to wield power, they can learn to do so responsibly. Without any experience with power, students are a sure bet to use it badly when it is available.

✤ when students are not constantly placed in competitive roles with each other, but function instead in collaborative relationships. Ideally, a good school strives to achieve something approaching a family feeling, in which each member is helped to grow in his/her own way, but not at the expense of someone else.

ACCOUNTABILITY TO THE PUBLIC

A school is good . . .

✤ when it moves away from bureaucratic paternalism and toward increased community participation. In the best arrangements, this means that there are established channels through which parents can express grievances against the school and also participate in its functioning. A school is bad when rancorous confrontation is the usual means by which parents call attention to their ideas and complaints.

✤ when it offers a variety of alternative programs to the many publics that comprise a community. At the present time, most schools are essentially monolithic, offering one kind of educational program to all their constituents—who, in fact, differ noticeably in their orientation to school. Of course, it is not possible for a school to offer a special program for each member of the community. But the best schools recognize that there are several respectable but contrasting arrangements for learning, each of which is favored by some segment of the community. The idea is to offer as many of these as feasible. In this way, each school becomes several schools, and most students can find a program which suits their particular life and/or learning style.

✠ when it is not afraid to be held accountable for its performance. The movement toward contract teaching and behavioral objectives is, in part, a reaction against the traditional resistance of teachers and administrators to being evaluated—sometimes by anyone. In the best schools, the staff tries to make explicit to parents and students what it wishes to accomplish (and what it does not); how it intends to do this; and what kinds of evidence it will accept as a sign of success. If school people refuse to do this, state legislatures will increasingly do it for them, probably to the detriment of everybody.

ACCOUNTABILITY TO THE FUTURE

A school is good . . .

✠ when its concept of knowledge, attitudes, and skills is oriented toward the future. This does not mean that a knowledge of the past is not useful. It means that a school has realistically assessed what students will need to know in the years ahead and is making some serious attempts to help students learn those things. For example, subjects like ecology, space technology, and urbanology are undoubtedly of great importance for the future. If they are not part of the curriculum, a school is probably making a serious mistake. Skills involving open-ended problem solving and the use of electronic media fall in the same category, as do attitudes that promote strength and intelligence in the face of continuous change. A school is bad—to put it plainly—when it has no viable strategy or plan to deal with vast cultural change. For example, schools that are striving to return to the "basics" are in deep trouble, and so are their students.

◄ when it interprets its responsibility to the future as a responsibility to its students first, and to other social institutions (e.g., college, business, the professions) only at a late and convenient hour. This does not mean that schools should ignore, or even treat lightly, the present requirements of college, industry, and business in designing their curricula. It does mean that a good school is careful to avoid serving *solely* as a processing and certifying agency, but balances the future economic needs of its students with their emotional and social needs as fully functioning adults.

There you have, in somewhat extended form, the thrust of most school change at the present time. Of course, there is no school anyplace that has achieved all these changes or is even trying to achieve all of them. In fact, a good school is simply one that is trying to replace many of the old conventions with many of the new. How many? That would be hard to say. In Chapter 7 we have tried to provide you with a method by which some kind of reasonable judgment can be made as to whether a school is good, bad, or in between. We have also included there a list of questions which presents in abbreviated form everything we have described above. In the end, any judgment about how good a school is will be both imprecise and subjective. But it can be well informed.

Our purpose in this chapter was to provide you with an understanding of what the present definition of "good" is—as formulated by the most intelligent and active school critics, administrators, and teachers. Why do they think these changes represent improvement? In some cases, because it can be demonstrated empirically that one procedure is better than another. For example, there is simply no question about the fact that positive reinforcement is a more effective way of changing behavior than is punishment. In other cases, a change is regarded as good because it appears more logical than some other procedure. For example, plain common sense dictates the inclusion in the curriculum of many subjects that did not exist fifty years ago but which are today the focal point of exciting research and new knowledge. But the main reason most of these changes are considered good is philosophical. More than any other social institution, the American school mirrors what we want to think we are as a people. But when we approach it to ask, Are we not the fairest one of all? it keeps replying, in the most irritating fashion, that we are not. And over the past twenty years or so, its replies have become nasty accusations. In some ways, nastier than ever before. Our schools have been telling us that we are becoming dehumanized, empire-building technocrats, and that we care more for our missiles than for our children. We are being told, by the *facts* of our schools, that we are racists, that we aim for mediocrity, that we cherish conformity, that we have no love of learning, that we have lost our moral fervor. It is an ugly picture, but being Americans, we still think all things are possible and all trends reversible. And so, we do what we have always done: reform our schools in the hope that they may help us to actualize what we fancy is the Great American Experiment in How to Live Honorably and Intelligently. And this entails asserting that school conventions should promote independence, creativity, egalitarianism, flexibility, and all the other stuff that graduation day speeches are made of. So ultimately, what is good about a good school is that it takes some of that seriously, even if everyone does not.

4

A FABLE, A PLAN, A REALITY

IN THE previous chapter we listed various changes that schools are undergoing. All those changes involve modifying impotent, inefficient, irrelevant, or bureaucratic conventions, and do not require attacking the essential functions of school. You will probably find it hard to believe—after you have read the fable below—but there is nothing contained in that fable that does not conform to the same general principle. At first reading, it will probably appear to you that we have concocted a fantastic, radical alternative, which requires overturning most or all of the particular mandates imposed on the school as an institution. We trust that on a second reading you will see that this is not true. The schooling process we have imagined here involves the structuring of time and activities, the defining of intelligent and responsible behavior, the evaluation of student behavior, differentiation between teacher and student, supervision of students, accountability to the public, and, above all, responsiveness to both present realities and future contingencies. While it is true that no school anywhere, let alone a school system, is contemplating such a pervasive re-creation of school conventions, it is also true that some schools—Parkway, for example—have made tentative moves in some of these directions. In any event, our school fable is included here to give you some idea of how much change might conceivably take place *within* the essential (and traditional) structure of the institution known as school.

A FABLE

ONCE UPON a time in the City of New York civilized life very nearly came to an end. The streets were covered with dirt, and there was no one to tidy them. The air and rivers were polluted, and no one could cleanse them. The schools were rundown, and no one believed in them. Each day brought a new strike, and each strike brought new hardships. Crime and strife and disorder and rudeness were to be found everywhere. The young fought the old. The workers fought the students. The whites fought the blacks. The city was bankrupt.

When things came to their most desperate moment, the City Fathers met to consider the problem. But they could suggest no cures, for their morale was very low and their imagination dulled by hatred and confusion. There was nothing for the mayor to do but to declare a state of emergency. He had done this before during snowstorms and power failures, but now he felt even more justified.

"Our city," he said, "is under siege, like the ancient cities of Jericho and Troy. But *our* enemies are sloth and poverty and indifference and hatred."

As you can see, he was a very wise mayor, but not so wise as to say exactly how these enemies could be dispersed. Thus, though a state of emergency officially existed, neither the mayor nor anyone else could think of anything to do that would make the situation better rather than worse. And then an extraordinary thing happened.

One of the mayor's aides, knowing full well what the future held for the city, had decided to flee with his family to the country. In order to prepare himself for his exodus to a strange environment, he began to read Henry David Thoreau's *Walden*, which he had been told was a useful handbook on how to survive in the country. While reading the book, he came upon the following passage: "Students should not play life, or study it merely, while the community supports them at this expensive game, but earnestly live it from beginning to end. How could youths better learn to live than by at once trying the experiment of living?"

The aide sensed immediately that he was in the presence of an exceedingly good idea. And he sought an audience with the mayor. He showed the passage to the mayor, who was extremely depressed and in no mood to read from books, since he had already scoured books of lore and wisdom in search of help but had found nothing.

"What does it mean?" said the mayor angrily.

The aide replied, "Nothing less than a way to our salvation."

He then explained to the mayor that the students in the public schools had heretofore been part of the general problem whereas, with some imagination and a change of perspective, they might easily become part of the general solution. He pointed out that from junior high school up to senior high school, there were approximately 400,000 able-bodied, energetic young men and women who could be used as a resource to make the city livable again.

"But how can we use them?" asked the mayor. "And what would happen to their education if we did?"

To this the aide replied, "They will find their education in the process of saving their city. And as for their lessons in school, we have ample evidence that the young do not exactly appreciate them and are even now turning against their teachers and their schools." The aide, who had come armed with statistics (as aides are wont to do), pointed out that the city was spending $1 million a year merely replacing broken school windows and that almost one-third of all the students enrolled in the schools did not even show up on any given day.

"Yes, I know," said the mayor sadly, "Woe unto us."

"Wrong," said the aide brashly. "The boredom and destructiveness and pent-up energy that are an affliction to us can be turned to our advantage."

The mayor was not quite convinced, but having no better idea of his own he appointed his aide chairman of the Emergency Education Committee, and the aide at once made plans to remove almost 400,000 students from their dreary classrooms and their even drearier lessons, so that their energy and talents might be used to repair the desecrated environment.

When these plans became known, there was a great hue and cry against them, for people in distress will sometimes prefer a problem that is familiar to a solution that is not. For instance, the teachers complained that their contract contained no provision for such unusual procedures. To this the aide replied that the *spirit* of their contract compelled them to help educate our youth, and that education can take many forms and be conducted in many places. "It is not written in any holy book," he observed, "that an education must occur in a small room with chairs in it."

Some parents complained that the plan was un-American and that its compulsory nature was hateful to them. To this the aide replied that the plan was based on the practices of earlier Americans who required the young to assist in controlling the environment in order to ensure the survival of the group. "Our schools," he added, "have never hesitated to compel. The question is not, nor has it ever been, to compel or not to compel, but rather, which things ought to be compelled."

And even some children complained, although not many. They said that their God-given right to spend twelve years of their lives, at public expense, sitting in a classroom was being trampled. To this complaint the aide replied that they were confusing a luxury with a right, and that, in any case, the community could no longer afford either. Besides," he added, "of all the God-given rights man has identified, none takes precedence over his right to survive."

And so, the curriculum of the public schools of New York

City became known as Operation Survival, and all the children from seventh grade through twelfth grade became part of it. Here are some of the things they were obliged to do:

On Monday morning of every week, 400,000 children had to help clean up their own neighborhoods. They swept the streets, canned the garbage, removed the litter from empty lots, and hosed the dust and graffiti from the pavements and walls. Wednesday mornings were reserved for beautifying the city. Students planted trees and flowers, tended the grass and shrubs, painted subways and other eyesores, and even repaired broken-down public buildings, starting with their own schools.

Each day, 5,000 students (mostly juniors and seniors in high school) were given responsibility to direct traffic on city streets, so that all the policemen who previously had done this were freed to keep a sharp eye out for criminals. Each day, 5,000 students were asked to help deliver the mail, so that it soon became possible to have mail delivered twice a day—as it had been done in days of yore.

Several thousand students were also used to establish and maintain day-care centers, so that young mothers, many on welfare, were free to find gainful employment. Each student was also assigned to meet with two elementary school students on Tuesday and Thursday afternoons to teach them to read, to write, and to do arithmetic. Twenty thousand students were asked to substitute, on one afternoon a week, for certain adults whose jobs the students could perform without injury or loss of efficiency. These adults were then free to attend school or, if they preferred, to assist the students in their efforts to save their city.

The students were also assigned to publish a newspaper in every neighborhood of the city, in which they were able to include much information that good citizens need to have. Students organized science fairs, block parties, and rock festivals, and they formed, in every neighborhood, both an orchestra and a theater company. Some students assisted in hospitals, helped to register voters, and produced radio and television programs which were aired on city stations. There was still time to hold a year-round City Olympics in which every child competed in some sport or other.

It came to pass, as you might expect, that the college students in the city yearned to participate in the general plan, and thus another 100,000 young people became available to serve the community. The college students ran a jitney service from the residential boroughs to Manhattan and back. Using their own cars and partly subsidized by the city, the students quickly established a kind of auxiliary, semipublic transportation system, which reduced the number of cars coming into Manhattan, took some of the load off the subways, and diminished air pollution—in one stroke.

College students were empowered to give parking and litter tickets, thus freeing policemen more than ever for real detective work. They were permitted to organize seminars, film festivals, and lectures for junior and senior high school students; and on a UHF television channel, set aside for the purpose, they gave advanced courses in a variety of subjects every day from 3:00 P.M. to 10:00 P.M. They also helped to organize and run drug-addiction rehabilitation centers, and they launched campaigns to inform people of their legal rights, nutritional needs, and of available medical facilities.

Because this is a fable and not a fairy tale, it cannot be said that all the problems of the city were solved. But several extraordinary things did happen. The city began to come alive, and its citizens found new reason to hope that they could save themselves. Young people who had been alienated from their environment assumed a proprietary interest in it. Older people who had regarded the young as unruly and parasitic came to respect them. There followed from this a revival of courtesy and a diminution of crime, for there was less reason than before to be angry at one's neighbors and wish to assault them.

Amazingly, most of the students found that while they did

not "receive" an education, they were able to create a quite adequate one. They lived, each day, their social studies and geography and communication and biology and many other things that decent and proper people know about, including the belief that everyone must share equally in creating a livable city, no matter what he or she becomes later on. It even came to pass that the older people, being guided by the example of the young, took a renewed interest in restoring their environment and at the very least refused to participate in its destruction.

Now, it would be foolish to deny that there were not certain problems attending this whole adventure. For instance, thousands of children who would otherwise have known the principal rivers of Uruguay had to live out their lives in ignorance of these facts. Hundreds of teachers felt that their training had been wasted because they could not educate children unless it were done in a classroom. As you can imagine, it was also exceedingly difficult to grade students on their activities, and after a while, almost all tests ceased. This made many people unhappy, for many reasons, but most of all because no one could tell the dumb children from the smart children anymore.

But the mayor, who was, after all, a very shrewd politician, promised that as soon as the emergency was over everything would be restored to normal. Meanwhile, everybody lived happily ever after—in a state of emergency, but quite able to cope with it.

Is it really possible for such a "radical alternative" to happen? Probably not; at least, not in our lifetime. Moreover, such an alternative would by no means be altogether desirable. In the first place, it imposes on all children a particular kind of schooling, leaving no options for those who could not or wish not to learn in this fashion. If the school reform movement has learned anything over the past two decades, it is that within any given school population there is enough diversity in learning styles to make diversity in learning programs a necessity. Thus, any school proposal—fabulous or otherwise—that does not offer alternatives is manifestly deficient.

In the second place, proposals like this one pose enormous problems in supervision; and require planning (of time and activities) of such care that most schools, or school systems, would realistically be defeated right at the start. In the third place, proposals of this kind have political and legal implications that go far beyond anything the schools have ever had to cope with. And yet, the fable is not so fabulous after all. In Chapel Hill, North Carolina, high school students are presently being given credit for teaching (eight hours a week) in elementary schools. Similar options are offered in Palma Heights, Ohio; Plattville, Wisconsin; and dozens of other places. In Vermont, the State Education Department, under a program called DUO (Do Unto Others), offers full academic credit to students who participate in legitimate political, social, or ecological organizations. We will be describing the Parkway program in Philadelphia, which takes an entire community as its school. Similar programs have been developed in Chicago (the Metro project), in New Rochelle, New York (the 3 I's program), in Cherry Creek, Colorado, and in at least ten other cities around the country. Work-study programs are becoming commonplace. What is happening, and what our fable is intended to reflect, is that school people are searching for *new models of student participation.* There simply is no question about the fact that listlessness, ennui, and even violence in school are related to the fact that students have no useful role to play in society. The strict application of nurturing and protective attitudes toward children has created a paradoxical situation in which protection of children has come to mean excluding them from meaningful involvement in their own communities. At the same time, educators of all persuasions are rediscovering the great capacities of children. Thus, it is hardly utopian for school reformers to try to invent or reinstate forms of youthful participation in society as a substitute for or a supplement to the schooling process. Pro-

fessor Martin Hamburger of New York University has catalogued various ideas for restoring to the lives of children a sense
of how they might learn by participating in real experiences.

Here's what he has come up with:

1. In elementary school: We might include a wide range of
manual, mechanical, even technical tasks, such as the use of
typewriters and office machinery, as well as cooking and baking.

2. More direct observation of the world at work, which
would take students out of school more than at present.

3. The early assumption on the part of children of responsibility for tutoring.

4. Participation in the care and governance of school and
community property, including a great range of safety responsibilities.

For junior high school students and up:

1. The wide use of camps all year round, and greater use of
community centers, to extend the concept of school.

2. The development of children's communes or of the
school as an economy; that is, a system in which students grow,
build, and manufacture products, if not for the general market
place then for their own purchase and use.

3. Participation, under supervision, in beautifying the city,
repairing homes and neighborhood facilities.

4. Participation in public safety tasks.

5. Participation in real work, in offices and shops.

6. The development of programs comparable to the Peace
Corps and Vista.

What is on Professor Hamburger's mind is also on the
minds of an increasing number of school people. For them, the
great school question of the 1970s and beyond, is, How can we
use the energy, idealism, and capacities of the young in ways
that will connect them directly to the functioning of their own
society? Nothing but convention defines a school as a building

to which students must be confined for six hours a day. Nothing but convention says that schooling must be circumscribed by "subjects." Nothing but convention says that the activities of school must be academic, i.e., not real.

Can such conventions be replaced? They can, and have been, as you can learn by reading the following article by Patricia Jeys and Janet Schraw who, as seniors in Monument High School, Fruita, Colorado, participated in a real "radical" alternative.

THE STUDENT SPEAKS . . .
PATRICIA K. JEYS
AND JANET A. SCHRAW

Students as Teachers

A SUCCESSFUL new course, "Students as Teachers," developed by a team of students, teachers, and other faculty members has been in operation for one school year (1971–72) at Fruita Monument High School, Fruita, Colorado. The purpose was to involve high school students in the realm of education and educating.

The Fruita community, the students, and faculty members of the school encouraged the formation of SAT for varied reasons. The community felt that students could be an important asset in involvement in community problems, perhaps by providing more meaningful interaction among high school, junior high, and elementary school students. The community members wanted to become more directly involved in the high school's function. This involvement would serve to build the community's confidence in FMHS.

Teachers felt that SAT would offer a challenge to the more capable students (who could help the less capable ones), that individuals learn best while they are teaching, and that these students could contribute valuable ideas and assistance.

Students voiced the opinions that they needed opportunities to learn about education, were interested in careers in education, and had a desire to become involved in creative and productive activities.

To fulfill community, faculty, and student needs the course objectives were formulated. They began with, "The student teacher will increase his knowledge both in teaching and learning which will help him understand student/teacher relationships, problems encountered by teachers, mechanics, lesson plans, physical plant, understanding teacher/administrative/public relations problems; and which teaching methods may be most effective."

It was decided that the student teacher will take upon himself certain responsibilities that were formerly taken care of by the supervising teacher. This would relieve a portion of that supervising teacher's work load, give him more time for individualized instruction, and allow him to become involved in the planning of departmental activities, new courses, and team teaching.

Necessary classroom skills will be developed by the student teacher. The mechanical skills include writing objectives, lesson and curriculum planning; researching and assisting in special projects. He will begin to handle responsibility in the form of supervising activities, organizational responsibilities, and the maintenance of efficient working relationships. The student will learn to communicate through the use of audiovisual media, large- and small-group presentation, and by using different language levels.

The potential student teachers were admitted to SAT by teacher and counselor interview, visited possible work sites early in the course, met the potential supervising teachers, and assigned themselves to one of these for field experience. They attended faculty meetings, departmental meetings, and other extracurricular activities that served to enhance their positions in the classroom.

COURSE CURRICULUM

During this period they participated in one 50-minute class session per week to supplement actual classroom experience. These class sessions were flexible enough to prevent boredom but provided the opportunity to fulfill objectives.

The students were introduced to current books and periodical literature dealing with different methods of teaching, viewed slides and films, and listened to guest lectures. The student teachers examined and evaluated methods of teacher evaluation, current problems, funding of public schools, effectiveness or ineffectiveness of public school systems, current alternative schools, and accountability. The student teachers while investigating teaching as a profession kept a personal folder of tests, evaluation materials, and written assignments.

Small problem-solving sessions involved student teachers in teaching ethics and philosophies of education which included their earlier and later definitions. Role playing was utilized in micro-teaching units, student-teacher confrontation, and for the understanding of the educator's varied roles. In addition to basic classroom teaching techniques (inquiry and diadactic approaches) with emphasis on cognitive, affective, and psychomotor domains, special techniques for helping problem and exceptional children were examined. This examination included information needed in spotting perceptual, behavioral, and learning difficulties in children.

SPECIAL PROBLEMS

Some student teachers took the initiative to create their own special learning projects. Such was the group of five girls who began a cultural living project by living in a migrant worker's home while continuing their regular school activities. At the same time they had a 75-cent-a-day budget and one change of clothes (during a Colorado winter). The girls discovered the meanings of isolation, being hungry, and prejudices. This helped them begin to understand the minority student.

Two students developed a new technique for teaching letters and numbers that was later implemented into the teaching methods of elementary classes. Another team of student teachers created learning materials for first and second graders. They investigated a child's vocabulary, interests, and favorite activities, thus learning what a teacher may encounter when selecting learning materials for the classroom.

Other special projects were reporting on and working in special schools such as street schools; working with exceptional children in local institutions; research of local problems and possible working solutions in developing extracurricular activities for elementary children; forming an elementary instructional library in the high school for the use of student teachers and the planning and performance of an alternative graduation ceremony. There are limitless possibilities and the use of local community resources is encouraged.

EVALUATION OF THE PROGRAM

Numerous tools for the measurement of the effectiveness of both curriculum and student were utilized. Each student was evaluated by his performance on objective measures of factual information, concept classification, participation in knowledge sessions, and the judgment of his supervising teacher. The tools used were quizzes, unit tests, and self-evaluation in an interview with the instructor.

Factors involved in course evaluation include the provisions made of fulfillment of original objectives, opinions expressed by student teachers and their supervising teachers, the students' interest shown beyond class work, interest expressed by the public, the student teacher's success, and flexibility of curriculum.

At the end of the course, one class period was used to seek out students' opinions about SAT's weaknesses. Some opinions were as follows: results were best at an elementary school level; some students experienced peer pressure from high school students; there were some problems arranging transportation for student teachers, too much responsibility placed on student teachers, and a lack of planning time between supervising teacher and the student teacher.

HOW TO SET UP THE PROGRAM

SAT was successful for those involved in FMHS's program. For developing SAT's curriculum, here are some suggested important guidelines. It would be advisable to obtain administrative support. Emphasize that such a course is very easy to organize and materials can be obtained at a low cost. Point out that students who are influenced by the course may begin to inform the community of its school activities and by participating in guest sessions, teachers, students, administrators, and community members may present their viewpoints to both a sympathetic and objective learning audience, thereby gaining insight and understanding of interaction among the groups.

Explore faculty, student, and community interests and check out work areas. Form a coordinating council, perhaps consisting of a media supervisor, two or three teachers (preferably those teaching different subjects), a local school administrator, and interested students.

Have the supervising teachers meet together with the course coordinators for a better understanding of what the course involves and what is expected of the student teacher. Ask them for suggestions as to what course material would enable the student teachers to function in their classrooms. Organize the scheduling, deciding on how often classes will meet, for how long, and how many students will be enrolled in the course.

Select students who have an interest in SAT, will work, are good experimenters, show self-confidence, and perhaps work well with children. This may stimulate needed community support. Write course objectives in a cooperative effort among student, faculty, and coordinating council.

Material resources can be obtained from the following with very little trouble or expense: resource people such as district and private psychologists, special-education personnel, the speech therapist, professional teachers, administrators, consultants, the media supervisor, and lay people; community resources such as local county library, instructional and professional materials library, social agencies, and private libraries; and local institutions such as junior colleges, homes for the mentally retarded, and the public health department. Students should be informed about the numerous available resources.

Begin writing lesson plans, but keep curriculum flexible. Publicize the formulation of courses and obtain public support, possibly with the cooperation of teacher-parent groups, the local chamber of commerce, and community action councils.

Be creative and adjust the course plans to the students and the environment.

5

PRESENT AND
FUTURE ISSUES

ON ALMOST any given day, you are likely to find in the newspaper some story about schools. It may concern racial conflict, violence, a taxpayer's revolt, a study which reveals student deficiencies, a dispute over busing, or a dozen other juicy alternatives. For example, on the day this is being written, the *New York Times* has a front-page story which reports that the governor of New York wants to have a "watchdog" to oversee elementary and secondary education. (Check out "Looney's Law," p. 70.) It is impossible to catalogue all the possible controversies about schools. What we have tried to do in this chapter is to explicate eight core issues, each of which is generating, and will continue to generate, a variety of perplexing controversies. The idea is to give you some background on each, so that you will be able to develop a reasonable point of view about what is happening the next time the hollering starts.

THE EQUALITY ISSUE

During much of this century, the issue of "equality" in school rarely surfaced. Most everyone assumed that equality meant equality of opportunity; and except for the 1954 Supreme Court decision on desegregation (see p. 251), which asserted that separate facilities for white and black were inherently unequal, the matter was not widely discussed. But in recent years, a question has arisen as to whether equality of opportunity is, first of all, a meaningful idea, and second of all, a just idea. The issue has developed along the following lines:

It has been argued that the schools can provide equal opportunity only if the children entering school come from roughly equal social and economic conditions. If, for example, some of them (as is the case) come from deeply deprived situations, then it is meaningless to say that school affords everyone an equal chance at success. The cruel irony of this matter is expressed, by analogy, in Anatole France's remark about the law. The law, he said, is fair in the sense that it forbids both the rich man and the beggar to steal bread. But, of course, the law can be fair only if the rich man and the beggar have equal legal access to bread, which they do not. And so, the argument goes, what is needed is not the concept of equality of opportunity, which is a sham, but the concept of equality of *result*. Translated into a policy for schools, this means that until such time as all children have equal backgrounds, we must try to equalize their situations by whatever reasonable methods we can invent. This might mean, for example, admitting to college students who might not otherwise qualify. Or allowing certain students to pass courses even if they have not met the same standards as other, more privileged students. Or offering special compensatory education programs for the deprived. In this way, it is hoped we might break the cycle of deprivation, failure, further deprivation (because of failure), more failure, more deprivation, and so on.

This mode of social engineering is, of course, based heavily on the assumption that one's environment is the principal, if not the sole, determinant of one's future. But what if that is not true? What if your genetic characteristics play an almost equally important role in determining what you can make of the opportunities afforded you? Then, wouldn't all this social engineering be mostly a waste of time and money? And wouldn't equality of opportunity then be the best anyone could reasonably expect?

These questions, and questions like them, have been recently raised by some psychologists, sociologists, and political scientists who assert that the trend toward equality of result is misguided, naive, and impossible to achieve. For the most part, they base their judgment on studies of the performance of various groups of people on IQ tests. (See intelligence tests, p. 171 and Arthur Jensen, p. 226). Such studies invariably arrive at percentages which claim to state how much of a role genetics plays in achievement, as distinct from the influence of environment. The figure varies from study to study; some say 25 percent, some 35 percent, some more. (William Shockley, the inventor of the transistor, says genetics is four times more important than environment.) How these percentages are arrived at is known only to statisticians and to those who are able to comprehend their dreamy, highly abstract world. But it adds up to this: social engineering has its limitations and genetics is one of them. Even if you could equalize social and economic conditions, you would end up with unequal people and even unequal *groups* of people. In fact, Edward Banfield, a political scientist at Yale, has been quoted as saying that "the situation of most Negroes would not be fundamentally different even if there were no racial prejudice at all." Why? Because he and others believe that the genetic endowments of Negroes, as a group, are less rich than those of other people. Thus, those with "good" genes will always achieve more than those with "bad" genes. Harvard psychologist Richard Herrnstein has said that "in times to come, as technology advances, the tendency to be unemployed may run in the genes of a family as certainly as bad teeth do now." Or presumably the tendency to do badly in school.

And so, the issue of equality begins to come to a head. Is equality of opportunity a reasonable objective of schools? Is equality of result a utopian concept which, in practice, cannot work? Here is our considered opinion:

In the first place, after examining the literature on the subject, we conclude that even when it can be shown statistically that there is a correlation between mean IQ and race (in the same way that there may be a correlation between bad teeth and race), there is simply no realistic way of knowing to what extent such IQ scores are affected by environment. There is, for example, no such thing as a culture-free IQ test. Neither is there a culture-free definition of intelligence. This being the case, we believe it impossible to say how much of the achievement of a group is influenced by its genetic characteristics. You may judge this question for yourself by reading H. J. Eysenck's *The I.Q. Argument* (1971), in which he advances the opposite view. In our view, the social, economic, historical, and psychological environment in which an individual or a group must live is not only of overriding importance to such matters as intelligence and achievement but far too complex to separate from genetic factors.

In the second place, even if it could be determined by surrealistic statistical abstractions that Negroes, for instance, have "bad" genes and Jews "good" genes, we fail to see how this would have any social significance in a just society. There are smart Negroes and dumb Jews, and the schools must, in any case, deal with each student as an individual, not as a category. So the question is this: In cases where children of any race have exhibited a pattern of failure, shall we continue to assume that environmental deprivation is the cause? In this matter we stand with B. F. Skinner, who believes that by changing environments we can change behavior. In other words, yes. If this means establishing procedures in which the school is less punishing to the deprived than are other social institutions, then that is something that must be done. To take any other position, it seems to us, leads in only two possible directions. The first—implied by Herrnstein, Jensen, Banfield, and specifically recommended by Shockley—is genetic engineering as opposed to social engineering. That is, don't let "bad" genes people marry each other. The less said about this, the better. The second is to continue to pretend that school offers everyone an equal chance at success, in which case, patterns of failure will continue unabated. The alternative to these positions, as we have said, is for the school to make a special effort to compensate, in its treatment of "unequal" children, for the dreadful consequences of racism, poverty, and isolation. We must not, however, be too optimistic. Both the Coleman Report (see p. 208) and the Jencks Report (see p. 225) give us good reason to believe that there is only so much the school can do in these matters. But that *something* can be done is fairly clear. For one example, see Edward Carpenter. (p. 207). For another, see Matthew Schwartz and Seymour Fliegel (p. 243).

THE PSYCHOLOGY ISSUE

At the present moment, two forces in psychology are exerting perceptible influences on school thought. One is called behavioristic psychology, and its chief proponent is B. F. Skinner. The other is called humanistic psychology, and to the extent that it draws its inspiration from one man, he is the late Abraham Maslow. As the name suggests, behaviorists are largely concerned with changing the behavior of people, and this, they believe, can be done without regard to feelings or other nonobservable events. Behaviorists do not deny that people have feelings, but they maintain that it is misleading to think of feeling as distinct from behavior. In fact, they come close to saying that we do not cry because we are sad, but, rather, we feel sad because we cry. In other words, in a sense, our behavior *is* our feeling, and we do not need to invoke such terms as *motivation* and *purpose* to describe human behavior, to explain it, or to change it.

B. F. Skinner has observed, in fact, that such disciplines as physics did not begin to develop into productive sciences until physicists stopped attributing purpose to physical objects. For example, early physicists (e.g., Aristotle) believed that the reason objects such as stones fell to earth was that the earth is where they naturally belong; and the reason objects accelerated as they neared the ground was that they were happy to be nearing their proper place. Skinner believes that if we stopped discussing the purpose and feeling of people and concentrated on what they actually do, we could begin to develop a productive science of man.

One obvious reply to this line of thought is that the analogy between inanimate and animate objects simply does not hold up. Rocks don't have feelings, but men do, and to ignore this difference would be fatal to any science of man. Another objection to behaviorism, especially by those who believe it to be a malignant philosophy, is that it is ratomorphic: it proceeds from the proposition that men are very much like rats, and that the behavior of men can be changed in much the same way as can that of rats. The behaviorists respond by saying that there is nothing in their point of view that demeans man, that they are merely trying to discover the principles by which observable change in behavior is governed. Moreover, their record in getting people to change behavior is not without some success. In laboratory experiments, behavioristic principles have been used effectively to manipulate people into certain kinds of changes.

For the most part, humanists do not deny that there are some similarities between men and rats, and that, to a certain extent, common psychological principles govern the behavior of both. But they insist that the differences are far more significant than the similarities. One main difference, they believe, is that the behavior of men is largely governed by the structure of their beliefs—i.e., their feelings, their purposes, their attitudes, their perceptions, etc. There is no great trick, they believe, in forcing people to behave as you wish them to, whether through the use of punishment or through benign manipulations. The idea, they insist, is to allow men the freedom to decide for themselves how they ought to behave. Psychology, they say, should not be the study of how to control people. Skinner says that, inevitably, it must be. For more details about these apparently contradictory philosophies, see the sections in Part II that discuss behaviorism, behavioral objectives, humanism, B. F. Skinner, Abraham Maslow, and Carl Rogers. Here we want to say something about how this conflict affects the schools.

At the theoretical level, most schools favor the humanist philosophy in that school people tend to believe that children have feelings, self-concepts, and modes of perception that govern the way they behave. Curricula are designed, in theory, to change inner states of mind. But at a practical level, most schools operate on behavioristic assumptions—for example, that a child is what he does—and little attempt is made to address what is causing behavior. But the schools' version of behaviorism is distorted. Skinner insists, for example, that aversive responses are not generally effective in changing behavior, but schools use punishment all the time. Skinner insists that reinforcement must be consistent and systematic, but schools reinforce haphazardly, usually on an ad hoc basis. In actuality, then, schools are not committed to any psychological system. Perhaps that is why Charles Silberman called schools "mindless." In the best schools, however, teachers are consciously eclectic rather than mindless. They use behaviorist methods *when they are applicable*, and humanistic assumptions the rest of the time. But most schools are not "the best," and at this juncture behaviorism is on the rise, largely because it appears to be more efficient in effecting change. Dealing with feelings and perceptions is a long, complex, and frequently ambiguous process, and the schools have never been very good at it, anyway. Moreover, the cult of efficiency would seem to demand that it is better to deal with students as if they were rats, rather than people—especially if one thinks of school as an investment on which one expects a decent return.

What does all this mean to you? Well, the issue can be seen in its most concrete form in the way you, and professional school people, make judgments about a school. For example, if you think the most important criterion for evaluating a school is the students' achievement on reading and math tests; if you define learning as meaning, exclusively, temporary behavioral change (feigned or otherwise); if your demand for accountability is linked to "objective" measurements; if you want the school to stress uniformity—then you are in the behaviorist camp. On the other hand, if you want the school to help increase a child's sense of self-esteem; if you think feelings can be changed and that it is worthwhile to help children clarify their values; and if you want less, rather than more, control over students' lives—you are in the humanist camp. Realistically, most people do not confine themselves to a single point of view. Nor should they. But wherever you stand, or want to stand, you ought to be fairly clear about the assumptions underlying your position.

THE INTEGRATION ISSUE

At the core of the present agonies over busing, neighborhood schools, and community control is the issue of integration. In 1954, when the Supreme Court ruled that segregated school systems were illegal, very few people clearly perceived the problem as essentially systemic; that is, that our schools were simply one part of a complex pattern of segregation that extended into every corner of the social, political, and economic life of the country. We know better now. It is unlikely that we can have integrated schools until we come much closer than we presently are to a society in which there is an equitable distribution of wealth and opportunity among all people.

Plainly speaking, the problem is something like this: In New York City, for example, the crime rate in Harlem is almost 300 times as great as the crime rate in Kew Gardens, a white, middle-class neighborhood. This means several things. One is that crime is a much greater affliction to poor blacks and Puerto Ricans than it is to middle-class whites. It also means that the middle class, regardless of race, is prepared to fight off the encroachment of the poor at almost any cost. The fight is not essentially about keeping the poor out of the schools, but about keeping them out of the neighborhood. Of course, much of the middle class has chosen to flee rather than fight: the decay of the inner city has been accompanied by the rapid emergence of a largely segregated white suburban culture. But the poor have now followed the middle class to the suburbs, and the time is rapidly approaching when an interface of the two cultures is inevitable.

The school is caught in the middle. It is an institution designed to foster upward social and economic mobility, and it can still do that when the children entering it come from homes in which there is a history, motivation, and pattern of life geared to support such movement. But the poor today are different from the poor of thirty or forty years ago, because the needs of our economy are different. We have come much closer than we like to think to a situation in which there is a permanent class of poor people. We no longer need the poor as workers, and unemployment and welfare are not temporary aberrations but an integral part of our way of life. The children of the poor understand this, although they cannot always articulate what it is they understand. The consequences, however, are all too clear: children who see little chance of being "lifted" beyond their present station are children to whom school and its various conventions are a meaningless charade. Make no mistake about it: the key to such success as any school has is an attitude of self-denial and an acceptance of delayed gratification on the part of students. If these ingredients are absent, school becomes a mere extension of the street.

Now, what does all this mean? Well, in the first place, it is surely unfair to label as racists those who fear the encroachment of the culture of poverty. We have noticed that those who are quickest to use that label usually live in the suburbs or, if they have stayed in the city, have placed their own children in private schools. This is not a small point. What we are talking about is the attitude of moral superiority that critics very often take toward "the people." We can do with a lot less moralizing about this problem, and some more realistic proposals.

Second, the middle class does not fear integration of schools so much as it fears being overwhelmed by the poor. Integrating a white school, especially in northern cities, has often meant turning it into a mostly segregated, lower-class, black school. The middle class, white *and* black, will continue to flee from this situation unless some arrangement can be made whereby integrated schools can remain integrated. (According to the Coleman Report, a ratio of 60 percent white middle-class to 40 percent black lower class is the mix beyond which the advantages of racial and economic integration begin to get lost.) Constructing new schools on the borderline between white and black neighborhoods will help to some extent, but it may be necessary to control the racial and economic mix in schools rather more carefully than has so far been done. And if it occurs to you that there might be a parallel between the heterogeneity of individual classrooms and the heterogeneity of a whole school, you're right. When a class has a balanced mix of low and high scorers, there are certain advantages to both. But when the mix skews too far to one side or the other, one (or the other) group seems to suffer.

Third, we could all do with a lot less panic than we have seen during the past decade. In many schools, white and black, middle class and poor, function quite well together. Mostly, this has happened where the middle class has not fled to the suburbs at the first sign of a black neighbor. Such situations do not get much publicity, and there is a powerful tendency toward a kind of xenophobia among both whites and blacks. How such fears can be allayed, so that white and black can begin to see each other as people, is a question to which we have no answer.

But the solution, we are sure, will have to come through social, economic, and political reforms. In other words, this is not a problem that the school as an institution can do much about. In a society in which there is a sharp social and economic division among people (e.g., where there is an absence of a viable black middle class), schools will always reflect that division.

THE ACCOUNTABILITY ISSUE

As you may have heard, there is a new form of natural law that has become especially visible under the Nixon administration (although it clearly has antecedents). We call it Looney's Law. Looney's Law states that as any governmental agency becomes more incompetent and inefficient, it also becomes more arrogant. The most common form this arrogance takes is that of demanding that everyone *else* demonstrate that *they* are competent and efficient.

The best manifestation around of Looney's Law is at the Pentagon, to which, several years ago, Robert McNamara introduced certain concepts of industrial efficiency. Specifically, the idea was to have Program Planning Budget Systems (PPBS) put into effect so that everyone would be "accountable." Accountable for what? Well, that gets a little tricky. McNamara faced the following situation: The Pentagon spends billions of dollars each year. For what? For "defense." And so officers at the Pentagon arrange with private industry to produce weapons we can "defend" ourselves with. Well, we should not be surprised by what they did. After all, if you have an addict and you give him some money to spend as he thinks most necessary, what will he buy? Right. And our Pentagon officers are weapons junkies of the first rank. And so, it appears, they were wasting billions of dollars to feed their habit. This is where the PPBS approach comes in. It was intended to give us the "biggest bang for our buck." The idea is to plan a system that defends a budget. The system has a built-in subsystem of accountability: those who run the system have to account to whoever gave them the money in the first place—not only for the money itself, but for the results produced by the expenditure of the money.

Now, there are two interesting points about all of this. The first is that the PPBS approach doesn't work at the Pentagon—after years of it, cost overrides are still 200 percent or 300 percent of the original contract (cf. Lockheed and Grumman). And the second is that the PPBS mentality is now, increasingly, being applied to schools. What this means is that the schooling process is being compared to industrial productivity, or even worse, the development of efficient (?) weapons systems. The idea is most commonly expressed through something called Performance Based Evaluation. PBE is supposed to tell you if you are getting the biggest bang for your buck. It is a system of evaluating teachers *not* on the basis of directly observing their work, but on the basis of the performance of students on standardized tests—from which the teacher's performance is inferred. (The Stull bill, in California, is an example of how an incompetent state legislature applies Looney's Law by enforcing accountability in the schools.)

The assumptions underlying Performance Based Evaluation could give you the bends. In the first place, it assumes that learning is a product whose dimensions can be specified, like the dimensions of a fighter plane. Second, it assumes that standardized tests reveal something worth knowing about children. Third, it assumes that teachers should spend most of their time training students to get higher scores on such tests. Fourth, it assumes that what teachers do is directly reflected in the scores students get on standardized tests. All these assumptions, and several more we have not catalogued, seem to us to be anywhere from unwarranted to exceedingly dangerous.

So, we have this curious manifestation of Looney's Law as applied to the schools: Generally incompetent bureaucracies such as state legislatures, state departments of education, and the U.S. Office of Education assert that the schools are incompetent. They then require the schools to be accountable. This means that teachers and students will be evaluated on the basis of performance or productivity. And performance turns out to mean a score on a questionable test. Moreover, for some curious reason, no doubt deeply imbedded in the logic of Looney's Law, teachers are not permitted to teach their students the answers to the standardized tests—which would be the easiest way for students to get to know what they are. This is considered cheating, although it is a mystery why. Further, teachers are not even allowed, in many cases, to use the methods and materials they feel will give them the best shot at succeeding: in many instances where PBE is in effect, there are mandated procedures by which teachers must operate.

All of this is most regrettable, if for no other reason than that the word "accountability" will suffer irreparable harm. (It already has.) There is no question that schools must be accountable to their constituents. But such accountability cannot be rationally achieved by using an industrial-military metaphor. To assume that the schools are in the business of training children to score well on standardized tests is to mock the schooling process, to reduce it to a single dimension at precisely that moment in time when school requires an imaginative widening of its perspectives. As a parent, you have every right to demand that a school be accountable to you. You have every right to ask why certain things are done or not done. You have every right to demand alternatives, and to seek change. But if the present movement toward a mechanistic and narrow concept of accountability continues, there may be nothing left to interest you at all.

THE TAX ISSUE

The subject of how schools are financed and the equitability of existing arrangements has been brought into the open by two landmark cases: *Serrano* v. *Priest* (in California) and *Rodriguez* v. *San Antonio Independent School District* (in Texas). (*Serrano* is discussed in some detail on p. 260.) In both instances state courts ruled, in effect, that the existing system of financing discriminates against the poor because it makes the quality of a child's education a function of the wealth of his parents and neighbors.

The problem runs something like this: Presently, local schools are funded by a combination of local property taxes and state aid. (Federal funding was not significantly present until the passage of the Elementary and Secondary Education Act in 1965, and is still a relatively minor factor in the total picture.) But property taxes, unlike income taxes, are not progressive. A family living in a $15,000 home is assessed the same *percentage* of the house's value as is the family living in a $150,000 home. Thus, two communities which tax at the same rate can generate vastly different amounts of revenue and will, of course, spend disparate amounts on education. To use the example detailed by New York State's Fleischmann Commission: Two towns ten miles apart—Great Neck and Levittown—tax at the same rate, but, because of the higher value of the homes in Great Neck, Great Neck is able to spend $2,077 per pupil, Levittown only $1,189. It is true that Levittown receives from the state (under an equalizing formula) more than twice the amount per pupil than Great Neck receives. But state aid can never equalize the situation. Great Neck gets $1,684 per pupil from local property tax, Levittown only $410. In order for Levittown to generate the revenue available in Great Neck, it would have to tax its homeowners right out of the county.

The problem is exceedingly complex. To some, the answer

lies in having the state assume the entire burden through state-wide property taxation and then statewide distribution of school funds. But wouldn't this mean the end of local control of schools? And what about the problem of the inequalities of wealth among states? Wouldn't statewide financing discriminate against those who live in poorer states?

Another solution has been put forth by Professor John Coons, who was instrumental in preparing the *Serrano* brief. In Coons's proposal, local communities would retain their power to set the *rates* of property tax, but the state would have the power to guarantee equal financial consequences for equal tax rates. For example, suppose two communities chose to tax property at 4 percent. In Community A, the value of real property per student is $15,000; in Community B it is $30,000. Community A will produce only half the revenue of Community B. At this point, the state would equalize the revenue either by making up the difference itself or by extracting funds from Community B. The proposal is rather more complicated than that, but its major feature is that richer communities support poorer ones (whose interest in education, as judged by tax rates, is equivalent). The trouble, of course, is that such a proposal is political dynamite. It is not hard to imagine a resident of Great Neck saying, "What is Levittown to me or I to it, that I should suffer so?" The state courts have taken the position that *someone, somehow,* has got to pay to correct what has been ruled an unconstitutional practice. However, on March 21, 1973, the U.S. Supreme Court upheld the constitutionality of the Texas school finance system in a 5–4 decision. This means that, for the moment, the financial structure of schools will remain intact. But since the *Seranno* case in California poses somewhat different issues from those of *Rodriguez* (the Texas case), most constitutional lawyers believe that the issue is far from settled. For this reason, we have provided a summary of the issues in the *Serrano* case.

THE SCHOOL INFLUENCE ISSUE

It has been documented a number of times, most notably in *The Imperfect Panacea* (1968), by Henry Perkinson, that the closest thing we have to a national religion is our faith in the public schools. Americans have always turned to their schools in time of crisis to solve all kinds of intractable social, political, economic, psychological—you name it—problems. Are there too many automobile accidents? Let the schools give driver education. Are there too many premarital pregnancies? Let the schools give sex education. How about the drug-abuse problem? Let the schools give drug education. And so on. Thus, it has come as something of a shock that a good deal of the educational scholarship of recent years has concluded, in one form or another, that schools do not now have, nor have they ever had, as much influence on the lives of children as we like to believe. The Coleman Report, the studies of Arthur Jensen, the Jencks Report, and several others have suggested rather forcefully that our faith in the schools is naive.

As we pointed out earlier in the book, we agree with this judgment—up to a point. We think it is a mistake for parents to believe the schools can do things to or for children that the parents themselves are unable to do. For example, parents who cannot communicate to their children the meaning of trust, or the value of knowledge, or even a sense of inner discipline can hardly expect teachers—no matter how committed—to accomplish that for them. There is a certain amount of truth to the idea that a school can do only what the home has already prepared children to do. But there is much more to the matter than this.

To begin with, the schools have historically promised much more than they can deliver. As the Jencks Report has shown, the schools cannot deliver economic success. The Coleman Report indicates that schools cannot even deliver improved cognitive skills. And the schools assuredly cannot deliver freedom from anxiety, or a love of good music or art or literature. Well, what can they do? The best answer we have is that we really do not know. All the studies we have are based on a system of schooling whose conventions, for the most part, have possibly outlived whatever usefulness they may once have had. It is time to address ourselves to two fundamental questions:

1. What can we *reasonably* expect the institution of school to do for our children?

2. What conventions will provide the best chance of achieving these goals?

All answers to these questions must be given as hypotheses, especially in the light of rapid technological developments and changing values. We have already given some answers of our own, and we offer some more in Chapter 8. Here, we want only to stress that the *potential* of the school as a powerful influence on the lives of children is still untapped, unanalyzed, and unknown.

THE REFORM VERSUS REVOLUTION ISSUE

Although we have made several oblique references to this problem throughout the book, it may be instructive to confront it head-on here, especially because in the years ahead it will almost certainly keep coming up. The problem is as follows: There are some fairly serious people who maintain that the schools are a kind of shadow institution, merely reflecting the main outlines of the economic, social, and political structures of society. They believe that while it is possible to make certain cosmetic improvements in school, nothing of substance can really change unless preceded by radical changes in the society itself. Thus, those who try to reform the practices of school are essentially conservatives (although they may appear radical) because they do not address themselves to the root causes of why things are as they are. For instance (so goes the argument), the problems of the ghetto school cannot really be solved by trying to make such schools more pleasant and interesting places for children to be. We have ghetto schools because our economy is structured in such a way that wealth and resources are distributed unequally. Those who get the least are trapped in dreadful, spirit-enervating circumstances and will naturally exhibit the most antisocial tendencies, including a vigorous resistance to any moral lessons their society wishes them to learn. The role of reformers in this situation, whether they acknowledge it or not, is to mollify the anger of the poor by sweetening the superficial trappings of their existence. But this is little more than a domestic pacification program, designed to distract everyone from looking at the real cause of inattention and incorrigibility in ghetto schools, namely, poverty. Do you want to eliminate the ghetto school? Then eliminate the ghetto. But to do that would require a major economic and political upheaval which most people are unwilling to undergo, let alone work for. The true revolutionary is willing to do both.

This line of thinking is by no means restricted to an analysis of the ghetto school. The orthodox radical critic sees every procedure and aim of the school as only a manifestation of some fundamental bias of the culture, and he concludes from this that all attempts at school reform are superficial. Only revolutionary cultural changes can really make a difference. Of the many people who have lately taken this line, Ivan Illich heads the list. But one can also find a half dozen or so young teachers and scholars who have written penetratingly, if not extensively, from a radical perspective: Michael Rossman, Michael Katz, Miriam Wasserman, Alan Graubard, Arthur Pearl, Joel Spring, and others. Moreover, some of them have done more than write on the subject; they have tried to involve themselves directly in the political process so that they might actually affect the forces that shape the school. For example, Arthur Pearl, who is a professor of education at the University of California in Santa Cruz, once ran for governor of Oregon. He lost. Which is not surprising and which also brings us to the first answer one may give to the challenging questions posed by the radicals. It is this: while much of what radical historians and analysts say is probably true, there is very little immediate prospect for a radical change in the structure of American institutions. Thus, if one is serious about helping to improve the lives of children, one must work at those levels where improvement can actually occur in the foreseeable future. In a way, the question is, What does one do about the schools until the revolution comes? The radical critic says: "Nothing. Spend all your time bringing the revolution about." The reformer says: "Spend your time improving schools as much as possible. There are real kids in the schools now who can benefit in significant ways from efforts at reform." But the reformer has more to say than that. In the first place, he maintains that the radical argument, when carried to its logical conclusions, amounts to little more than a copout. The argument says in effect that since nothing of significance can be done about the schools until the new order arrives, why try to do anything? The reformer's reply is that, obviously, schools will always reflect the inequities of society, but this fact does not preclude the possibility that a child's life in school can be made richer and more agreeable. If this be pacification, so be it. But it is worth noting that parents at all levels of our society, especially those parents whose children suffer the most from inequities, deeply desire such pacification. Radical critics may be willing to wait until there are no poor people, but they do not speak for the poor, who by and large want as much improvement as they can get in the present circumstances. Moreover, radical critics do not speak for any people, poor or no, who are dissatisfied with the ways in which their children are presently dealt with in school. In fact, the radical critic turns out to be the enemy of all those who seek relief, improvement, or enrichment for their children because the logic of his own abstractions frequently prevents him from engaging in the hard, sometimes tedious, always frustrating job of making real (as against hypothetical) change.

In the second place, much of what the radical critic has to say is based on the assumption that most or all of the cultural biases of America are mistaken, misguided, or destructive; and, it follows from this, that almost everything about school is equally bad. For example, much has been written on how schools promote attitudes of delayed gratification, respect for authority, respect for property, sexual inhibition, even good manners and soft voices. It is usually charged that such teachings are antihumanistic (or antibiological or antidemocratic), and that they are practically impossible to dislodge under the present system (because they form part of the hidden curriculum). But it is far from settled that such teachings are, in fact, mistaken or misguided in any sense. It is true that some radical critics have been liberated from such attitudes and behaviors, but when they offer themselves as illustrations of the benefits that will accrue from such freedom, their argument is almost always irreparably damaged. In any case, the reformer rejects the idea that a revolution (particularly of the kind advanced by some radical critics) is required to save America from moral decadence, economic slavery, political depravity, or whatever. The reformer's position is this: In order to do my work, I assume that America is a culture of great vitality, worthwhile tradition, reasonably sane institutions, and morally acceptable prospects. Within that framework, I can proceed to holler and otherwise criticize what appear to be wrongheaded procedures, especially when such procedures are amenable to change. I need not wait upon a revolution. Indeed, I need not even desire one. I want only the satisfaction of knowing that for some children somewhere my efforts made a difference.

To sum up the issue (our own position must be fairly clear by now), we might say that the radical tends to be a utopian who like Mr. Nixon forgoes the "easy solution" (i.e., the practical and sensible) and speaks to and for posterity. The reformer tends to be a pragmatist who will take what he can get (if it's better) and speaks for and to people.

THE SEXISM PROBLEM

Before Betty Friedan, Germaine Greer, Kate Millet, and the rest, the problem of sexism in the schools was, believe it or not, the subject of considerable discussion. But most of it was concerned with the unreasonable ways in which *boys* were treated. For example, the best work on the subject was done by Patricia Cayo Sexton, who demonstrated how boys got caught in a kind of Catch-22 situation. On the one hand, the culture expected (demanded?) that boys be aggressive, spontaneous, physical, exuberant, etc. But on the other hand, when boys were in school, they were expected to be passive, reflective, intellectual, and so on. As a consequence, those boys who could not manage the school's expectations were considered troublemakers—arrogant, intractable, uncooperative. And those boys who could—especially if they also showed an interest in poetry or art—were considered effeminate. The evidence offered to support the supposition that boys were badly damaged by this contradiction included some astonishing statistics—for instance, the fact that boys have reading difficulties at a rate five times that of girls.

It was assumed, of course, that girls had something of a picnic in school, largely because there was some consistency between the culture's expectations of girls and the school's expectations of them. But now that everyone's consciousness has been raised, we can see fairly clearly where the problem is in that view: consistent or not, the expectations of girls and the concomitant constraints imposed on them are simply unreasonable in today's world and serve to cut off millions of young women from taking advantage of exciting possibilities in life. There are many well-documented cases, for example, of girls with extraordinary intellectual gifts being encouraged to settle for less than boys with less ability.

Happily, though, this is one problem that can be solved and is being solved in the schools, without an upheaval. An increasing number of school people (many of them, after all, women) are reexamining textbooks, counseling procedures, curriculums, subject matter, and everything else they can think of in an effort to eliminate as much sex bias as possible. The boys, of course, will benefit from this almost as much as the girls. Ten years ago, it was extremely rare for a boy to take a course in cooking. Within five years, it will probably be commonplace.

But at the present time, the revolution is far from finished. There are still pockets of resistance, or more accurately, indifference, and the pressure will have to continue for many years to come. Of course, it is apparent that the pressure is in no danger of drying up at its source. There lurks ahead, however, at least one interesting question that will have to be answered—in the school and elsewhere. It is this: Assuming that beyond obvious biological differences, there might also be real psychological differences between boys and girls, how should these differences be dealt with? The question is undoubtedly premature; before turning to it, most of our institutions have much work to do to correct obviously wrongheaded biases against females. But it is there, nonetheless, and eventually the schools will have to confront it.

6

THE READING PROBLEM

IN THE previous chapter we tried to describe a series of school issues that must be resolved in the years ahead. Here we want to discuss one more—this time, in some detail—because it has been given so much attention by almost everyone who thinks about schools. We are talking about the reading problem. And what we have to say about it may entail a bit of hollering, largely because it seems to us that so many people have an unbalanced perspective on this issue. We'll try to keep the hollering soft, but we feel it necessary to present a definite point of view.

We start with this observation: In America today, illiteracy comes very close to being a psychiatric diagnosis. It is not uncommon for children of seven, eight, or nine who have not learned to read to be labeled emotionally disturbed. Among some people, illiteracy is even assumed to reflect a mental deficiency. At the very least, illiteracy is thought to be a kind of social disease, something like syphilis—especially endemic among the poor, and vaguely immoral. It would be tedious to document the prevalence of these attitudes. There are very few prominent educators who have not said *something* like, "Reading is our most important problem."

Now this is quite odd. Why, at this juncture in communications history, are the schools making such an all-out assault on illiteracy? After all, more than half a millennium has passed since the invention of the printing press with movable type. And more than half a century has passed since electronic media broke the monopoly of print and began to remake the world in their own images. Even if Marshall McLuhan did not exist, the electric plug would. And one need not be a media determinist, apostle, or anything else to point to the obvious fact that print has less importance in the conduct of our lives today than it has ever had. Why, then, the frantic pursuit of literacy?

To begin with, when one takes a close look at what our schools are actually doing, it turns out that they are not very interested in *literacy* at all. What they care about is teaching *reading*. Literacy is to reading what mathematics is to counting. Learning to name numbers does not ensure that one will understand their operations; nor does it imply that one can use those operations effectively. Learning to correlate spoken words with the symbols that represent them on a page does not ensure that one will understand the operations of the spoken or written language. Both mathematics and language are systems of propositions about the world and the relationships within it. *Literacy* means a high degree of competence in analyzing linguistic propositions, evaluating them and correlating them with reality. Anything less than that is *letteracy*, not literacy. By this definition, one may be able to read and still be hopelessly illiterate. And the opposite is also true: many people have developed sophisticated abilities in evaluating the uses of language who have not learned how to read.

If schools were teaching *literacy*, they would in effect be educating students in the rational uses of language. By teaching only letteracy, they may, in fact, be rendering their students more susceptible to the irrational uses of it. Perhaps that is why school boards sometimes get so upset about "dangerous" books showing up in school libraries or classrooms. Letterate people believe that "if it is in the book, it is true." Literate people do not. That is perhaps also why school boards and administrators are fearful of permitting students to *hear* "controversial" speakers. Letterate people believe something is true because it has been said. Literate people do not—no matter how elevated the speaker or his platform.

The question, then, is not, *Why do the schools want literacy?* but, *Why do they want readers?* The most obvious answer is that one must read well to be successful in school. While this is undoubtedly true, it is not so much a rationale for teaching reading as it is a description of the rules of the school game. In effect, it says we must teach reading because we require reading. But why require reading? Because one cannot learn unless one can read? Not true. The most significant learning human beings ever do occurs in the first six years of their lives—*before* they know how to read. Such learning is by no means confined to the development of motor skills, but includes the most sophisticated abstracting and conceptualizing processes. Is reading required because children find it the most efficient means of acquiring knowledge? Somewhere between 10 percent and 30 percent of all children with normal and above average IQs have difficulties in reading, and the percentage increases substantially among children with IQs below 90. Thus, for at least half of our children, reading is an *inefficient* means of acquiring knowledge. Moreover, it is entirely possible, through the use of electronic media, to minimize reading skill as a prerequisite to the acquisition of knowledge. At present, there already exist several bookless curricula which use tape recorders, records, film, videotape, lectures, drama, music, film projectors, photographs, group discussions, and the like for the dissemination of knowledge.

In short, "cumulative academic retardation," which is what many school people contend happens to poor readers, is not a necessary result of reading disability. It is the result of the *assumption* that people who read badly cannot learn well. And that assumption is false.

But of course there are other reasons offered by those who run the schools, and those who pay for them, for making reading skill the backbone of the schooling process. Foremost among these is the economic argument—which, incidentally, is at least 3,500 years old. An Egyptian document dating from the New Kingdom admonishes the young to master reading and writing:

> Put writing in your heart, that you may protect yourself from hard labor of any kind, and be a magistrate of high repute. The scribe is released from manual tasks; it is he who commands. . . . Do you not hold the scribe's pallette? That is what makes the difference between you and the man who handles an oar.

These words have a contemporary ring because it is still commonly assumed that unless one can read well he is denied access to gainful and interesting employment as an adult. There are two important questions about that assumption. One is, How well does one have to read to make a successful entry into our economic system? There are probably very few jobs, even professions, whose performance requires reading skill much beyond what is called "a seventh-grade level." And those few jobs that *do* would scarcely justify the massive, compulsory, and unrelenting reading programs that are inflicted on all children. The second question is, Even if twelfth-grade reading levels were required for many jobs and professions, do we want all our schools to be devoted to vocational preparation? Should one's childhood education be largely concerned with one's future employment? After all, one could argue that the teaching of reading is no more important than the teaching of skill in question asking or the exploration of the emotional problems of children or the development of competence in the uses of electronic media of communication. Such goals as these have a bearing on one's life, not just his livelihood. Moreover, they are not without value in the marketplace. There is, after all, growing evidence that even industry, at its higher levels, is not so much interested in good readers as it is in people who are effective problem solvers, who have a high degree of sensitivity to others and understanding of themselves, and who have a perspective on the impact of new technology on business and culture.

Other arguments almost as old as the economic one are that the basic purpose of reading instruction is to open the student's mind to the wonder and riches of the written word; to give him access to great fiction and poetry; to permit him to function as an informed citizen; to have him experience the sheer pleasure of reading. Now, these are certainly worthy goals of education, but they are functions of *literacy*, not reading skill. There are no reading tests that are designed to discover whether someone enjoys the pleasures of reading or has had his horizons widened as a result of it. For the most part, the tests used to evaluate a student's ability are concerned with what is called comprehension, and nothing more. (In fact, considerably less.) And as for good citizenship, to the extent that this phrase implies tolerance, rationality, and humanity, there is no evidence whatsoever that the better you are as a reader, the better you are as a citizen. Dr. Joseph Goebbels, minister of propaganda of the Third Reich, received his Ph.D. in Romantic Drama from the University of Heidelberg at the age of twenty-four. He and all the others convicted of crimes against humanity would have passed the Metropolitan Reading Tests with flying colors.

Because the obvious reasons for the preoccupation with teaching reading are based on so many questionable assumptions, one begins to suspect more sinister motivations. For instance, it is surely true that in a highly complex society one cannot be governed unless he can read forms, regulations, catalogues, road signs, and the like. Thus, some minimal reading skill is necessary if you are to be a good citizen. But good citizen, here, means one who can follow the instructions of those who govern him. It also means one who believes in the myths and superstitions of his society. Since these are presented most systematically in the schools' basic books, one needs a certain minimal reading skill to learn what they are or to have them reinforced. If our children do not read, how will they know what they will find in their textbooks: that our flag is sacred, our history noble, our government representative, our laws just, our institutions viable? A reading public is a responsible republic—by which our schools mean it believes most or all of these superstitions.

Moreover, there *is* an economic argument to be made for reading skill, but not quite the one usually advanced. Industry does prefer those who have successfully completed school to those who have not. This preference derives not so much from the actual requirements of jobs, but from the evidence a diploma provides of one's obedience to the rules of a system. Your learning to read, whether you want to or not, tells industry you can be relied upon to behave yourself. In this context, it is worth noting that the Egyptian scribe and the Egyptian oarsman were *both* slaves.

But surely these conjectures are entirely too Manichaean. The true reasons for our reading mania may not be so rational or intelligent. For one, the stewards of our schools are people for whom reading and writing have been their most important means of expressing intellectual interest and competence. They are apt to be relatively incompetent in the uses of film, videotape, audiotape, LP records, even photography—and therefore place no great value on literacy in these media. In this respect many of our teachers are very much like those students for whom the printed word is neither an exciting nor an efficient medium: both refuse to learn the unfamiliar code. The difference, of course, is that the students have no power to assign their teachers to remedial film-viewing classes.

It is also possible that, to those who run our schools and those who pay for them, skill in reading and writing represent a firm connection with what they construe to be a viable tradition. The generation gap is, to a considerable extent, a product of the conflict between an old technology and new technologies, between an older learning style and a newer one. As we all acknowledge by now, things are changing more rapidly than human beings can adapt to them. In the process of attempting to stabilize themselves, people transform necessary activities of the past into rituals whose repetition provides a comforting illusion of permanence. The practice remains, even though the context which gave it its meaning is gone. Like the colonial administrator who dressed for dinner and high tea in the jungles of Africa, our older generation holds on to its equation of reading and education, for just that reason: to hold on. One has the feeling that even if there were no children in school, the teaching of reading would persist.

This is another way of saying that in the midst of unprecedented technological and social change, the schools have committed themselves to conserving the past. In a curious way, this commitment represents the abandonment of a traditional responsibility of educational systems—ironically, of that very responsibility which led to the teaching of reading in the first place: to prepare the young to cope with the dominant media of communication in their society. By abandoning that responsibility, the schools have implicated us all in a hazardous gamble with the future. At stake are not just the skills, but maybe the lives, of a generation of children. Here are some plain facts and projections that might help you to figure the odds:

✠ Electronic media now play a more important role than print media as a source of aesthetic satisfaction to the young. Youth still read, but not as much as they attend to LP records, transistor radios, films, and television. (By the time one graduates from high school, he has spent more time in front of a television set than he has in school.)

✠ Electronic media now carry the major burden for the dissemination of information in the culture. And it will soon be true, if it is not already, that more information is stored electronically than in all the books ever printed.

✦ The major political influences in our society, especially on the young, are exerted through electronic media. Bear in mind that the gurus of the peace movement—Bob Dylan, Pete Seeger, Joan Baez, Phil Ochs, for instance—are known to their constituency mostly as voices on LP records. Bear in mind, too, that probably not one American in ten thousand has ever *read* anything that Richard Nixon wrote.

✦ As youth becomes more oriented toward electronic media and away from print, the reading problem will become more acute. By equating intellectual competence with reading ability, we condemn *by definition* perhaps half a generation to failure. Especially males. At present, five times as many boys as girls have reading difficulty.

✦ Almost all studies show that remedial reading programs, when they have any effect at all, have only short-term positive effects.

In the face of such odds, many schools are betting that reading skill is the basic survival mechanism for the future—and that they can teach it. They may be right. But there are certain conditions to this bet that should be made clear. For one, the schools are backing their bet by diverting their resources from other possibilities—education for emotional health, education in electronic communications, education in problem solving, even education for literacy itself. Thus the risk is doubly high. We may find, sooner than we think, that reading abilities—at the levels the schools shoot for—will be irrelevant. But even if they are not, in the process of shooting for them we may produce a generation of readers who are otherwise disabled. Second, if the schools are wrong, the students lose, not those who made the bet. And finally, the gamble is not even necessary. Every curriculum is based on predictions of what students will need to know about and do. It stands to reason that, the more varied the predictions—the more avenues there are to success—the greater the number of winners. It goes against reason to make the game so loaded that a substantial number of students are guaranteed to lose. There are at present over 1 million dropouts; even "bright" students drop out at a rate of 100,000 a year—many of them shot down by the reading bullet in the curriculum gun. At that rate alone, reading roulette is costly enough. If we put a reading bullet in almost every chamber, how many can win?

The solution to this problem is, conceptually, not very difficult. To begin with, we are not suggesting that reading skill is unimportant. We probably ought to repeat the last sentence to avoid misunderstanding: we are not saying that reading skill is unimportant. What we are saying is as follows:

1. It is a mistake to *equate* reading skill with intelligence (which is now the case in many schools).

2. Schools must elevate the value they presently place on nonprint communication skills so as to give all students a fair chance to learn and to express what they know through the media they most favor.

3. Schools should undertake a realistic analysis of exactly what society's requirements are in relation to reading skill.

4. Schools should start questioning their obedience to the concept of reading grade levels. Without such a concept, it is quite possible that more students would learn to read competently than presently do, although they would do it in their own time at their own rate.

In other words, we are saying that the schools, to a large extent, have *created* the reading problem by making reading skill (almost) the only key to a successful experience in school. Within a year, we could create a similar problem with almost any subject in the curriculum if the schools insisted that a particular form of behavior was exclusively preeminent. For example, suppose schools demanded that every student had to learn to speak one foreign language competently before being allowed to graduate. And suppose once the foreign language were introduced in the first grade, all subjects from then on were taught in that language. And suppose all students were tested at every grade level to see what progress they were making. And suppose that a student's progress being insufficient, the student was judged to be dumb. And suppose that such a student was then assigned to a remedial foreign language course. And suppose the *New York Times* published the foreign-language-speaking grade levels achieved in all schools. What would be the effect of all of this? Obviously, we would discover we have a "foreign language problem." We would be shocked at the number of failures we had. We would condemn our schools, and demand they redouble their efforts. And the schools would comply. And the situation would grow worse.

Now, one answer to all this supposing is that, yes, we might create a problem in foreign-language achievement, or for that matter, in physical education (e.g., every student must be able to do fifty push-ups in order to graduate) by singleminded insistence on achievement in that area, but, after all, the plain fact is that reading skill just happens to be the most important intellectual behavior any one needs. Thus, it is necessary to do this with reading. We are saying, of course, that it is not; that many behaviors can reasonably be judged to be as important, or more, than reading; and that a more balanced view of the matter might even help more children to learn to read well. Moreover, we do not maintain that our view is in any way radical. As we said a moment ago, the problem is not difficult at a conceptual level; that is, many people would agree that it is desirable to offer students not one key, but several, to success in school. But the problem is difficult at a practical level. At this writing, the schools seem caught in an almost neurotic spasm in regard to reading. There is very little parents, or even teachers, can do to protect individual children who get low scores on reading tests from being victimized by the situation. Except to be persistent in challenging it. Of course, if you are a parent whose child is successfully handling reading, you may have no strong motivation to do so. But if you are concerned about children who are having a bad time of it (either because it is your own child or because you care about children other than your own), here are some questions you might raise at PTA meetings, faculty meetings (if you're a teacher), and other forums for the discussion of school matters:

1. Why does a child have to begin reading instruction in the first (or second) grade?

2. How do we know this is desirable for all children? Or even for some? Why not start in the third or fourth grade?

3. Has serious consideration been given to harmful side effects of reading instruction? For example, does it interfere, as Jean Piaget suggests, with the development of cognitive skills?

4. What communication skills are being neglected in deference to reading?

5. Why doesn't the school give tests in listening? Does anyone know how well the children listen? Or talk?

6. Why doesn't the school give tests in the question-asking ability of students? Isn't that considered important?

7. Why aren't children grouped according to their ability as talkers, or artists, or musicians, or actors? Doesn't it hurt children who are good artists to be in the same class with children who are bad artists? If not, why group according to reading ability?

8. Why doesn't the school have a program in visual literacy?

9. Has the school made a careful analysis of the standardized reading tests it uses?

10. What are the reading scores of the teachers and administrators in the school?

11. What is their record in teaching children to read?

12. Does the school make any useful distinction between letteracy and literacy?

13. What does the school do to promote critical thinking?

7

HOW TO EVALUATE A SCHOOL AND WHAT TO DO ABOUT A BAD ONE

THE PURPOSE of this chapter is to give you help, if you need any, in making judgments about a school, and in doing something constructive about a deficient school. Let's start with evaluation. In Chapter 3 we tried to supply a definition of a good school. But we were careful to say that our definition was biased. It represents the thinking, as we understand it, of many school critics, as well as informed teachers and administrators. By specifying that bias, we were trying to say that whether or not a school is good depends on who is looking at it. After all, some people think school critics and progressive teachers are subversive, misguided, ill informed, crazy (choose one or more). And so the process of evaluating a school must begin with your making some judgments about yourself. We see things not as *they* are, but as *we* are.

Below, in parallel columns, are two sets of assumptions about learning and schooling. The set on the left side of the page is a series of beliefs that have been, and still are, the basis of most existing school programs. We might call these beliefs a traditionalist's creed (although we have not tried to be exhaustive). The set on the right side of the page represents an alternative point of view. That is, many popular and influential critics hold these beliefs to be true, or mostly true, or certainly plausible. We might call these beliefs a progressive's creed (again, by no means an exhaustive list).

Check yourself out. The point is not to find out if you are a traditionalist or a progressive. Such labels needn't be very important. The idea is to help you sharpen your consciousness of your own assumptions. In this way, you become prepared to evaluate a school. Of course, each statement is an oversimplification and, unless you are drowsy, you will probably react by saying "Yes, but . . ." or "No, but . . ." to each one. Fair enough. But when you are done assessing all of them, you should have a clearer sense than before of your own position.

ASSUMPTIONS

For someone to learn something properly, he must be taught it in a systematic way. The function of a good teacher is to organize what is to be learned in such a way that it *can* be learned—thoroughly and efficiently. Learning is too important to be done haphazardly.

Teaching can be a serious obstacle to learning. All significant learning is self-appropriated—a do-it-yourself job. The less teaching, the more learning.

If a student is interested in what he is supposed to learn, everyone is better off. But interest is not a prerequisite to learning. There are many things that must be learned whether the student wants to or not. Life's demands do not always await student interest.

For someone to learn something, he must be aware of and interested in solving some problem or answering some need; he will then organize his own learning experiences in his own way. Enforced, teacher-dictated learning results in bitterness and alienation.

Since efficient learning must follow an orderly and logical line, it is necessary to divide what is to be learned into discrete subjects, each with a specific and stable content.

The learning process, at its best, rarely follows a logical and sequential pattern. It is spasmodic, random, integrated, simultaneous, and spontaneous —the way it is with children before they go to school.

While it cannot be denied that children vary in interest and ability, the school must try to get all children to learn roughly the same things in roughly the same way. Without such an effort, you cannot have a coherent school program.

Why do we need a coherent school program? Each child should be allowed to investigate the problems that most interest him, *when* they interest him, through a learning medium he feels most comfortable with. A coherent school program may be necessary for bureaucratic efficiency, but it has nothing to do with individual growth.

Learning takes place best when the student is in a specially designed environment, generally one that is isolated from the community in a centrally located building.

Learning takes place most effectively when the learner is immersed in the environment where the problem is that he's investigating. A school is an artificial setting which often stifles real inquiry and rarely permits spontaneous and dynamic experience.

Learning takes place primarily when a classroom is quiet and orderly, and when the learner

Learning takes place whenever and wherever the learner is involved in solving a problem.

is sitting still, either reading or listening to the teacher.

How he is sitting, or *if* he is sitting, has nothing to do with it. A quiet classroom may be the last place any significant learning can occur.

Children learn best from adults, especially from adults who are not connected with the child's social life but who are experts in specific subjects.

Children learn best from their peers, and from those adults with whom they have a strong, positive, emotional relationship. They also learn from anyone they think is experienced with some problem they are trying to solve.

Competition and anxiety have a positive aspect. They are among the best spurs to learning. Moreover, competitive school environments prepare students for the realities of life.

Cooperation and relaxation are among the best spurs to learning. Real life would be vastly more agreeable if children were encouraged to learn in non-threatening situations.

The experience and expression of emotions interfere with the learning process. There is a place for everything. School is for learning. Teachers have no business practicing psychotherapy.

Feeling cannot be separated from thinking. Any attempt to divorce one from the other ends in disaster. A child's feelings are as much a part of the school's business as anything else.

The best way to determine whether learning has taken place is by giving a paper-and-pencil test which requires the student to answer questions the teacher has posed.

The best way to determine whether the student is learning is to observe how he deals with real problems. If this means students cannot be graded by A, B, Cs, so much the better.

No one can deny that we are living in times of great change, but the best way to prepare for this is to teach the basics thoroughly, and to reaffirm time-tested truths and values. With everything else in a state of flux, school should communicate stability, order, and sound tradition.

We are in a changing culture. The traditional schooling process is designed for a stable culture. We need new conceptions of what the basics are, and we must discover new truths and values. School should be a testing ground for new life and learning styles. If it is not, then it will become increasingly irrelevant until it loses all credibility and influence.

School has its defects and limitations, but there is nothing wrong with it that *careful*, systematic reform cannot fix.

School is dreadful for most children. Tinkering with the curriculum won't help much. We need to try radical alternatives now. Sure, there will be mistakes, but timidity will get us nowhere.

Teaching is a profession, which means that it requires extensive and rigorous training. While it is probably true that teachers are not as "professional" as doctors and lawyers, that is the best reason why amateurs and dilettantes should be prevented from entering teaching.

With a little practical experience, almost any sensitive, alert person who likes children can become a good teacher. Extensive training (four years in college) is unnecessary. A good mind, a good heart, commitment, and a willingness to learn are the basic ingredients.

If you have read our book this far, you will not be surprised to know that many (not all) of the statements comprising the progressive's creed make sense to us—that is, if one is allowed to make suitable elaborations and explanations. There are some statements in the traditionalist's creed that also make sense. In fact, in a few instances, we can accept two seemingly contradictory statements because each could be true in a particular set of circumstances. The schooling process is too complex to be judged by a single set of unified assumptions. At least that is our opinion. It is not necessary that you share it. It is only necessary that you are aware of what your own biases are.

It is also necessary, in evaluating a school, that you have some mechanism to make visible the conventions of the school you are looking at. Below, we have tried to provide such a mechanism. It is in the form of a list of slightly more than one hundred questions, each designed to evoke some descriptive and then some evaluative statement about a school. Of course, the questions themselves are not entirely unbiased. But we have tried to make them useful to people of varying points of view. Their purpose is to help you *see*.

QUESTIONS

Where is the school located? Is it easy to reach? Is it isolated from the center of community activities? Do its surroundings have any aesthetic merit? Are there locked doors, fences, No Trespassing signs? Bars on the windows? Does the building itself have any interesting architectural features? If so, is there any discernible purpose to them? What purposes in general does the architectural structure seem designed to serve? Control over students? Safety of students? Openness and freedom?

What kinds of special facilities does the school have? Are there rooms designed for specific purposes? Is there a music room, or an art room, or a theater? If not, why is there a gymnasium? What kinds of equipment does the school provide for aesthetic education? for learning about new media? What does

the interior of the school most remind you of? an office building? a factory? a prison? a hospital? a home?

How are the classrooms arranged? What lines of communication does the seating arrangement suggest? What objects
decorate the walls? Is there any evidence of student creativity or
even effort? Artwork? Photography? Sculpture? If there are mottoes, flags, trophies, etc. in evidence, what do they tell you
about the kinds of people and values the school honors?

Does the school have a dress code? If so, what is its real
purpose? Who designed it? In what sense is it necessary? Are
students required to line up? For what purposes? Are they required to carry hall passes or bathroom passes when they leave
their classrooms? Who makes the rules in the school? Are teachers consulted? parents? students?

What kinds of rites and rituals are performed at regular
intervals within the school? What cultural values do they reflect? To what extent do these values reflect your own?

What kinds of models of adult behavior does the school
provide? How do the teachers dress? behave? speak? How would
you characterize their personalities? Who are the adults who
have been invited to speak at school assemblies and club meetings? What do they do for a living? What points of view do
they represent? Who are the people pictured in the halls and
named on plaques in the school? For what reasons are they
honored?

Are some students taught things that others are not? How
are the students organized for instruction? If they are grouped,
what is the basis of the grouping? Does the grouping promote
homogeneity or diversity? What cultural assumptions underlie
the basis of the grouping? In fact, is there economic, social, or
cultural segregation?

Who or what poses most of the questions in the classroom?
The teacher? the textbook? the students? Do the students raise
substantive questions at all? In what circumstances? Who decides what issues will be discussed? Who decides what books

should be read, what projects undertaken? Who decides what is a "serious" comment?

Once a question is raised, who is responsible for finding answers? Are students usually urged to accept one right answer, or to consider a number of possible answers? Who or what is recognized as a source of authority for answers?

Who does most of the talking in the classroom? Who needs permission to talk? from whom? To what extent are students prodded to question their own statements, attitudes, beliefs? Do students address most of their statements and questions in class to the teacher or to one another? Do students listen as attentively to their classmates as to the teacher? If not, why?

Are students encouraged to be accepting or critical of the views expressed in their textbooks? of the views expressed by teachers? expressed by classmates? Are there particular sources of authority which students are *not* encouraged to question?

What attitudes toward authority is the school training students to accept? What attitudes toward obedience? What attitudes toward toleration? What attitudes toward criticism?

What kinds of information do the students spend most of their time studying? For what purpose? What institutions in the culture most benefit from this situation?

What kinds of activities do the students spend most of their time performing? What habits or skills do these activities develop or reinforce? What assumptions about learning underlie the encouragement of these activities? What relationship is there between school activities and what's happening—or will happen—in the world?

Do the students ever leave the school as part of a learning activity? If so, what do they do? To what extent, if any, is the community involved in student activities?

Is there a parents' room in the school? If you don't know what a parents' room is, why hasn't the principal discussed it? How are parent dissatisfactions dealt with? In what ways do teachers indicate their sense of accountability to parents? to students? Can you *do* anything to improve the school? If you could, is there a way for you to get "plugged in"? Do you *want* to do anything?

If all the questions above are too unwieldy for you to use—if you need a simpler instrument—then try this. Next time you visit a school, ask yourself these questions:

What are the RULES operating here?
    (In what sense are they good or bad for children?)
What are the ROLES students are expected to play?
    (Do they promote independence, self-discipline, creativity?)
What are the RIGHTS granted to students?
    (Do they protect a student's dignity and sense of well-being?
    And do they protect your sense of dignity and well-being?)
What are the RESTRICTIONS imposed?
    (Are they reasonable? Who is best served by them?)
        and finally,
What are the possibilities of meaningful CHANGE in this school?

Of course, if you think you share our biases about school and learning, then you may also find it useful to use, as a basis for making your judgments, the definition of a good school we supplied in Chapter 3. That definition consists of thirty-five statements concerning the conventions of the schooling process. Here is a simplified version, in the form of questions, of that model:

Are the school's time sequences related to the reality of student activities?
Are children allowed to learn at different rates?
Are children allowed to structure their own time?
Are rational or empirically based reasons advanced for what the children are asked to do?
Are children allowed to structure their own activities?

Are the activities related to the psychologies of learners?
Are most of the activities *student* oriented?
Do students get a chance to use the resources of the community?
Are students of wide cultural diversity brought together?
Is problem solving encouraged?
Are involvement and independence encouraged?
Is the application of knowledge valued?
Is there a concern for a wide variety of communication skills?
Are "new" subjects taught?
Is there an interest in self-knowledge?
Are most of the responses to students positive?
Is the evaluation system individualized?
Is there a respect for a wide spectrum of abilities?
Does the school make clear what it wants its students to learn?
Is testing individualized?
Are there constructive procedures for evaluating teachers?
Are students given responsibility for supervising themselves?
Is the school sufficiently small to permit humane interaction?
Are nonprofessional teachers brought into contact with children?
Do students play a role in determining school policies?
Is competitiveness played down?
Are there nonemergency procedures through which parents can
     express grievances?
Are there alternative programs offered?
Is the school accountable to parents?
Is there a concern for the future?

You may have noticed that our numerous questions have not included several of the most important ones that many parents tend to ask when evaluating a school: Will my child be physically safe? Are there too many nonwhites in the school? (asked by a white). Are there too many whites in the school? (asked by a nonwhite). And, Will my child be bused into some "alien" neighborhood? We add those questions now, with the following comments:

1. *Will my child be physically safe?* Naturally, if there is any way to avoid it (for many poor people, there is no way), a sane parent will not send a child to a school that cannot assure his or her safety, including reasonable protection against drug pushers. In fact, most schools *can* give such assurance, although in large cities like New York and Detroit, many schools (not all) have daily instances of violence. Moreover, a 1972 report of the drug situation in New York City high schools asserted that half the students had easy access to drugs. But it is also true that there is more than a little exaggeration about the extent of both drugs and violence in school, and a wise parent will check the situation out personally. How? First, spend a couple of days hanging around the school. Note who comes and goes. Note also whether doors are kept open or shut. If the school doors are kept open, this could mean there is no danger. It could also mean that there is danger, but that the administration is careless. Note the extent of police presence, and be sure to pay attention to the attitudes of the students as they come to and leave school. That will tell you a lot. (A sure sign of a well-protected school would be your being picked up for loitering while making your observations.)

Second, talk with the principal, teachers, and students. From their statements and your own observations, you probably can build a reasonably accurate picture of the situation. Neighborhood gossip is generally unreliable. And keep this in mind: There are 54 million children who go to school in America. Almost all of them get there safely, stay there safely, and come home safely each day. If any group is in physical danger, especially in ghetto areas, it is teachers, not students.

2. *Are there too many nonwhites or whites in the school?* No one will have trouble determining what the racial distribution is in any school. The real question is whether or not you feel your child will be at a disadvantage because of the nature of the distribution. Although you wouldn't know it from reports in the media, many parents feel that their children will benefit

from a school characterized by wide racial and cultural diversity. Nonetheless, it is a melancholy fact that even when there is a close to equal distribution of white and black students, a system of voluntary social segregation exists, each child staying with his or her "own kind." (This is generally true in junior and senior high schools, not in elementary schools.) The system is even more rigid when the groups are not evenly represented. Thus, a parent must try to weigh the questions, How much integration is there in an integrated school? How much am I projecting my own fears on my children? What does my child lose by being isolated from children of different races? Few parents are willing to sacrifice their children to make a philosophical point, but keep this in mind: if we in America have any chance at all to develop a nonracial consciousness, it will come because schools are the meeting ground of white and nonwhite children. This is an enormous burden to place on the schools, and on our children, and if they come through, it will not be without pain.

3. *Will my child be bused into an "alien" neighborhood?* As we stress in our discussion of busing, people do not object to the bus but to its destination. At the present time, no more than 3 percent of all children in school are being bused *specifically to accommodate court-ordered desegregation rulings.* Of that percentage, a substantial number represents black children going into white neighborhoods. So it is not easy to understand why the bus-fuss has occupied so much attention. (See p. 136 on busing and p. 180 on neighborhood schools.) Keep in mind that it is an old story for politicians to try to generate divisiveness, suspicion, and even hatred, if it suits their purposes.

We come now to the final question of this chapter: If you judge a school to be deficient, what can you do about it? This is difficult for us to answer without knowing the specific change you want. But it is possible for us to give some useful advice at a general level. The points listed below derive from the assumption that you are serious about wanting to change something in school. This means that you know specifically what you want to happen, what change you want to make, and *why* you want to make it. If you can't be explicit about this part of the process, you have some second-thinking to do.

In general, when you confront some bureaucratic functionary with a problem, you should also provide one possible (i.e., feasible) solution. If the solution seems feasible to him (because it requires no modification of his perception of the system), the probability that your solution will be implemented is pretty high. But if your solution requires a departure from a deeply rooted convention, you have a serious problem. Its solution requires that you have access to power at least equal to, and preferably superior to, the power of the bureaucratic functionary. One immediate advantage you have in dealing with schools is that parents have more power than school administrators, although they frequently don't know it. At least, parents seldom *act as if* they know it.

This leads to the first point:

1. You cannot expect to do much about changing the system all by yourself. You need the help of others. You need a pressure group. A group of parents automatically has power, because it is one of the essential functions of school that it be accountable to its constituents. This accountability is the source of your power. So:

2. Organize a group of like-minded parents, and extend the group to include members of the community who automatically have additional influence by virtue of their role or position: lawyers, businessmen, ministers, politicians, etc. If they are also parents, so much the better.

3. Draw a diagram of your communication lines both to the members of the group and among the members of the group. The purpose of organization is to produce cooperative action, and both organization and cooperation depend upon good communication. You can tell how good your communication is by the degree of agreement that exists among the members of your

organization. Good communication does not happen by chance. It is difficult enough to achieve with a good deal of careful attention and effort. So, first figure out what the existing channels of communication are among the members of your potential organization, and use them. If they are not adequate or accurate enough, you will have to supplement them by developing new channels. But first make sure you know what the existing channels are, and that you are using them to the utmost before getting into the business of developing new channels.

4. The unifying element in your organization is consensus—agreement on *what* the organization's specific purpose is, and *why* it is important for that purpose to be achieved. It is equally important that you understand what the organization's purposes are *not*. This allows you to distinguish between issues on which consensus is necessary and issues on which it is irrelevant. If your organization's specific purpose is to change the elementary school's grading system, the members of your group do not need to agree on the conduct of U.S. foreign policy or on the values of communal living. Attempting to create consensus on such issues simply dissipates the energies of the organization—and it changes the point. The point is for your group to focus pressure on the system you want to change, not on your own members. So Point 4 is to establish *relevant* consensus on the organization's purpose and the reasons it is important. This permits the organization to focus, in the right place, the pressure it brings to bear.

5. The next step is to do just that: bring pressure to bear on the part of the system that is both most vulnerable and most responsive to the pressure. This leads to Point 6, which is very easy to forget, ignore, or just let slide:

6. Keep the pressure up. There are all kinds of bureaucratic strategies for resisting change. The most common forms include some kind of verbal agreement with the pressure group—that is, agreement in principle only, leaving no room for procedures to be developed—or some kind of overt delaying tactic, such as

"forming a committee to study the problem." You get the idea. Any one of several responses such as these generally has the effect of taking the pressure off, and as soon as the pressure is off, the system reverts back to its original state—like a plastic object with a built-in memory. That might be a good metaphor for thinking about systems and how they change: systems are like plastic, and will change shape only in response to sustained heat and pressure. This leads to the next point:

7. The kind of pressure your group brings to bear is good if it produces the desired effect. While you certainly don't want to use a form of pressure that is counterproductive, you also want to make a realistic assessment of the degree to which the form of pressure you elect to use will produce a perceptible effect. The judgment you make must be pragmatic: if you get the desired results then your tactics are good. If you don't, they aren't. If that sounds too hard-nosed for some of your group, you have another problem to deal with: getting them to agree with this criterion.

8. Know the sources of power and the way in which it is used in the system you wish to affect. This point underlies all the other points. Be careful about succumbing to some romantic illusion about how the system "ought to work." What you have to deal with is the reality of *how it does work.*

9. Remember: Anything you propose that is likely to produce real change may be regarded as outrageous, unpatriotic, irresponsible, immoral (choose one or more) by those who have power. Expect resistance. And make sure you know, before you start out, what price you are willing to pay for what results.

10. As was noted earlier, what is right is defined by those who have the power to define what is right. Period. Talk loudly and carry a big stick. When you have generated enough power to define what is right, you are on your way to effecting substantive changes.

11. People cannot make a choice they do not know exists.

One of the important messages to reiterate through your communication efforts must concern feasible alternatives to the existing system. You will have to educate not only those who resist your proposals, but also those who support them. As Jefferson noted, the price of democracy is the continuing pursuit of the common good by the common people. Implicit in this effort is an adequately and accurately informed common people. The probability is that your supporters, actual and incipient, are not adequately and accurately informed. You have to find out what they "know" and believe, and then you have to make available knowledge and information they do not have. (See Resources, p. 274.)

A final note: The best example of an existing medium of communication through which parents can work to change and improve schools is the PTA. By and large, the PTA, for all its organization, publications, and national and local representation, seldom deals with substantive matters in the schools. We suggest that careful consideration be given to ways in which you, as a PTA member, can enlist the potential power in that organization to begin to effect changes that you are convinced need to be made in the schools your children attend. If you do not have a lawyer among your supporters, you should give serious thought to arranging for your group to retain one, or at least have one available as circumstances require, since another potent source of power is the courts. If the bureaucracy that you are trying to affect remains insensitive to your status as mere parents, institute litigation against the school board and school administration. As the review of litigation on pp. 250–273 reveals, the probability of your losing your case in the lower courts is high, but your chances are good as you go on to higher courts.

The significant power in resorting to legal action resides in the fact that the bureaucrats whose power you wish to affect are no longer in a position to be arbitrary. They *must* respond to judicial decisions because of the power of the courts. Remember, though, that even with a favorable court decision, you will have to keep the pressure on to minimize the erosion of the advances you acquire through it.

8

SCHOOLS AND
THE FUTURE

CHARLES KETTERING once said that he was interested in the future because that was where he was going to spend the rest of his life. Most people are interested in the future, if not for Kettering's reason, then because of a pervasive feeling of anxiety produced by our old friend, uncertainty. Perhaps that is why we endow with such high value any attempts to reveal the future—no matter how improbable or implausible such revelations might be. Uncertainty is intolerable, and even in the second decade of the nuclear space age, Americans spend about as much money on attempts to predict the future (from horoscopes to tea leaf or palm reading, to phrenology or tarot cards) as they do on any other speculative venture (such as medical treatment).

All of which leads us to say that in this chapter we want to take a shot at the future of our schools. Almost everything we have said in this book so far (and will continue to say in Part II) has been about schools as they are now, and are likely to be in the next decade. But we wish to show here that our imaginations are no less excitable than those of others, and that we are quite aware of the possibility that by the year 2001, what is called schooling (if the word is used at all) may be unrecognizable to those of us who think we know what it means. So we'd like to construct a scenario of what schooling might mean at, say, the turn of the millennium. Our scenario will probably turn out to be completely mistaken, because if there is one thing that we know about predictions, it is that predictors (ourselves included) are more or less compelled to assume that the future will be an analogic extension of the present. After all, what else do we have to go on? Unfortunately, though, there is always a joker in the deck. There inevitably emerges something or other that no logical thinker could anticipate. The world, in sum, does not proceed like an Aristotelian syllogism. The damnedest things keep happening.

Arthur Clarke, author of 2001, gives an example of this point in his book *Profiles of the Future*:

> One can only prepare for the unpredictable by trying to keep an open and unprejudiced mind—a feat which is extremely difficult to achieve, even with the best will in the world. Indeed, a completely open mind would be an empty one, and freedom from all prejudices and preconceptions is an unattainable ideal. Yet there is one form of mental exercise that can provide good basic training for would-be prophets: Anyone who wishes to cope with the future should travel back in imagination a single lifetime—say to 1900—and ask himself just how much of today's technology would be, not merely incredible, but *incomprehensible* to the keenest scientific brains of that time.

Well, we have tried to keep an open mind, and to maintain a sufficient respect for the incomprehensible. If you will do the same, perhaps you will find what follows stimulating. We will start with a metaphor for the schooling process that is almost familiar. (Later, we'll use one that isn't.)

Since the most common role of the schools is to teach subjects, and since the most common form of this activity is communicating subject matter, let's look at the school first as a *medium of communication.* This will permit us to see a future role for schools that other metaphors might not allow. To bring that role into focus, we need some generalization about communication that will help us to make some judgments about the function of the school as a medium. The generalization we find most useful is that *two media of communication cannot exist at the same time if they are trying to do the same thing.* That is, if more than one medium exists at a given time to fulfill a certain function for a certain audience, the one that does it best (i.e., with the least expenditure of time, effort, and money) will survive, and the others will not. The others will not survive, that is, unless one of two things happens: (1) they find a patron who, for whatever reasons, is willing and able to subsidize their operations; or (2) they change their functions in some significant way.

A recent example of our generalization is provided by what happened to movies after the appearance of television. As soon as TV began to fulfill the function that movies had fulfilled for about forty years, and in a way that made it easier and more economical for the audience, the movies were in trouble. They were in trouble because the audience stayed home to watch TV rather than getting dressed, hiring a baby-sitter, and driving to the movie house. Since a patron with sufficient funds did not emerge to subsidize the movies, they had to redefine themselves—to fulfill a function that TV did not—in order to survive. And, after various misbegotten efforts at gimmicks to attract audiences to the old thing, movies did redefine themselves, by becoming "adult," that is, more "realistic." (Most people thought they had just become "dirty.") In any event, as movies changed, they attracted a new audience. And with the new audience, they not only survived, they flourished. Movies even became "cinema" and "film."

Our point in mentioning all this is that, in its present form, the school as a medium of communication, as a source of information, is bankrupt. There have just been too many developments in electronic information-handling media for conventional schools to make any sense in this role. James Coleman described the basic problem in an article titled "The Children Have Outgrown the Schools" (*Psychology Today*, February 1972). He put it this way:

> When the child lived in a poverty of information, the family and the school shaped the child's cognitive world by the selectivity of information they imposed. As the environment has become rich in information, the child's cognitive world has begun to be shaped by neither family nor school, but by comic books, television, paperbacks, and the broad spectrum of newspapers and magazines that abound, from the *Chicago Tribune* to the *Berkeley Barb* and from *Reader's Digest* to *Ramparts*.

The schools, then, are a kind of time machine. One enters them and is transported back in time to a preelectronic communication era in which print is dominant and teachers still labor to impart bits of information through methods that are anachronistic. At present, the schools can still afford to act this way, but only through increasing subsidies from patrons like the state and federal governments. But as the money crunch intensifies, the inefficiency, costliness, and obsolescence of the present form of schooling will become more visible. And as it becomes more visible, the demand for more efficient methods and media for imparting information will increase—to the point where schools will really begin to utilize computer based instruction. Programmed instruction—with television, typewriters, film, audiotape and videotape, and computers "married" into an information-access system (i.e., a teaching-learning system)—is already in use in business, industry, the military, and professional training. It is not only feasible, it is economical and efficient.

Lest we be misunderstood, we must say that we are not

talking here about a more widespread use of what is called educational television. In our view, the present forms and uses of educational television make about as much sense as using 747s to collect and transport garbage. About the only thing that educational television does now is to make a teacher audible and visible in the home, in just about the same role as the teacher fills in a conventional classroom. This isn't a *use* of television, it's a gross *misuse* of television. If a teacher talking at students in a classroom is the most inefficient way for students to learn (and there is an endless amount of evidence to support this dismal conclusion), what basis is there for supposing that merely reproducing that situation electronically, in another room, will make a difference? There is, we admit, some evidence from conventional testing of recall that teacher-talk via TV is retained better than teacher-talk in the classroom, but this is such a tiny gain as to scarcely warrant the use of the hardware involved.

Educational television aside, if you think about various ways to use the new media for the purpose of making information available, easily and inexpensively, to anybody who wants it, when and where he wants it, you might come up with several possibilities. We'll describe our vision in a moment, but first we'd like to stress two points. The first is that the conventional forms of schooling, because of the very structure of a school, violate just about everything that is known about how human beings learn. Basically, the structure of a conventional school requires that everyone be there when the school is ready, that everyone learn what the school teaches *when* it teaches it, and *where* it teaches it—all together, at the same time and in the same place. This is simply not the way human beings learn—anything. That's Point 1. Point 2 is that electronic information systems, because of *their* structure, can move information *to* the person who wants it, wherever he is. Moreover, they move it to him when, as, and if he wants it. In short, electronic information systems turn the whole environment into a library of information with unlimited access.

Given those facts, and the fact that the conventional school cannot long survive economically in competition with electronic media, how can we redefine the school so as to fulfill its information-imparting function economically, efficiently, and in a way that does not alienate its audience?

Well, what we propose is a school which, in part, looks and functions pretty much the way present neighborhood laundromats do. Laundromats are open, or can be open, twenty-four hours a day. The machines work when you put a coin in them. You put a coin in them when you want to wash some clothes.

The future school we are talking about would consist of a series of teaching-learning stations that would permit access to anything anyone wanted to learn, which would or could include not only all of the subjects presently included in common school curricula, but a good deal more that are not. Moreover, the stations would permit the student to have access to the information wanted *whenever* he wanted to try to learn it. The schools would be scattered about local neighborhoods and would be open twenty-four hours a day. If, for example, someone who wanted to learn algebra couldn't sleep at 2:00 A.M. on Thursday, he could go do algebra to his heart's content. Not only could anybody who wanted to learn anything try to learn it whenever he wanted, he could redo lessons as many times as necessary, without failing any tests or being subject to ridicule from teachers or other students for being dumb. Another advantage in this kind of school is that, as with most programmed instruction, everyone gets an A in whatever course he takes via the program—simply by virtue of completing it. Finally, the pernicious use and effects of grades will be eliminated.

How do we get the teaching-learning system to provide the desired lessons? Insert the appropriate tokens, to be distributed to students pretty much along the lines laid out for a voucher system. (see p. 195). Each student could be issued tokens worth a fraction of what it now costs to provide a year's worth of conventional schooling. Why not? Arrangements could be made for

adults to have access to the new schools too. Those are just cler-
ical details, not matters of substance. The point is that anybody
could go to school to learn whatever he wanted to, whenever he
wanted to, for as long as he wanted to.

Not only does this kind of school system eliminate the need
for school buses, it does not ever get tired, or sick, or pregnant,
and it doesn't shut down for the summer, and it doesn't need
cost of living increments, or retirement benefits. It just makes
instruction available as, when, where, if, and however some student wants it. And the funny part about it is that a system such
as this, sometimes decried as inhuman, is actually more humane
to the student than is the conventional classroom. At the same
time, it makes individual instruction possible to an extent that
simply cannot be achieved in any conventional school.

So much for instruction and imparting information. Our
learning laundromats can do it all better, cheaper, with less pain
and greater variety and richness. Moreover, teachers would then
be released to do some real educating. And that brings us to
these questions: What purpose should the school—as a *social*
institution, not an information medium—attempt to fulfill that
will not and cannot be fulfilled by any other medium? What
kinds of people do we want our schools to help our youth become?

To answer these questions, we employ our second metaphor: school as an environment for the development of healthy
egos. In other words, once teachers are free of the dominating
imperatives of information distribution, they would be available
to develop an environment (a school) in which all the processes
of interaction, questioning, and inquiring are supportive of realistic and positive self-concepts in students. We are *not* talking
about school as a mental institution. We are talking about
school as an analog for mental health. If that sounds peculiar,
it may be because at present there *is* no formal social institution
whose purpose is to help strengthen the egos of normally developing people. A mental institution is supposed to fix you up if

you are crazy. The school we are imagining here would be designed to enhance mental health, not restore it.

Let us begin our exploration of this idea by stating the obvious fact that intellect and emotion can be separated only verbally. They cannot be separated in reality, within any real human being. As Plato noted, "In order for education to accomplish its purpose, reason must have an adequate emotional base." And the base upon which all healthy learning is built is a feeling of adequacy, competence, and confidence. Anyone who feels inadequate and incompetent in the face of whatever is to be learned cannot learn it, because he has judged himself incapable of learning it—whatever "it" is. Each of us carries emotional—and so, intellectual—wounds of this kind. Almost everyone has at least one statement that goes, "Oh, I'm no good at that." Or, "I've never been able to learn that." Or, "I've always been dumb in that." What is odd about such statements is that they are made by people of verifiable academic intelligence and learning ability. People who are "good" in English, for example, are commonly "dumb" in mathematics. Engineers, who are "good" in mathematics, are commonly "dumb" in English. And so on. Whole areas of "dumbness" seem to pattern out along personality and professional lines.

What are we to make of this? Is what we are dealing with a genetic condition? While this possibility exists, the probability is that areas in which we think of ourselves as good are simply those in which we have not *learned* to think of ourselves as bad or dumb. Yes, these are *learned* beliefs. The invisible curriculum is that which profoundly affects each of us emotionally, and in the process teaches us that we are dumb in one way or another. It might have been the expression on the face of a teacher (whom we desperately wanted to please) just at the moment when we made a mistake. Nothing need be *said* to teach us that we are dumb. A change in expression or body tone, or even just a sigh of disappointment or disapproval—even just once, at one crucial moment—will produce the most durable kind of learning. And once we are taught that we are dumb or incompetent in something, we seem unable to forget it. It is so charged with emotional meaning that it is indelibly printed on the top layer of our memory.

What this means to us, then, is that in order to make children good at learning, we must design schools systematically to be supportive, rewarding environments, rather than disparaging, punitive ones. They must be designed—quite simply—to make children *feel* good about themselves.

How can this be done? Well, there are at least two approaches that we can envision, each one reinforcing the other. The first is to design all school conventions in such a way that they are, in sum, structurally consistent with the healthy attitudes we would want students to learn. For example, one reason that present schools fail to develop students' inner resources is that school conventions are organized in the manner of totalitarian states rather than democratic republics. If we spend twelve or more years in an autocratic environment, we are ill equipped, upon leaving school, to begin functioning as responsible individuals. Assuming, as we do, that an ability to judge for oneself is a characteristic of mental health, then our school of the future would have to be organized so that students are continually making decisions that affect their own lives. This would entail students' structuring their own time and activities, evaluating and supervising themselves, developing their own conceptions of relevance and intelligence, and so on. Such a place sounds more like a social club than a school, but remember, in this chapter we are not limiting ourselves to present realities. Remember, too, that young people form or join a social club precisely because its structure is designed to give solid support to developing egos.

Here is another example: Change is the dominant fact of our times. No one can be mentally healthy who does not have the inner resources to deal with change. This would mean that our students would have to learn to think in terms of probabilities rather than absolutes, of processes rather than fixed states, of contingencies rather than certainties. Our school of the future must, therefore, free itself of any language, procedures, or methods of organization that promote any of the following ideas: that there is a single, correct answer to problems; that authorities and experts always know what is best for you; that authorities and experts never know what is best for you; that intelligence is something you "have," that courses are something you "take," that education is something you "get"; that teachers have a right to punish; that labels provide understanding; or several more that are implicit in the structure of present-day schools.

But lest you think we have, ourselves, mistaken a process for a fixed state, we must acknowledge our understanding that an ego is not a thing but a mode of responding to the world. The ego only becomes visible when one is in the process of solving a problem. Thus, it would be insufficient—in fact, impossible—to create a school with a psychologically healthy structure that does not also have a substantive content. After all, even a social club has an agenda. A youngster may join a social club to find support for his ego, but if all that its members ever do is sit around supporting each other's egos, then they will find nothing to support. Therefore, our school of the future requires an intellectual focus that complements the structure of mental health. And since mental health is not a thing, but a process of responding to reality with courage, hope, realism, and intelligence, we suggest that the subject matter of our school of the future be the process of interaction itself. That is, what students would spend their time doing is studying (and that would include *participating in*) all the modes of transactions between various systems, in an attempt to identify what might be called techniques of healthy transactions. Below is a short list of some of the interactions that might form a curriculum:

◄H ◄H ◄H

1. The relationship of an individual to realities outside his skin (How does perception work? How do we make meanings? Is some meaning-making healthier than others?)
2. The relationship of various symbol systems (e.g., language, mathematics, music, painting, etc.) to reality (In what sense do symbolic statements represent the world? Do different symbol systems serve different purposes? Are they equally useful? For what?)
3. The relationship of an individual to various symbol systems (What constitutes a "healthy" use of a symbol system? How can we check out the reliability of our symbolic world?)
4. The relationship of individual to individual (How can I understand another person? And help him to understand me? How should I handle my feelings toward someone else?)
5. The relationship of individual to group (Where and how do I fit in? Do I want to? Do I have to?)
6. The relationships among individuals in a group (What are the lines of communication between the members of the group? How is power delegated? How are decisions made? What kind of group structure is "healthiest" for what purposes?)
7. The relationship of group to culture (How does our group connect up with the larger groups we're part of? How does our group conflict with them? For what purposes?)
8. The relationship of machine to reality (How does a machine —e.g., microscope, telescope, computer—organize reality? How can we judge the reliability of the machine's reality representation?)
9. The relationship of machine to machine (How is information transmitted from one machine to another? What happens to the information in the transmission process? Is there a limit to the number of machines information can be transmitted through before it becomes so distorted as to be totally unreliable?)

10. The relationship of machine to man (How do the machines we use alter our perception of reality? How do they affect our sensorium? Is there a point at which a machine begins to shape our behavior more than we control its "behavior"? How can we recognize that point?)

11. The relationship of technology to culture (What happens to the institutions in a culture when a new technology—e.g., the automobile, television, behavioral technology—is introduced? What happens to the physical environment in which the culture exists? What happens to all the other interactions between man and reality, man and symbols, man and man?)

What would be the intellectual perspectives from which these subjects and questions might be viewed? Well, there are many available, even now, although they are not easy to catalogue. For example, the approach developed by Alfred Korzybski, called *general semantics*, is demonstrably useful in helping people to understand the relationships among perception, symbol, and reality. The ideas developed by Edward DeBono, which he calls *lateral thinking*, provide a similarly revealing perspective on symbol and reality, as do the concepts of I. A. Richards. Materials have been developed by Sid Simon and Howard Kirschenbaum to assist young people in clarifying their own values, and thus their relationships with others. Transactional Analysis is a useful tool for understanding the process of interaction between individuals. So are sensitivity training, in its various forms, and transcendental meditation. Both can be used—in fact, already have been used with success—as instruments for increasing self- and other-awareness. Francis Driscoll, superintendent of schools in Eastchester, New York, has reported that students who have practiced transcendental meditation—which has been installed, believe it or not, as a secondary school subject—have markedly improved their relationships with their teachers, their peers, and their families. He also has reported, please note, a significant decrease in drug abuse.

But it is not our intention here to provide an outline of a curriculum. Perhaps it is sufficient to say that the following people have each provided a perspective, a style of thinking, or a set of questions that constitute useful instruments for the study of interactions: Marshall McLuhan, Buckminster Fuller, Alvin Toffler, Margaret Mead, R. D. Laing, Saul Alinsky, Lewis Mumford, Carl Rogers, B. F. Skinner, Erik Erikson, Abraham Maslow, Arthur Clarke, and many, many others. In our school of the future, there would be no shortage of substance.

In addition to a psychological structure and an intellectual perspective, our school has a philosophical point of view as well. That point of view has been given various names during the past decade, but it is most commonly referred to as the "ecological" or "systems" or "organismic" perspective. The ecological perspective has been elaborated on by writers in such diverse fields as psychology (Abraham Maslow), biochemistry (Ludwig von Bertalanffy), and philosophy (Ervin Laszlo), but, in general, it is characterized by the following assumptions: (1) no phenomenon or event or process takes place in a vacuum, but is integrally related to every other process and event that makes up the human environment; therefore, (2) what is most important in the generation of knowledge is the study of the relationships which unite the different pieces of a system into a whole which is *greater* than the sum of its parts; and (3) the purpose of such knowledge is not primarily to control the behavior of men or environments, but to understand their workings.

In short, the school of the future would add up to an environment in which students would study the principles of healthy interactions, within a structure based on the metaphor of a healthy ego.

What we have tried to suggest in this chapter is that the future might include a two-phase opportunity for redefining the role of schools. We propose, as the first phase, that the conventional function of schools to impart information and so-called cognitive skills be given over to electronic information (teaching) systems. The second phase would turn the resulting catastrophe—putting present schools and teachers out of business—into an opportunity. It would permit the school to focus *all* its attention on the development and support of healthy, well-integrated human beings.

PART TWO

LANGUAGE

THERE IS AN old story about a mother who was boasting of her son's academic achievements to a neighbor. At one point, the mother called her son into the room and insisted that he demonstrate his brilliance at once. "Harold," she demanded confidently, "say something in geometry for Mrs. Green."

The point of the story is supposed to be that the mother succeeded in demonstrating not her son's brilliance but her own ignorance. But if Harold were as smart as his mother believed, he *could* say something in geometry, and quite easily. For example, "Equals added to equals are equal." He could also say something in physics, chemistry, biology, and almost any other subject. The fact is that subjects are languages. Biology is not plants and animals, but a way of talking about them. History is not events; it is a language for describing or interpreting events. It is the same way with education. Education is not schools, students, and teachers. It is a language for talking about all of these. If you do not know the language, you cannot know the subject. We have included, therefore, a small dictionary of those terms that comprise the bulk of contemporary school talk. As you will see, each explanation is a small essay intended to be *read*, as against merely referred to. We have tried to write, not so much a glossary, but a report on the state of the subject. As you will also see, that state is far from satisfactory, but it is our hope that when you have finished reading our report, you will at least know where the subject is thriving and where it is most feverish.

Once again, we want to remind you that, in order to avoid

even the appearance of pedantry, we have been very sparing in the use of footnotes and cross-references. The index will tell you where to find a discussion of any name or term that is unfamiliar to you but important to the school scene and that you want to know more about as you read along.

❊   ❊   ❊

AFFECTIVE DOMAIN

In the good old days, teachers talked about the "emotional life" of children. Today, they talk about the "affective domain." It amounts to the same thing. But, unfortunately, by either name not much, until recently, has been done about the matter. For a long time, the schools have been largely indifferent to the feeling life of children. Here's Fred Rogers (of "Mister Rogers' Neighborhood") on the subject: "It's easy to convince people that children need to learn the alphabet and numbers. . . . How do we help people to realize that what matters . . . is how a person's inner life finally puts together the alphabet and numbers of his outer life. What really matters is whether he uses the alphabet for the declaration of war or for the description of a sunrise, and his numbers for the final count at Buchenwald or for the specifics of a brand new bridge." The plain fact is that there are thousands of children who have been rendered intellectually impotent and socially destructive by rage, fear, and confusion. The schools cannot deal with this problem by hiring a few guidance counselors. Many school critics feel we must make the study of one's own feelings a legitimate school activity, invested with an importance at least equal to that presently given to map-reading skills and spelling. People like George Brown (who uses the term "confluent education"), William Glasser, Sid Simon, and Mario Fantini and Gerry Weinstein have shown fairly clearly how this can be done, and an encouraging number of schools have become involved in the affective domain.

ALTERNATIVE SCHOOL

This widely used term has several distinct meanings. We have dealt with some of them under the terms *free schools, school within a school,* and *cooperative school.* But in general, an alternative school is one whose conventions are entirely different from those we associate with most public schools. An alternative school may be private or public. It may be Summerhillian or not. It may be good or bad. What makes it an "alternative" is that it offers an arrangement for learning that is in sharp contrast to what is offered in the "regular" school. Harlem Prep is one of the best known, and best, alternative schools in the country. Summerhill, in Leiston, England, is probably the best known alternative school in the world.

The growth of alternative schools in the United States is one of the most encouraging educational developments of the past five years. As these schools proliferate, we will have the best opportunity we have had in forty years to design and experiment with different kinds of learning environments. The plain truth is that in spite of the statistical razzmatazz produced by some of our reputable schools of education, we know very little about the conditions under which different kinds of learning best take place. B. F. Skinner, who claims to know more about this than anyone else, is also quick to say that the present state of his science is primitive. Jerome Bruner, who is certainly Skinner's leading intellectual competition in this country, concedes that he has only made a beginning toward formulating a theory of instruction, and recently has all but repudiated some of his speculations of only a few years ago. And Jean Piaget, who may indeed know more about the whole matter than anyone else, has not seriously studied the effects of social conditions and social conditioning on learning. It is possible that the social distance from his laboratory in Geneva to the streets of New York or Chicago may be greater than even he can presently calculate. In fact, it is even possible that the street urchins Maria

Montessori set about to educate in Rome at the turn of the century are sufficiently different from your average street urchins today to warrant a complete revision of *her* theory of instruction.

The point is this: There are, of course, some things we do know about learning, but they are mostly theoretical constructs, and we need to test their validity in real life situations. The emergence of alternative schools of all kinds will make this possible.

AUTO-DIDACTICS

This pretentious term means "self-teaching." An auto-didact is a person who is self-taught, which means, of course, that we are all auto-didacts, including you. Congratulations. The term has been introduced to education discourse by people who have become discouraged by the failure of schools to help students increase their competence as self-teaching learners. In fact, some believe that schools actually retard one's development as an auto-didact. And some even feel that there is something inherently wrong with having an institution control what, where, when, and how a person should learn. The alternative to school, they imagine, is a kind of nonbureaucratic, nonpunitive, informal system which would help any person—regardless of age, sex, race, mentality, or previous condition of servitude—make contact with other persons who can help him learn whatever he wishes. Such an arrangement is sometimes called a *free-learning system*. Of course, adult education programs are free-learning systems. So are libraries. And television and radio. And newspapers and magazines. In a sense, the entire culture is a free-learning system, and one may wonder what the fuss is about. Nonetheless, all the talk about auto-didactics is useful because it calls attention to the bureaucratic orientation of so many schools, and is a reproach to those schools that do very little to aid students in becoming better self-teachers.

BASIC FUNDAMENTALS

These two words always appear together, although one may reverse their order, as in *fundamental basics*. In either case, one or the other of the words is redundant. But redundant or not, the phrase refers to those skills that were essential for upward social mobility in the nineteenth century: reading, writing, spelling, good diction and arithmetic. In times of rapid change, schools are supposed to offer relief to teachers and help to students by "returning to basic fundamentals." This will certainly work if the nineteenth century comes back. If it doesn't, check with Alvin Toffler.

BEHAVIOR MODIFICATION

Until fairly recently, it was generally assumed by professional educators and psychologists that the best way to change people is by helping them perceive the patterns in their own behavior, helping them understand why they behave the way they do, and offering some alternative models of behavior that would be more appropriate. Thus psychologists labored to produce diagnostic instruments like the Rorschach, and Thematic Apperception Test, and talked about "personality patterns." Psychiatrists and psychoanalysts spent expensive hours helping people to explore the causes of their behavior, and talked about "insight." Teachers led their students through reams of world literature, and talked about "developing an understanding of human values."

Meanwhile, back at the laboratory, Pavlov, then Watson, and later Skinner were discovering that you can change animal behavior in astonishingly direct and efficient ways, without bothering about "personality patterns" or "insight" or "understanding" or "values." By applying such relatively simple techniques as operant conditioning and positive reinforcement, for example, Skinner and other behavioral psychologists could get rats, pigeons, dogs, and the like to perform tasks as elementary as pressing a lever to get food or as complex as playing Ping-Pong. To emphasize that they were operating on behavior *directly*, and to distinguish between their methods and those of teachers and psychiatrists, the behavioral psychologists called their work *behavior modification*.

So long as the behaviorists confined their experiments to rats, pigeons, and dogs, behavior modification remained in the relative obscurity of the laboratory. Inevitably, however, they began to investigate whether the same technology that worked on laboratory animals wouldn't work just as effectively to change human behavior. It did. At least, it did within highly controlled environments. And within a very short time, behavior modification began to move out of psychology textbooks and into the schools, where it now plays an increasingly important—and increasingly controversial—role.

The techniques of behavior modification are described in some detail under *operant conditioning,* on p. 183. It is enough to point out here that the argument for their application to classroom learning is based on two assumptions. The first is that people *are* only what they *do.* An "intelligent" man, for example, is simply someone who *behaves* in particular ways in particular situations. That's how we know he's intelligent. And the second assumption is that any behavior, no matter how complex, can be broken down into a mechanical sequence of steps small enough for any learner to handle—given the proper training. Therefore, the behaviorists argue, if the schools want to produce intelligent children, what they must do is define how intelligent people behave, break those behaviors down into component behaviors simple enough for the particular children in a given classroom, then apply operant conditioning techniques to get the children to perform those behaviors. This approach has the advantage, the behaviorists add, of making learning a highly controllable and predictable process—in fact, an inevitable one, since behavior modification techniques do not require the learner's cooperation or understanding or willingness to learn in order to work.

The objections to behavior modification as a teaching technology are as numerous as they are heated. They boil down to this: Behaviorist objectives and methods will produce automatons, not autonomous people. The characteristics of a creative, humane person cannot be reduced to simple observable behaviors, such as can be reinforced in the manner of animal training; and helping children to be more human (as opposed, say, to better spellers) is the main function of education. Thus, behavior modification avoids the important issue, makes promises it cannot fulfill, and comes frighteningly close to brainwashing in doing what it can do.

BEHAVIORAL OBJECTIVES

One of the most significant consequences of the current demand for accountability in the schools has been the involvement of school people in a frantic effort to convert what used to be called "instructional goals" into what are now called "behavioral objectives." As the term suggests, behavioral objectives are an important part of the process of behavior modification which is in turn a new concept of teaching derived from behavioral psychology. In brief, the rationale for behavioral objectives goes something like this: School has a responsibility to the community to provide young people with certain skills, information, and attitudes. The only way to tell if students are learning what the school is supposed to teach is by evaluating their behavior before and after the school has done its work. If those evaluations are to have any validity, they must be based on objective standards, so that everyone can agree on whether or not the students have in fact changed. The only way to have objective standards for measuring change is to spell out exactly what, after being taught, the student should be able to do that he couldn't do previously. This implies that what you want him to *do* has to be observable, and preferably measurable, as well. If, for example at the end of a year, 90 percent of the kids in a school can demonstrate 90 percent of the behaviors the school was supposed to teach, then the school is doing its job. If not—then someone's fouling up and ought to be replaced.

Sounds perfectly reasonable, doesn't it? And it might be, too—if not for a couple of major problems. The first arises from the unhappy fact that the behaviors which are easiest to specify, observe, and measure (as well as modify) usually turn out to be trivial. A typical behavioral objective in "language arts," for example, might specify that "at the end of six weeks of instruction, the student will be able to identify correctly, in a sample of ten sentences, fifteen words which function as nouns, ten which function as verbs," etc. A specific goal? Yes. Observable and measurable? Obviously. But is that really what we want kids to learn? And there's the trouble—the question that the movement to behavioral objectives does *not* address—namely, What's worth teaching? Inevitably, the behaviorally oriented curriculum is based, instead, on the answer to the question, What can we measure? And since the instruments available for measuring behavioral change are extremely limited, so are the behaviors such curricula set out to teach. So there's problem one. It could be solved, some say, by inventing more and better instruments for objective evaluation. Easily said. But the plain fact is that the most significant learnings cannot be translated into narrow behavioral objectives or measured on any standardized test. How would a school test, for example, whether its students are learning to rely on their own judgment, rather than on the pronouncements of authority? ("At the end of twelve weeks of instruction, 90 percent of the students refused to follow the school dress code 90 percent of the time"?) Or whether they are learning to be open-ended and tentative in their solutions to problems? Or whether they are enjoying the process of learning? The point is, of course, that where attitudes are concerned, change shows up in ways that are unique to each learner, and over times that range from a moment to a lifespan. Such change cannot be measured then, even in theory, by regularly scheduled standardized tests. And that's problem two.

There is, of course, much more to say about behavioral objectives—pro and con—than we can go into here. It is worth pointing out, though, that the danger in the current plunge toward behaviorism is *not* in the limitations of behavioral objectives, but in the schools' failure to recognize those limitations. In their efforts to be "scientific" about teaching, many school people are moving perilously close to the position that "If it can't be measured, it's not worth bothering about," or even worse, "If it can't be measured, there's nothing there." It would be difficult to imagine a view more *anti*scientific, or more deadly to the learning experience, than that.

BEHAVIORAL PSYCHOLOGY

Since all psychology is a study of human behavior, this term might seem at first redundant. In current usage, however, the words "behavior" and "behavioral" refer specifically and exclusively to *activities which can be directly observed*. In these terms, thinking about something is not a behavior—but talking about it is. Loving your children is not a behavior—but hugging them is. Enjoying a movie is not a behavior—but applauding it is. Behavioral psychology, then, is the study of what people *do*, and the patterns in which they do it, and the conditions in which what they are doing will change. This last concern of behavioral psychology—to spell out the conditions and techniques by which behavior can be changed—has given it substantial impact on the current school scene. Its influence is especially visible in the areas of goal definition (see behavioral objectives) and evaluation (see criterion reference tests), and is continuing to grow in the areas of activity structuring (see programmed instruction) and teaching methodology (see behavior modification).

For a brief outline of the dispute between behavioral psychologists and humanistic psychologists, see B. F. Skinner and Carl Rogers.

BUSING

Without doubt, busing is the most explosive, controversial, dramatic, emotional—you name it—issue on the entire school scene. Presidents have commented on it, candidates have made it part of their platforms, judges have lost reputations over it, friendships have ended because of it. One thing is clear: Americans, in general, are not against busing children to school. As pointed out in the explanation of neighborhood schools, for forty years a majority of children in this country have been bused to school without much objection. The problem with busing, as the term is currently used, is that it represents an attempt to use the schools as a means of achieving racial *and* socioeconomic integration. The issue really arose in 1954, when the Supreme Court ruled, in *Brown* v. *Topeka*, that *de jure* segregation (i.e., segregation by law) was unconstitutional. ("Separate but equal facilities are inherently unequal" was the decisive concept.) That decision affected only those states where such laws existed. Since no northern states had such laws, the *Brown* v. *Topeka* case was hailed in the North as a giant step toward the achievement of a free and equal society. But then, through a series of subsequent court decisions, the principle was established that *de facto* segregation is also unconstitutional. This meant that even if there were no *law* insisting upon segregation, there were still patterns of social and economic life that made segregation just as real. The courts ruled that where such patterns were being deliberately enforced, you had an illegally segregated school system. This principle means, in effect, that almost every school system in America is illegal, since there are very few racially integrated communities in the country. And it is that way because most Americans (white Americans, certainly; and maybe even black Americans) evidently want it that way. So we are faced with a monumental contradiction: our towns and cities are segregated—both racially and socially—but the courts have ruled that our schools may not be. Northerners have been in a particular panic about this situation, since it has forced many of them to question their customary rhetoric about freedom, and in some cases, to adopt a different stance altogether (one uncomfortably similar to the position of white segregationists).

What does it all mean? Probably this: There is no solution to this problem, as long as the social and economic structure of our society remains as it is. Racial segregation is so intertwined with economic segregation that it is difficult to know if the objections to busing are based on racial antagonism or on an aversion to poor people and the consequences of poverty. We suspect it is at least as much the latter as the former. Perhaps more. Not many white parents would object to their children going to school with rich black kids, or even being bused into an affluent black neighborhood with a low crime rate. But there aren't many rich black kids; neither are there many affluent black neighborhoods. To be black in America means to be poor. And to be poor means to live in a poor neighborhood. And to live in a poor neighborhood means that you and anyone else who goes there will be exposed to a high incidence of crime. And so, even if the hollering about busing is about economic, rather than racial differences, you still end up with the same problem. Can the schools do what the society in general has been unable to do? We personally doubt it. The problem of "busing" will remain until such time as poverty is largely eliminated. In the meantime, everyone will act out his part. The courts will try to dislodge *de facto* segregation. Many whites will continue to flee from blacks. Blacks will press for a reasonable piece of the economic pie. And the issue of busing will be a constant reminder that we are, as a people, not quite what we think we are, and very far from where we ought to be.

CERTIFICATION REQUIREMENTS

Every state in the union has a State Education Department, whose main function is to certify teachers. This function is based on the assumptions that (1) not just anybody can be a teacher, and (2) it is possible to train people to perform competently as teachers. The first assumption is undoubtedly true. Some people do not like children, or have no interest in their development, or are poor listeners or bad question-askers or regular point-missers. Such people do not make good teachers—no matter what is done with them—and should be barred from the profession. At present, however, there is no way to do this, because the certification requirements of most states have nothing whatever to do with these things. Instead, state certifying agencies assume that graduation from college and the accumulation of credits in education courses serve as adequate preparation for a teaching career. Of course, this assumption simply sidesteps the question of whether or not people can be trained to be competent teachers. The fact that someone has passed college courses says nothing—one way or the other—about his abilities as a teacher, and in no sense constitutes training for such work.

The situation is comparable to what the Pittsburgh Pirates would get if their requirements for making the team were that an applicant pass a paper-and-pencil test on hitting, running, and throwing, and submit a transcript showing that he has successfully passed such courses as Great World Series Pitchers and The History of the National League. Undoubtedly, some applicants could do this *and* also hit .310. But you would get a high number of .185 hitters. And you would never really find out how to prepare men to survive in the big leagues. Happily for Pittsburgh fans, the Pirates do not certify competence in this way. The teaching profession is not yet so enlightened. The fact is that the certification requirements of most states do not reflect the realities of what it means to be a good teacher. There are, however, some encouraging signs. In some states, student teaching is a requirement for certification, and where this is done in more than a perfunctory manner, it is possible to find out if someone is suited to teaching, and how you might train him to do it better. There is also a growing trend toward the use of performance criteria in evaluating teachers. Just for the record here, performance testing is the method of evaluation used by the Pittsburgh Pirates.

CHILD-CENTERED CURRICULUM

This phrase, popular in the 1920s and 30s, was much abused by the progressives, thereby fell into disrepute, and then just about disappeared by the 50s. It has been resurrected in recent years but seems as if it's headed for the same cycle. The phrase is intended to communicate the simple and irreproachable idea that what you do in school ought to grow mostly out of the needs and interests of children. The problem is that some people have difficulty locating the line that separates responding to the needs of children from being destructively indulgent toward them. Children are not small adults. That fact has been confirmed by the history of the human race. And for those who keep forgetting it, there is always Jean Piaget to remind them. Nonetheless, more than a few promising progressive schools have been ruined by the assumption that children can thrive in an environment in which they are treated exactly as adults. The effect of this is to deprive them of their childhood, which is the reverse of responding to their needs. In the best schools, teachers have a realistic grasp of what kinds of information, skills, and attitudes children need, and these become the basis of the curriculum. Curiously, the worst traditional schools and the worst progressive schools exhibit the same fatal tendency: dealing with children not as they are, but as someone wishes them to be.

COLLEGE ENTRANCE EXAMINATION BOARD (CEEB)

One of the most fear-filled games ever played by high school seniors (and their parents) is known as "Whadja get on your College Boards?" A solid winner can get a score as high as 800, a wretched loser, as low as 200. Winners tend to have easy access to colleges of their choice. Losers can end up pumping gas and changing flats. The tests that comprise the College Boards may include the Scholastic Aptitude Test and/or the Scholastic Achievement Test (which deals with a mountain of trivia about such subjects as English, modern history, and science). These are generally referred to as "the SATs." A similar test known as ACT (American College Test) is also widely taken by high school seniors, especially in the Midwest and Far West, but this test is not used by the CEEB.

The CEEB is a nonprofit organization which has approximately 1,600 colleges and other educational institutions as members. In effect, the CEEB helps them screen applicants by administering entrance tests (i.e., the College Boards). Their tests are prepared mostly by the Educational Testing Service in Princeton, New Jersey.

The assumption underlying the SATs (and other entrance tests) is that there is a strong correlation between high scores on the tests and success in college. This is greatly to be doubted, and there are some who believe that the College Boards have about as much validity as your horoscope in the daily press. Nonetheless, about 40 percent of the colleges in the country require that applicants take them. Part of the reason is undoubtedly economic. It's expensive for a college to design and administer its own entrance exam. It is also expensive (in time as well as money) for college admissions officers to deal directly with everyone who may wish to go to their college. Therefore, many colleges establish a certain score on the College Boards which any applicant must surpass to merit consideration.

The whole system is somewhat archaic and certainly bureaucratic. Happily, a few colleges (e.g., Bowdoin and Brown) have begun to question the entire procedure, and it will not be surprising if, in the years ahead, the College Boards diminish in importance.

COMMUNITY CONTROL

When segregationist southerners want to keep black children out of white schools, they holler, "Community control!"

When stylish northern liberals want to keep black children out of white schools, they holler, "Community control!"

When despairing militant blacks want to keep white teachers and administrators out of *their* schools, they also holler, "Community control!"

Obviously, community control is one of the most flexible terms we have in the language of school politics. What it means depends on how you feel.

In theory, American schools are a product of the local communities in which they reside. But they are also financed and overseen by state governments. (About three-fifths of the total elementary and secondary school budget now come from sources other than local property tax.) And since they are bound by Constitutional restraints, they are influenced to some extent by federal law. It's quite a hodgepodge of overlapping regulations and interests. In general, however, most people favor the idea that whenever possible (assuming, for example, there is no conflict with state and federal law), school policy should be formulated by the people who are directly served by the school. But that's just the beginning of the problem. Who *is* "the community"? Very often, it turns out that the community is only what some particularly aggressive person or group says it is. Any three people demanding to fire a teacher or principal can say they represent the community—and who can prove them wrong? At the same time, any outdated or timid teacher or principal can justify a policy by saying it represents the will of the community. And it probably does—since you can always find ten people to support any damn thing. The truth is that every community is dozens of communities, and the only way to resolve who should control what is through the ballot. Fortunately, in most towns in America people can vote for members of a school board and for school budgets. In this way they can express, in a highly abstract form, the community will. But in large cities, such as New York and Chicago, it is much more difficult for people to give coherent expression to their views. Decentralization has helped to some extent, but the fact is that at the moment most large-city dwellers have inadequate access to the formulation of school policy. And since so many blacks, Chicanos, Puerto Ricans, and other minorities live in our large cities, they are particularly vulnerable to the will of other people—for example, teachers, bureaucrats, appointed school board officials, and so on. Thus, it is not surprising that many of them feel that community control is a mockery, in its present state at least. The same opinion is presently held by those whose children are being bused against their will. So we end up where we started: what community control means depends on where you are, what you want, who you're afraid of, and how much power you've got.

COMPUTER ASSISTED INSTRUCTION (CAI) / COMPUTER BASED INSTRUCTION (CBI)

The difference between CAI and CBI is one of degree. In CAI, computers are used as supplements to teacher-directed classwork. In CBI, computers virtually replace teacher-directed classwork.

Most teachers are apprehensive, to put it mildly, about the intrusion of teaching machines and computers. It is worth noting that teachers who see their main function as that of imparting information have good reason to be apprehensive: programmed instruction via computer *is* much more efficient and effective than any teacher, when the purpose is solely to cover content or impart information.

While the use of CAI or CBI is still by no means common in the schools (mostly because of what seems to be an unprecedented expense at the outset), it is probably inevitable that at some point computers will assume most instructional information handling tasks.

CONTRACT TEACHING (PERFORMANCE CONTRACTING)

Since education is America's biggest business, it is understandable that American business wants a healthy piece of the action. Private educational consulting firms (many of them subsidiaries of publishing companies or communications conglomerates) are the most interesting new angle. School systems unable to accomplish a particular teaching objective can now employ such private firms to do the job—on a (more or less) money-back-guarantee basis. The contract usually specifies the precise behaviors that must be achieved by the students if the company is to get paid. For example, the contract might specify that 80 percent of a particular student population must score better than 75 percent on a particular spelling or reading or arithmetic test at the end of a certain period. The company usually supplies the teaching materials, and the tests, and even trains the teachers. If the specified goals are not achieved, the company loses (i.e., does not get paid or is paid only a partial sum). If the goals are achieved, the taxpayer loses—on two counts. In the first place, he has paid twice for the same service—once for his public school teachers and once for the "help" they get from private industry. And in the second place, the service he's getting is often not worth paying for at all. Since most good businessmen are disinclined to make high-risk contracts, they tend to specify learning objectives that can be achieved with a good measure of reliability. And such goals usually turn out to be trivial, short-range, and mechanistic. This is not to say that good business is inevitably bad education. But the more rigid the terms for doing business are, the less likely it is that the schools will profit in any significant way from their interaction with private enterprise.

In any case, the development of contract teaching has, naturally, led a number of politicians to demand more *teacher* accountability—their point being that if an outside agency can be held accountable for its success (or lack of it) in the schools, why not public school teachers as well? If some teachers fail to accomplish what they were hired to do, some people argue, why should they be paid in full? The teachers reply that, sometimes, you just can't make a silk purse out of a sow's ear. Besides, they add, education is a very complex process; its results may not be observable for many years and, in some cases, are not at all measurable. These are strong points, but in some communities around the country (most notably in California) people are insisting that teachers specify objectives and be held strictly accountable for their achievement.

The argument in favor of strict teacher accountability goes something like this: In most lines of work, if you perform incompetently, you lose money or prestige or even your job. In teaching, you fail the student. The more students you fail, the greater grows your prestige. When almost everyone fails, you are said to have "high standards." If no one can learn anything from you in any circumstances, you are "rigorous." Such a state of affairs is horrendous. Teacher accountability implies that the well-known equation of performance and payoff be applied to teaching: student failure equals teacher failure.

Albert Shanker's objection to this line of thought—namely, that in such a system teachers would inevitably give students the answers to all their tests—can safely be ignored. That's what teachers are supposed to do anyway. But the objection that strict procedures of accountability would force teachers into specifying trivial, short-range, mechanistic goals is serious and can be ignored only at our peril.

COOPERATIVE SCHOOL

In the best populist tradition, parents who disapprove of available public schools, and particularly of elementary schools, are increasingly starting their own schools. Such schools are called cooperatives. Parents rent space for the school, administer it, finance it, clean it, and even teach in it. In this way, they believe they can get exactly the kind of school they want. But the price is high—in time, energy, and money. As a consequence, the life span of most cooperatives is short. Moreover, parents frequently run into intractable philosophical problems. They sometimes discover, for example, that the only thing that binds them together is their distrust of the public schools. Beyond that there may be very little agreement among them about what makes a school good. This inevitably leads to conflict, and it is not uncommon for a number of parents to split off from the original cooperative and form their own. This process of disaffection and affirmation can occur two or three times within a year, until everyone is so exhausted that they return their children to the public schools, or to professionally run private schools, and take a vacation.

CORPORAL PUNISHMENT

In a historic decision in 1943 (*West Virginia State Board of Education* v. *Barnette*), the U.S. Supreme Court clearly defined the school's responsibility to adhere fully to Constitutional standards. The key sentence in the decision was: "That [the schools] are educating the young for citizenship is reason for scrupulous protection of Constitutional freedoms of the individual, if we are not to strangle the free mind at its source and teach youth to discount important principles of our government as mere platitudes." Despite that decision, the courts have taken no clear-cut steps to prohibit teachers and administrators from inflicting bodily harm on students as a punishment for "bad" behavior. In fact, the legal right of public school officials to inflict violent bodily punishment without being guilty of assault and battery is so well established in common law that many state codes do not even mention it. Moreover, at the present time, at least thirteen states explicitly *do* mention it, and permit it (California, Delaware, Florida, Hawaii, Michigan, Montana, Nevada, North Carolina, Ohio, Pennsylvania, South Dakota, Vermont, and Virginia). There are several court actions pending whose purpose is to challenge the legality of corporal punishment. But it would appear that the courts will continue to uphold the practice.

One of the more depressing features of the whole situation is that most school people favor corporal punishment: In a 1969 survey conducted by the National Education Association, 65 percent of the elementary school teachers polled, and 55 percent of the secondary school teachers, said they favored "judicious use" of violent bodily punishment. A comment made by the president of the Pittsburgh Teachers Federation tells an awful lot about where things are at—the school reform movement notwithstanding. He said: "Until somebody comes up with an alternative, we'll support it [corporal punishment]. It's a quick way to show disapproval—like the city giving me a ticket when I park illegally."

For the most up-to-date information on the legal background of corporal punishment, write to the American Civil Liberties Union, which has prepared some readable documents on the subject.

CRITERION REFERENCED (OR BASED) TESTS

Criterion referenced tests, CRTs, are used for assessing the effectiveness of conventional classroom teaching in which behavioral objectives and accountability are dominant concerns.

A CRT consists of test items so constructed as to verify or estimate the degree to which behavioral objectives have been achieved, and particularly to distinguish between students who have mastered a subject and those who have not. Conventional standardized educational achievement tests do not do this; they merely rank testees on the basis of their comparative scores. They do not clearly distinguish those who have achieved mastery from those who have not.

The student behavior described in the objective for a unit of instruction comprises the criterion on which both the teaching and the testing are based. But not all student behavior constitutes a criterion for testing. For example, the statement "The student will read five novels" states an activity, not an objective, and therefore cannot be used as a criterion. The statement "The student will learn to understand and appreciate literature" sounds like an objective, and it is still commonly used in English courses, but since it does not describe what kind of observable behavior the student is intended to be able to engage in, it is not a behavioral objective, and is useless as a criterion for testing.

At this point it is necessary to note a crucial observation made by Robert F. Mager, an expert in the writing of behavioral objectives. Mager reminds us that "it is true in general that the more important an objective is the more difficult it is to state."

How to word an objective to permit a criterion referenced test to determine whether a student "understood" a work of literature, much less whether he "appreciated" it, has yet to be determined. It is because of this limitation that those concerned with "affective education"—teaching intended to affect attitudes and beliefs and feelings—are skeptical about the indiscriminate use of behavioral objectives and criterion referenced tests.

Once upon a time, "curriculum" was one of the most boring words in the school vocabulary. In recent years, however, it has been enlivened by the placement of several provocative adjectives before it. For example, we now have the "relevant curriculum," "sequential curriculum," "spiral curriculum," "new curriculum," and "hidden curriculum." Frequently, a progressive school will dazzle its PTA with a fireworks display of such adjectives, proclaiming that some new course of study constitutes a "sequential and spiral relevant new curriculum." When this happens, duck.

Sans mumbo jumbo, a "relevant" curriculum would be a program of studies that is extremely interesting to students. In practice, this often turns out to be a program of studies that concentrates on what students already know about, not on what they might be interested to know about. As a consequence, some awfully repetitious and generally nonilluminating courses have been given in the name of "relevance." In any case, the term "relevant curriculum" is not very useful, precisely because the word relevant has been inflated out of all meaningful shape. Nonetheless, the phrase has made one small contribution: it has invited school people to look at what's happening *from the students' point of view*. This does not mean that one must pander to ephemeral student interest. It does mean that teachers must ask themselves seriously if their reasons for teaching something are based on student needs or their own.

The phrase "sequential curriculum" is somewhat redundant, since it is supposed to mean a program of studies that proceeds in an ordered way from "lower" to "higher" skills, with each lesson building on skills and concepts learned in previous lessons. Of course, any curriculum—"sequential" or otherwise—is supposed to do something like that, although in practice many do not. Most commonly, a curriculum is a random collection of subjects, tenuously alleged to have something to do with culture or education. The term "sequential curriculum" is supposed to remind teachers that a curriculum ought to have some coherent organization.

A "spiral curriculum," as the metaphor suggests, is a curriculum which moves from "lower" to "higher" skills, but which systematically turns back to review and consolidate previous learnings before going on. Any good teacher will also try to do something like that, and one may well wonder what all the new labels are about.

In point of fact, the terms "sequential" and "spiral" both derive from the period of curriculum reform (late 1950s and early 60s) when "new curriculums" were sprouting like weeds. You've probably heard of the New Math. Well, in addition to that we now have the New English, the New Science, the New Social Studies, and so on. In general, the idea underlying all the new curriculums is that the study of a subject ought to engage students in *doing* what the scholars in that field *do*. The old curriculums were mainly concerned with getting students to remember the facts that those scholars had already discovered. The problem there, as everyone knows, is that students forget the facts. And so do the scholars themselves—by which we mean that the facts in any given subject *change* at a remarkably rapid rate. The new curriculums have tried to overcome this problem by emphasizing how facts are discovered in any discipline. By engaging students in the *process* of scholarship, the new curriculums teach them (in theory, at least) how to ask questions, how to define terms, how to seek answers—all of which knowledge should stand the learners in good stead no matter how much or how fast the *content* of the discipline changes. In practice, unfortunately, the new curriculums have quite often turned out to be modified versions of the old. However, in some schools one can find exciting applications of the "process approach" to curriculum.

According to some school critics, notably Ivan Illich, no school curriculum—whether old or new, spiral or sequential, relevant or irrelevant—has the impact on children's lives that the "hidden curriculum" of school has. By "hidden curriculum," Illich and others mean the essential structure of the schooling process itself. In other words, the particular conventions used to order the lives of children in school are insignificant when compared with the basic fact that the children are supervised and evaluated, that their time and activities are structured, and so on. The medium, in short, is the message. And the message of the hidden curriculum is that school is for the purpose of processing children so that they can fit into society. So what else is new?

CUSTODIANS (NÉE JANITORS)

It has been pointed out by a number of school critics, including Charles Silberman, that the role of custodians in advancing or retarding school reform has been generally overlooked. We wish here to correct that oversight. Custodians have all kinds of power in a school, since in many ways they control the use of space, the arrangement of furniture, the availability of certain materials and media, and so on. Along with school secretaries, custodians provide a certain texture—sometimes appealing, sometimes not—to a school environment. And it is not unusual for them to exert a more powerful presence than even a principal. Almost everyone in the school business has at least one horror story concerning custodians. There are instances, for example, where custodians have objected to the rearrangement of chairs in classrooms or the use of facilities before and after school hours, and have thus effectively blocked some interesting innovation. But the situation is not all that bleak. Many school custodians are cooperative and imaginative, and their efforts have helped teachers to get important things done.

DECENTRALIZATION

During the past fifty years, the school and almost every other public institution has become increasingly large, impersonal, and bureaucratic. The word "alienated" is commonly used to describe how people feel toward some of their basic institutions. In the case of school, decentralization is supposed to represent the cure. Through decentralization, it is believed, people will get in closer touch with their schools, and thus be able to participate more meaningfully in decisions affecting their own children. It is a consummation devoutly to be wished. But there are a few problems.

Let's start from the beginning. In the liberal ideology, it has been widely asserted that centralization—yes, even bureaucracy—is one of the best protections we have against the tyranny of provincialism. There can be no doubt that this is true in many ways. What prevents a community from deciding that it will prohibit, by law, blacks or Jews or Catholics or you name it from attending its schools? The answer is, the largest centralized agency in the country—the U.S. government. In fact, it is probably true to say that, insofar as civil liberties are concerned, the federal judicial system has done more to protect against their infringement, in this century, than any other institution. And so the argument against large, concentrated power is by no means clear-cut. Such power can be used, and has been, to protect people from the whimsical, idiosyncratic, and tyrannical exercise of localized power. Moreover, centralized authority can undoubtedly accomplish many things that diversified authority cannot. A serious crisis arises, though, when centralized authority runs amok—as in the case of the Vietnam war—or when its bureaucratic structure gets so congealed that change becomes almost impossible—as in the case of many centralized school systems. At that point, movement toward decentralization is almost always healthy.

But the question is, How can decentralization be achieved

without losing, at the same time, all the benefits of centralization? This is the puzzle at the center of most of the controversy over decentralizing schools. In New York City, for example, it was obvious that a school system of over 1 million children and 50,000 teachers could not be administered intelligently, let alone efficiently. Inevitably, decentralization was required. But many questions remain unanswered. The teachers worry that autonomous communities might disregard hard-earned protections against arbitrary dismissals. Administrators worry about how funds will be distributed. Some parents worry about the schools becoming overly politicized. These are worries particularly relevant to large-city systems. Outside the cities, you do not find much centralization—at least not of the type that causes alienation and gross inefficiency. But since most American children go to city schools, the issues of decentralizations are in urgent need of resolution.

The issues can be summed up like this: If we really want neighborhood schools, then neighborhood people must decide what kinds of schools they want, including who should teach in and administer them. But how can we protect administrators, teachers, and students from the exercise of irresponsible authority? How can we ensure a minimum degree of quality if some local authority fails to supply it? How can we ensure an equitable system of financing? In other words, if there is true decentralization of authority, will there be true decentralization of financial responsibility? And if a community has to pay for its own schools, won't inner-city schools be at a serious disadvantage? On the other hand, can we ask taxpayers to support school systems over whose policies they have no control?

It must be said, of course, that from the standpoint of many black and Hispanic parents, such questions are maddeningly irrelevant. They believe that their children are being victimized by an uncaring, remote bureaucracy, and they feel justified in using whatever means are at their disposal to wrest control of the schools from such centralized authority. This means inevitably that there will be no quiet solutions in the years ahead.

DIDACTIC TEACHING

This is a technical-sounding term for a situation that is perfectly familiar to almost everybody: a classroom in which the teacher is at the front of the room telling students, straight out, what he thinks they ought to know. The teacher may ask few questions or many, but they are usually of the "What Am I Thinking?" variety; that is, the student is expected to give an answer that the teacher has previously determined is "right." If the student can say what the teacher wants to hear, he has answered correctly. If he says something different, the teacher tries to find someone else who can say the right words. A didactic teacher may, of course, use provocative materials, and may even give interesting talks. He is almost always well organized, and some of the most memorable teachers on any school faculty are essentially didactic. But the point is that didactic methods do not require much thinking on the part of the learner. The learner is supposed to "absorb" the knowledge of the teacher. In most cases, knowledge absorbed in this manner is retained for about one marking period.

DIFFERENTIATED STAFFING

Differentiated staffing is another old idea that seems new because a lot of new people have never heard of it. It refers to a process by which a teacher's work is assigned according to his or her ability, much as it was in the old craft guilds, where one went through stages from apprentice to master. The terms used in differentiated staffing are even similar to those used in the old craft guilds, ranging from "novice" for a beginning teacher to "master teacher" for one who ostensibly has more capability after some years of experience. Differentiated staffing is merely an attempt to recognize that with all the virtues of a "single salary schedule" (which most school systems have) there are differences between and among teachers, and that not all teachers can do everything equally well. It is also an attempt to recognize the fact that not all teachers become better merely as a result of longevity.

Differentiated staffing will make teachers nervous, probably because it smacks of another old school problem, "merit" pay. The problem with distinguishing important differences between the abilities of different teachers is that no one has yet succeeded in stating the criteria by which to make this judgment, much less a process by which the criteria can be employed.

As such devices as performance-based criteria become part of the school process, some attempt at developing criteria and methods of judging will have to be made. You will hear the hollering that accompanies these attempts, because it will be loud, for both good and bad reasons.

DYSLEXIA

Your son has trouble reading. He is in fourth grade, and he reads *was* for *saw*, *dog* for *god*. He spells *girl*, *gril*. You are worried, especially because his sister was reading well when she was ten. You go to see your son's teacher. The teacher says, "Perhaps he has dyslexia." What's she talking about?

The sentence "He has dyslexia" is to the diagnosis of reading problems what the sentence "He has a cold" is to medical diagnosis. When someone has a cold, you know he is not well, but the precise cause of the problem is unknown—to you, him, the doctor, and everyone else. When someone has dyslexia, you know he has a problem, but you don't know why, and neither does anyone else. Dyslexia, in short, is a catchall term. In its narrowest and most technical sense, it frequently implies a neurological dysfunction, but in its general use, it means simply that a child is experiencing some unusual difficulties in learning to read. The symptoms may or may not include the reversal or inversion of letters; may or may not include a refusal to try to read; may or may not include an inability to see certain words; may or may not include similar problems in the perception of numbers or of any figures drawn on paper.

Since 1896, when an English physician named Morgan described for the first time a condition he called "congenital word-blindness," more than 20,000 books, articles, and papers have been published on the subject of dyslexia. All this activity has been in search of a common behavior pattern in dyslexic children, and of hard evidence of a common neurological cause. At the moment, there is no clear-cut evidence of either.

Nonetheless, the term dyslexia is being increasingly used by school people as a kind of general diagnosis of reading disability. It's not much good as a diagnosis, because the term does not imply any special teaching strategies for remedying the problem. Moreover, many children are having difficulty learning to read because they are subjected to bad teaching. To label them dyslexic is not only inaccurate but also obscures where the real problem lies.

In summary, dyslexia is a technical-sounding but nonetheless vague term referring to a wide range of reading difficulties for which the causes are unknown. If a teacher suggests that your child might have dyslexia, don't panic. She is probably wrong—but you should check with a doctor anyway, and preferably with a neurologist.

EDUCATION KONFERENCE/EDUCATION CONFERENCE

The first phrase describes a meeting of free school advocates, during which there will be several radical caucuses, continuous expression of solidarity with "the people," and an almost total preoccupation with financing. It is not entirely clear why *konference* is spelled with a *k*, except that it indicates a certain contempt for the establishment way of doing things. Which is why the konferees are always short of money.

The second phrase refers to a meeting of establishment teachers and administrators, during which nothing happens at all—except in the hotel bar.

EDUCATION RESEARCH

This is a process whereby serious educators discover knowledge that is well known to everybody, and has been for several centuries. Its principal characteristic is that no one pays any attention to it. This is unfortunate because it is quite important that school people be reminded of simple and venerable truths. For example, in spite of our attempts to make teaching into a science, in spite of our attempts to invent teacher-proof materials, and even in spite of our attempts to create "relevant new curricula," one simple fact makes most of this ambition quite unnecessary. It is as follows: When a child perceives a teacher to be an authentic, warm, and curious person, the child learns. When the child does not perceive the teacher as such a person, he has difficulty learning, or does not learn what is being taught. There is almost no way to get around this fact, although technological people such as ourselves try very hard to. We believe in experts and expertise, and we tend not to trust any activity that does not involve a complex technique. And yet, increasing the complexity of the act of teaching has not really made much difference, for there is always the simple fact that teaching is the art of being human and of communicating that humanness to others. Believe it or not, that's what most of our education research adds up to.

EXTRACURRICULAR ACTIVITY

An activity that is not required, on which students are not graded, in which students have an intense interest, and where instruction—when needed—is informal and personal, is called "extracurricular." Such activities would include swimming or playing basketball, putting out a newspaper or magazine, performing in a play or orchestra, doing a science or art project. If you are thinking that such activities are dynamic, creative, and altogether educational in the best sense, you are in good company. In fact, some educators have even argued that since extracurricular activities promote more wholesome learning than curricular (i.e., mandated) activities, the simplest way to improve schools is to make all activities extracurricular. The idea is not altogether unserious. The characteristics of an extracurricular activity form a useful model for almost any system of learning: there is no compulsion, relatively little fear of failure, continuous self-evaluation, almost no record keeping, many options, informal relationships, clear objectives, indisputable relevance, no distinction between work and play. Think about it.

FIELD-TESTED PROGRAM

When a publishing company is ready to sell a textbook or other school material, it almost always announces that the stuff has been field-tested. This is supposed to mean that during and after the preparation of the book (or whatever), real teachers tried the material out with real kids in real situations and everyone found everything superb. In those rare cases where things don't work out, revisions are carefully made until everyone is satisfied.

Naturally, no one believes any of this, but the charade persists, sometimes with ingenious elaborations.

The plain fact is that publishers produce materials that some editor thinks will sell. On rare occasions such material will turn out to be of great interest to both students and teachers, and something of value will be learned from it. When this occurs, everyone is surprised, especially the publisher.

FREE SCHOOLS

The "free" refers to the atmosphere, not the tuition. In fact, free schools are essentially private schools, but with this difference: the people who start and run them generally reject the entire gamut of traditional school conventions. This includes the grades, the lectures, the tests, the competition, the courses, and especially the authoritarianism. As a consequence, in many free schools, the children have as much to say about what happens as the adults, which has the effect, sometimes, of helping the children to grow up—and sometimes of making the adults more childlike. Mostly the latter. There is no telling exactly how many free schools there are in the country, but estimates run somewhere between 1,500 and 2,000. Most of these schools are in a financially shaky condition from start to finish, and they go out of business at an uncommonly high rate. Jonathan Kozol's book *Free Schools* (1972) is the most comprehensive statement we have on the meaning of the Free School movement. In it he denounces the irrelevant romanticism and dilettantism that characterize many free schools, but he sees a clear need for the continued vigor of the movement. Essentially, the case for free schools runs something like this: Free schools, in general, do not have to cope with the bureaucratic restraints and demands that face public schools. Therefore, there are practically no limits to the variety and depth of experimentation open to them. From such experimentation, we can find out much about how children learn, some of which could be applied to the schooling of all children. Moreover, a healthy system of free schools would serve as a safety valve for those who simply cannot function or do not believe in public schools. Whether or not we will get a healthy system of free schools depends on many factors, not the least of which concerns how they can be securely financed (see voucher system, p. 195). Another factor concerns the quality of the teachers who are attracted to them. With some notable exceptions, the quality has so far been exceedingly poor. We shall see.

GOOD SCHOOL

We have given a definition of this term in Chapter 3. We have also provided a handy evaluation chart on pages 102–103 which may be used as a basis for making judgments about the quality of a school. Here we want only to point out that, for many people, what makes a school good has nothing whatever to do with what we have been saying. For example, there are parents for whom the proper definition of a good school is a school with few or no blacks, and not threatened by integration—forced or otherwise. There are black parents who regard a school as good only if it has black teachers and a black administrator. Some parents think a school is good if a high proportion of its students go on to college, and some think a school is good if the halls are quiet. There are even people for whom the concept of a good school is wholly dependent on whether or not prayers are said in the morning. There are, in short, almost as many definitions as there are people. This is a point you might think is hardly worth making. But the fact is that in their search for "good" schools, many parents are too easily satisfied with superficial evaluations, as against detailed descriptions of what happens in a school. A typical conversation might go something like this:

"We've been looking for a house in your town. How're the schools?"

"The schools? Really good. Our kids go to the elementary school, which is excellent—but the high school is good, too."

"That's nice to hear. We're moving, you know, because the school our kids go to is really bad."

"Well, I think you'll find that the schools here are good. Not perfect, of course, but very good."

Unless someone inquires, *at some point*, into the criteria being used for "good," this kind of conversation can have disasterous consequences. Of course, if your aim is primarily to establish amicable social relationships with your neighbors, it is probably best to let the term "good school" go undefined. But if you really need to know about the schools, you'd better ask, What do you mean by "good"?

GRADING SYSTEM

Just about everyone knows what this term refers to, and there is no point in describing it here in detail. However, it is worth saying that the standard variety of grading (whether letters or numbers) appears to be the bedrock on which many other school conventions rest. Take away the grading system and a general collapse would probably follow. For example, without grading, there would be no need for midterms, finals, tracking, courses, and a dozen other dubious practices. This is why school reformers have discovered the grading system to be the most difficult of all school conventions to dislodge. Still, the effort to do so must continue. In almost all cases, the grading system tends to diminish the value of learning. Students rarely (would you believe, never?) ask at the end of the term, "What did you learn?" They ask, "What did you get?" The grading system teaches them that competence and pleasure in learning are not as important as getting a good grade. And getting a good grade is not necessarily related to either. In fact, it is not too much to say that the grading system institutionalizes cheating in the schools and in many ways corrupts the meaning of evaluation.

Unfortunately, the various alternatives to grading that have so far been proposed have not been practical, and the search continues frantically. In general, the search is an attempt to replace an intimidating, cabalistic, abstract symbol with a non-punitive, constructive, and concrete means of evaluation. For a status report on the search, see *Wad-Ja-Get?* by Sid Simon *et al.*

A final point: Since a grade is at least a quasi-public document, and since a poor grade can have the effect of damaging a student's reputation and limiting his future income, some critics have charged that the assignment of a poor grade constitutes libel. It is doubtful that any court would sustain that view, but the issue will certainly arise in the near future.

GUIDANCE COUNSELOR

As secondary schools became larger and larger, they became more and more impersonal and factorylike. One result of this was that students really did not have any extended association with any teachers. They never got to be known as individuals themselves, and they didn't ever get to know any school personnel as individuals. For this reason, along with several others, such as the increasing use of standardized tests, a new function was added to the high schools, that of guidance. The original intention seems to have been to provide *someone* a student could speak to about some specific personal problem, and in the process be guided to a choice or decision that would be better than one made for emotional reasons on the basis of inadequate or inaccurate information.

But, the way things worked out, guidance counselors—despite their professional training—turned out to be clerks whose job it was to straighten out scheduling problems (for the convenience of the school, not the student) and to keep file cabinets full of records relating to students. The records included students' grades, the scores they made on tests, information about jobs and colleges, and assorted information from one agency or another about adolescent problems. As the quantity of paper they had to file increased, guidance counselors had less and less time and energy to devote to dealing with students. If you have ever had any dealing with a governmental agency, such as the employment service, or the Veterans Administration, or a free clinic, or the Internal Revenue Service, you know how students feel when they go to the guidance office. In most schools, this is the last place any kid would go for help or guidance.

HOMOGENEOUS GROUPING/HETEROGENEOUS GROUPING

The first phrase refers to the practice of assigning children to classes on the basis of their similarity in reading ability, IQ score, or general academic achievement. This is sometimes called *tracking*. And many school critics believe it to be an educational caste system which has the effect of teaching arrogance to those at the top and despair to those at the bottom. The second phrase refers to the practice of *not* doing this—that is, of forming classes indiscriminately, so that each class will have a random distribution of "good," "average," and "poor" students.

The major argument in favor of homogeneous grouping is that children of roughly equal ability can be taught more efficiently than children of varying abilities. Some people even believe that "smart" children will be held back if there are "dumb" children in their classes, because the teacher will naturally have to spend more time with the latter than the former. They also believe that "dumb" children will be made to feel even dumber if they are put together with "smart" children.

The replies to this argument are many and, in our opinion, decisive: All children are both smart and dumb at the same time. For example, a child who reads poorly may have extraordinary musical talent and artistic insight. A child who reads well may be disinclined to think independently. A child with poor performance in mathematics may be a natural leader, with unusually developed persuasive powers. A child with a high IQ may have no aptitude for solving real-life problems. And so on. Therefore, when a school groups homogeneously, it is saying in effect that it values certain aptitudes and skills more than others. But this preference is arbitrary. Why should artistic ability, social effectiveness, or leadership qualities be rated lower than, say, reading ability? Thus, the first objection to homogeneous grouping is that it is based on a limited concept of ability, talent, and intelligence.

The second objection is that even if you group homogeneously you really have a mixed lot anyway—although you may not realize it. Just because twenty-five children have roughly the same reading test scores does not mean they are similar in other respects. For all practical purposes, there will be as many real differences among the students in a homogeneously grouped class as in any other kind of class. Thus it is a snare and a delusion to think that homogeneity makes for more efficient instruction.

A third objection is that research indicates that officially designated "smart" children do *not* perform any better or worse because of how they are grouped, and that officially designated "dumb" children benefit, rather than suffer, from heterogeneous grouping. And a fourth objection is that there is evidence that the process of labelling children "dumb" (whether or not they are called "Bluebirds") can have serious consequences in their lives, because they ultimately accept and internalize the school's judgment of them.

All things considered, then, homogeneous grouping would appear to be at best unfair and ill founded, and at worst, malevolent. Still, many people favor it. Why? One reason is that, to a considerable extent, homogeneous grouping divides students among social and economic lines, since success in school, as the Coleman Report showed, is largely a function of a student's background. Thus, homogeneous grouping is a practical and legal way of maintaining segregation, and there are people who desire that outcome. Another reason is that many teachers believe, in spite of research findings to the contrary, that they can "do more" with homogeneously grouped students. And as long as they continue to believe this, the practice will continue.

Parents tend not to object to homogeneous grouping so long as their children are in a "high" track. When their children are in a "low" track, they begin to understand how damaging it can be.

(For more, see nongraded classroom, p. 181)

HUMANISTIC EDUCATION

This is another one of those terms, like "relevant curriculum," that has as many different meanings as there are people who use it. Most often, though, school people who call themselves humanists mean to distinguish themselves from behaviorists. The humanists believe that behaviorist objectives and methods are mechanistic and will produce automatons, not autonomous people. They believe that the characteristics of a creative, humane person cannot be reduced to simple behaviors such as can be reinforced in the manner of animal training. And they believe that helping children to be more human (as opposed, say, to being better spellers) is the main function of schooling. Moreover, they tend to believe that conventional schooling is so structured that it is virtually impossible for a student to learn how to relate authentically and sensitively to other people. As a consequence, many humanists have abandoned conventional schools altogether and have become involved in free schools.

The humanists have consistently encountered two formidable problems which have not been adequately resolved. First, they have been unable to design an environment, or even a program, that can demonstrably contribute toward making a child more humane (even assuming that everyone could agree on what that means). And second, inevitably, humanists have had to offer themselves as illustrations of what a humane, creative person is like. If you have ever met an avowed humanist, you probably know what a problem this is.

Nonetheless, the best expressions of the humanist point of view come from such substantial people as Carl Rogers and the late Abraham Maslow. Their ideas of what a real education could be like stand in sharp and inspiring contrast to the one-dimensional conception of the behaviorists. And it is important, it seems to us, that the humanist ideal, if not the humanists themselves, be considered with the utmost seriousness.

HYPERKINESIS

Children who are excessively restless, cannot concentrate, and are difficult to control are sometimes labeled "hyperkinetic." This means that the child is assumed to have a chemical abnormality that affects the brain and causes his disorganized behavior. The label can be trusted if it has been assigned by a competent neurologist, who has given the child a battery of tests. In that case, amphetamines and other drugs may be prescribed, and some children have apparently been helped by them. Under the influence of drugs, they are able to control their desire to wander, both physically and mentally. Of course, the physician and parents must decide together if the administration of drugs giving temporary relief outweighs the risk to the child of possible long-term addiction. It must also be borne in mind that the hyperkinetic syndrome ordinarily disappears at the onset of puberty.

If the label hyperkinetic is assigned by a teacher, principal, school nurse, school secretary, custodian, school superintendent, school board member, or anyone else but a neurologist, *it is not to be trusted.* John Holt, Nat Hentoff, and others have uncovered a practice in some schools of almost indiscriminate labeling of troublesome children as hyperkinetic. They have even reported cases where, on the basis of totally inadequate diagnoses, parents were pressured into consenting to the use of drugs to make their children more tractable in school. It cannot be stressed too heavily that many children who are difficult to handle may have nothing whatever wrong with them. Considering how boring many classrooms are, it's a wonder that more children do not wander, turn off, and exhibit restlessness.

Some physicians, for example, William Glasser in *The Identity Society* (1972), suggest that the symptoms of hyperkinesis are made more pervasive by the lack of personal involvement experienced by children of the TV era. He claims that prolonged television viewing can actually cause children to act out their frustrations in the classroom, and thus appear to be hyperkinetic.

In any case, a wise parent will not trust any layman's diagnosis of hyperkinesis. More often than not, the problem is not that children are hyperkinetic, but that their classrooms are hyperlethargic.

INDIVIDUALIZED INSTRUCTION

This will sometimes occur when a teacher acknowledges that not all biological and intellectual needs of children can be satisfied by collective action. Then, if it's possible, the teacher follows the line usually taken by any sensible parent—namely, that each child is singular in his/her development and requires special attention. The problem is that in most schools, individualized instruction is not possible because there are simply too many students for the teacher to cope with. Thus, only those students who distinguish themselves, as scholars or as troublemakers, earn individual attention.

In schools that have made it possible for teachers to deal on an individual basis with students' needs (usually as a result of a government grant), students inevitably do better than they have previously done. In most schools, however, about the only good example of individualized instruction you can find is exhibited by athletic coaches or drama teachers. Some schools claim to have individualized instruction when they use programmed learning materials or machines. In such cases, the materials and machines are designed to indicate to students, on an individual basis, whether or not they had the right answer to a certain problem. Any administrator who believes this represents individualized instruction has an impoverished idea of what a real, human teacher can do.

INDUCTIVE TEACHING

This is a method of instruction that goes by many names. Sometimes it is called *discovery learning,* sometimes *inquiry training,* sometimes *the Socratic Method,* and sometimes *heuristic teaching.* It amounts to a learning situation in which the student, not the teacher, carries the burden of intellectual effort. What usually happens is that the teacher poses a problem for the students, for which the teacher may or may not have an answer. (Socrates, in spite of his claims to the contrary, *always* had an answer.) The point is for students to come up with adequate answers to the problem by using their own powers of questioning, observation, and generalization. When the technique is used well, it can often help students learn how to solve problems, which is another way of saying, to think for themselves. Unfortunately, the technique does not always work, especially if the problems hold no interest for the students, or if the teacher is inexperienced in using such methods. When this last is the case, the problem generally is that the teacher does not know the difference between *convergent* and *divergent questions.* A convergent question is one which narrows thinking; a divergent question broadens thinking. For example, "What is the capital of Illinois?" is a convergent question because its answer leaves no room for speculation or, in fact, for any kind of thinking process other than memory. You either know it or you don't. On the other hand, "What are some of the ways we might solve our pollution problems?" is a divergent question, because it requires students to use analogies, contrasts, metaphors, and other instruments of thinking (including facts). It is also the kind of question that leads to other questions. In this way, the process of learning becomes a continuous and dynamic experience, as against an artificial and static one.

In a classroom in which inductive methods are used, the main emphasis is, naturally, on *how* students are doing their thinking, not on *what* they think. That is why an inductive teacher is often called "process-oriented." Process-oriented teachers not infrequently get into trouble with both administrators and parents, who are sometimes more interested in the content of a student's learning than in the methods by which a student is acquiring content. Some parents believe that anything less than traditional fact-oriented teaching will make it difficult for their children to get into college. For what it's worth, all the evidence we have indicates that there is no truth to this belief whatsoever.

INNER-CITY SCHOOL

This is a school located in what we conventionally call a city, and one which has mostly poor children in it. Such a school used to be called a ghetto school, and, before that, a slum school. Apparently, "inner-city" sounds nicer and is presumably more descriptive. The same antiseptic linguistic process has occurred in relation to the kids themselves. In the old days, children of the poor were called poor children, sometimes slum children or ghetto kids. In more recent times, their label has been elevated to "culturally deprived," "culturally disadvantaged," and even "culturally different." It is doubtful that this semantic hocus-pocus has made much difference to the kids, although some teachers might feel better about working with "the culturally different in an inner-city school" than they would about working with "poor kids in a slum." One thing is clear: children of the poor, and especially of the despairing, are different in important ways from children of the aspiring middle class. When you are poor, you do not have adequate access to experiences that the culture values. When you are poor, the exigencies of survival divert your attention from learning the conventional wisdom and the appropriate schoolhouse demeanor. None of this should be new to anyone who is operating at a level somewhat above Archie Bunker. But it is surprising that so many people who appear to perceive the dimensions of the psychological devastation of poverty, racism, and hopelessness also believe that the school can adequately deal with the problem. While it is true that empathetic, knowledgeable, and dedicated teachers can make a difference of sorts, the problem of the ghetto school will continue largely unattended until the ghetto itself is eliminated. This is no argument against improving ghetto schools. We are talking about distinguishing between causes and symptoms. The ghetto school is bad because the ghetto is bad. Ghetto schools can be made better, and have been, but we must not mistake making the patient more comfortable for curing the disease.

INSTRUCTIONAL TECHNOLOGY

In the days before bureaucratic double-talk (if there ever were any such days), instructional technology would have been called teaching equipment.

If you were to visit twenty or thirty or forty classrooms at random, in any kind of school from first through twelfth grade, the chances are that the most sophisticated instructional technology you would see is a chalkboard. And, chances are, there won't even be any chalk.

INTELLECTUALLY GIFTED

Children whose IQs are somewhere around 125 and above are considered to be intellectually gifted, and are thereby thought to be worthy of special treatment. It is not entirely clear why. Some people take a political tack, asserting that such children are a precious national resource and, like all precious resources, need to be carefully nurtured. That is to say, the development of these children is viewed as providing America with certain advantages in the future, such as ensuring a full complement of scientists, physicians, engineers, writers, and the like. Other people take a psychological approach, claiming that the intellectually gifted cannot learn in the same way that "normal" children do, and therefore require special classes. The psychological argument applies equally to retarded children, and one will sometimes come upon the phrase "exceptional children," a term that refers to any child who requires special attention, whether the child is exceptionally bright or exceptionally slow.

From the standpoint of public policy, both these arguments are controversial, especially when they imply that a school should invest extra time and money in helping exceptional children. In the first place, every parent regards his or her child as exceptional. If a school proposes to treat certain children as special, often at the expense of others, the reasons ought to be compelling. Most parents will, of course, acquiesce to special assistance for retarded children, on the grounds that such children are, from the start, at a serious disadvantage in life. If they can be helped in any way to function on an equal basis with others, it is generally urged that this should be done. But the intellectually gifted, in theory at least, begin school with a considerable advantage. By definition, a high IQ means that your chances of being successful in business, the professions, and other important fields are excellent. Why, then, should this advantage be increased, particularly if it is done at the expense of others? The answer that these children are likely to be more valuable to our country will not appeal to many parents—perhaps only to those who are superpatriots. In any case, the political argument is just that—a political argument. And like all such arguments, it is made up of conflicting ideas about the meaning of democracy, egalitarianism, justice, and the like. So much depends on what you think is valuable, and whether or not you think a school has the right to make that judgment.

The psychological argument is, in theory, easier to resolve. Essentially, the question is, Do intellectually gifted children learn differently from other children? If the answer is yes, then the school is probably obliged to make the appropriate arrangements, even if it means incurring unusual expense. At the present time, however, we do not have a clear answer to the question, and it is not likely that we will get one in the near future. In fact, we do not even have sophisticated knowledge about how "ordinary" children learn. And so, the issue of whether or not we should have, at public expense, programs or schools for the intellectually gifted will continue to be decided on the basis of political philosophy.

INTELLIGENCE TESTS

In order to make any sense out of this term, you must first know the meaning of two other terms used in testing: "reliability" and "validity." A test (or any measuring device) is *reliable* when you get consistent results from it upon repeating the test. If you get on and off your bathroom scale three times in succession, and you get the same reading each time, your scale is reliable. If you get three different readings, it's not. But validity is something else. A test is *valid* if it measures accurately what it says it's supposed to measure. Suppose some salesman sold you your scale to help you check your height. No matter how many times it reads 135 pounds, it's never going to tell you how tall you are. In that case, your scale is still reliable, but it's not valid. So a test can be reliable without being valid. But if it's not reliable, then it cannot be valid.

Now, the simplest way to get valid results is to measure things *directly*—for example, the way we measure height with a standardized ruler, or weight with a reliable scale. But many things that scientists want to measure cannot be measured so directly as height or weight, and this will always cause problems in assuring validity. What they have to do is measure something *else*, under the assumption that there is some correlation between that and what they want to know. In the field of medicine, for example, there is no way to measure "health" directly. Instead, we measure such things as body temperature, blood pressure, and the like, on the assumption that these things correlate with the presence or absence of disease. In psychology, "intelligence" falls in this category. To get an indirect measurement of intelligence, psychologists have constructed a variety of tests of what they call verbal ability, verbal fluency, numerical ability, spatial ability, perceptual ability, memory, and inductive reasoning. These tests tend to be fairly reliable. Of that there is little doubt. Most people will get roughly the same scores each time they take them. The question is, How *valid* are they? Do these tests measure intelligence? The psychologists say they do, because high scores on such tests have a correlation with success in school, or in business, or in the military. (The earliest significant work in the field of intelligence testing was done by Alfred Binet and others during World War I, in an attempt to predict who would make good officers and who wouldn't.) In other words, the psychologists *define* intelligence as success in school, business, and so on, and have designed tests whose scores correlate with performance in these areas. Thus, from a practical standpoint, intelligence tests have been useful, particularly in industry and the military, for predicting with some accuracy what your chances are of making it.

But does this mean that they are really defining intelligence? Most people in the field of testing will give an answer something like this: Intelligence is a term so vague that it is difficult to get any two people to agree on a definition. But it is fairly obvious that success in school or business is considered by most people to require some degree of intelligence. That is, the *culture* defines intelligence, to a considerable extent, as being successful in these fields. In addition to that, there are some fairly specific criteria for judging success in school or business— for example, high grades or promotion to executive status. Therefore, we feel justified in using such standards as a basis for establishing the validity of our tests.

There are, of course, some objections to this line of thought. One is that success in school or business does not imply intelligence, but only a willingness to be amicable and to conform. The psychologists reply that many people who desire to be amicable and to conform nonetheless fare badly in school or business. Something else is at work, and that something is intelligence. The objectors come back with: Maybe so, but this is at best a very limited concept of intelligence. True, say the psychologists. We never claimed anything more for it.

The trouble is that many people, including teachers, *do*. They have somehow got it into their heads that intelligence tests measure a fixed thing called intelligence. *This is not true.* An intelligence test gives you a score comparing your performance on certain tests with the performance of other people on those tests. And the social significance of your score is that it roughly estimates your chances of succeeding, in certain ways, in certain fields.

What does it all mean? Generally speaking, intelligence tests are reliable. How valid they are depends on whether or not you accept the definition of intelligence used. One thing is sure: no reputable psychologist would claim that an intelligence test measures a "thing" called "intelligence." And even the staunchest defender of the validity of intelligence tests will admit that the definition of intelligence expressed by the tests themselves is sharply limited (For more, see IQ, below, and Arthur Jensen p. 226.)

IQ (INTELLIGENCE QUOTIENT)

An IQ is the ratio $\frac{\text{mental age}}{\text{chronological age}} \times 100$. "Mental age" is determined by the number of "correct" answers which the "average" child of a specified age can give on a particular intelligence test. (There are many different publishers of intelligence tests, and school systems vary in which ones they prefer). For example, suppose a certain intelligence test has 100 questions on it, and 50 percent of all the ten-year-olds who take the test get 60 questions right. Those 50 percent, of course, would then represent the average ten-year-old, and a "mental age of ten" would be defined as 60 questions right. From then on, *anyone* who takes that test and gets 60 questions right is said to have a mental age of ten, no matter how old he really is. If he happens to be ten years old, his IQ would be 100, since $\frac{10 \text{ (mental age)}}{10 \text{ (chronological age)}}$ $\times$ 100 = 100. If he is five years old, his IQ would be 200 ($\frac{10}{5} \times$ 100 = 200). If he is twelve years old, his IQ would be 83 ($\frac{10}{12} \times$ 100 = 83). By definition, the "average" child at any age has an IQ of 100.

It was once widely believed that a child's IQ was stable—that is, that it could not be increased. We know now that this is untrue. An IQ can be increased, not only through normal maturation, but through specific learning programs which teach how to take IQ tests. The idea behind giving IQ tests in school is that it is supposed to tell the teacher what a student is capable of. If, for example, a child gets an IQ of 50, the teacher is supposed to know that the child is mentally retarded. But of course, if the teacher has not already noticed that there is anything retarded about the child, then the test is simply inaccurate. If the teacher *has* noticed, then the test is irrelevant. In short, the way a teacher responds to a child should be based on the way the child actually behaves, not on the way some test says he is likely to behave. Which is why some school systems (New York City, for example) have stopped giving IQ tests altogether. Another reason is that it is just about impossible to construct a culture-free IQ test; that is, a test which measures intelligence instead of cultural background.

In places where IQ tests are still given and respected, one sometimes comes across the terms "underachiever" and "overachiever." The first term refers to a student with a superior IQ score, whose performance in school is below someone's expectations. The second term refers to a student with an average or low IQ score, whose performance in school is above someone's expectations. The latter term, overachiever, is particularly ridiculous because it amounts to asserting that a child has skills or understandings that he is not supposed to have. Who says he's not supposed to have them? The IQ test. You would think it might occur to someone, in such cases, that the test is faulty. Well, it does. But not to everybody. Actually, we are probably all underachievers, in the sense that—life being what it is—none of us ever performs quite up to our best.

KINDERGARTEN

A few remarks need to be made about this venerable institution. Kindergarten is supposed to be a child's initial experience in school, occurring at about the age of five—which some people think is rather too early. But it now appears that many American parents are more eager to relinquish their children to the care of others than one would have supposed. By the time they get to kindergarten, some children have been going to school for years. Nursery schools are now an established part of the school industry, and some of them will accept children as young as three years—and have no trouble finding customers.

It is hard to know what such a trend signifies. To begin with, it probably says something about the decline of the extended family. In the good old days, a child was educated not only by father and mother, but by an ample supply of accessible and involved adults—grandparents, uncles, aunts, older cousins, and so on. In today's situation, most often the mother is left alone to cope with the insatiable curiosity and relentless energy of the child, and a preschool school comes as a welcome—maybe even a mind-saving—invention. After all, can anyone teach for fourteen hours a day without relief? Then too, the preschool school is simply a necessity for parents who must work, and is rapidly becoming one for families in which the mother wishes to pursue a career. The preschool school is also being utilized by anxious middle-class parents who fear that their children might "fall behind" in reading or arithemetic without a little head start. And speaking of head starts, the preschool school is increasingly being used by non-middle-class parents whose children will almost certainly have difficulty in school unless they get a running start on the system.

What does it all mean? Well, the school has always been shaped by the economic and social conditions of the society that supports it. The kindergarten as the five-year-old's entry point to institutionalized learning will probably disappear, replaced by a prekindergarten structure that will take children at four, three, two, maybe even younger. What will be the price? It's hard to say. Of necessity, a school must segment and regulate the learning process in ways that frequently run counter to the natural inclination (learning style) of young children. More than one educator has speculated that an institutional setting tends to reduce rather than increase a child's curiosity and malleability. As a medium for learning, there is no adequate substitute for the informality, warmth, fluidity, spontaneity, and individuality of the home. But if no one's home, what can you do?

LEARNING STYLES

In everyday conversation about schools, the terms "good student" and "bad student" come up all the time. When this happens, it is important to know that the use of either term always implies a *particular* kind of learning environment. In other words, there is no such thing as a "good" or a "bad" student in the abstract. Any good student you might know is good because he can accommodate himself effectively to a certain kind of arrangement for learning. The same student might be bad if put into an entirely different situation. This observation might seem perfectly obvious, but only recently has it been given any serious attention in school. The use of the term "learning style" is intended to help everyone remember that children vary widely in the ways in which they learn. Some, for example, thrive in a situation that is open-ended, with plenty of room for student initiative, but become moody and anxious in a tightly run, teacher-directed classroom. Others thrive in a conventional arrangement, but are irresponsible and confused in open classrooms. Unfortunately, we know very little about the various learning styles of children, and in fact we do not even have a decent vocabulary for talking about the matter. But this much is pretty clear: Very often, what we mean by a "discipline problem" or an "emotionally disturbed child" is a child who is being forced to accommodate himself to a situation that is simply unreasonable from his point of view. Naturally, such a child appears to be "bad" or "stupid," when in fact, the only thing holding him back is the absence of a situation that supports his way of learning. In other words, the learning situation is the problem, not the child.

There are, of course, children who seem unable to function well in *any* reasonably ordered learning environment. But there are probably not as many as we are led to think. Any school that is not providing at least one alternative structure will have a number of children who are being falsely labeled and judged. That's why we need more talk about "learning styles."

MINI-COURSES/MODULAR SCHEDULING

Mini-courses are simply courses that are shorter than the usual semester-long (twenty-week) ones. They are relatively new in the schools, and they seem to be the result of two parallel but disparate influences. The first is a lack of interest and disenchantment on the part of students that teachers find unnerving. The second is fallout from modular scheduling, another innovation in planning the school day. "Modular scheduling" is the result of research into the old educational assumption that all courses should meet for the same length of time, regularly, every day for twenty weeks. The research seemed to indicate that the school day could more profitably be arranged in "mods" (periods) of twenty minutes or some multiple of that time, depending on the material to be covered. Modular scheduling thus made more time available during the school day, and teachers began thinking about offering courses in subjects that kids were already interested in outside of school. This meant that many of the new electives had to do with subjects like ecology and witchcraft and Oriental philosophy and astronomy. As it turned out, not all these courses could sustain themselves for twenty weeks. And so was born the mini-course. At first, it was of varying lengths, depending upon all kinds of things. Then, as experience was gained, some sense of the length of time courses of this kind could sustain themselves was developed, and they were planned for three or six or eight weeks or whatever. Because of the variety that mini-courses provide, they seem to have a salutary effect.

MONTESSORI METHOD

The Montessori Method refers to a series of techniques developed by Maria Montessori. The aim of the method is to help children develop what she called their mental, spiritual, and physical personalities. Originally designed to be used with what we currently call "disadvantaged children" (Montessori called them "deficient children"), the techniques require careful teacher observation of the child and carefully kept records of his or her physical growth, motor skills, and cognitive development.

The physical environment in which learning takes place is an integral part of the Montessori Method, and the setting is supposed to include an open-air playground with enough space for gardening, as well as for active play. The classroom itself should contain movable furniture and equipment especially chosen to stimulate sensory experience. Through such arrangements, children are encouraged to learn self-discipline in their movements, and to observe the things in nature that surround them.

One of the most important components of the Montessori Method is its emphasis on sensory training. This is accomplished through a variety of means—for example, through gymnastics, coloring, and playing with specially designed toys. On this foundation, according to Montessori, children build their cognitive skills. These are further developed through a series of highly structured lessons during which the teacher tries to limit the child's focus to a specific learning task. Throughout the process, the teacher tries to avoid intervening more than is absolutely necessary.

In this country, Montessori schools or Montessori-oriented schools have flourished, particularly in recent years. Unfortunately, considerable confusion about them has flourished as well. To many people, "Montessori" suggests a kind of informal, free-wheeling environment. To others, "Montessori" suggests tightly organized lessons with well focused objectives. In a sense, each conception is correct, although each is incomplete without the other. On the one hand, the Montessori Method stresses what she called "the prepared environment." That is, the teacher controls the learning experience by carefully designing what the environment will contain. The teacher also has a well-formulated idea of how sensory experience helps to build intelligence, and of what the stages of cognitive growth are. In this sense, then, the Montessori Method *is* well organized with clear objectives. On the other hand, Montessori also insisted that teachers not correct a child who is making a mistake, not interrupt a child, not direct a child unless asked to, and, in general, be "invisible" as much as possible. She even urged teachers (if you can believe it) to animate the classroom by their *silence*. In short, she wanted her method to represent "freedom in a prepared environment." In this sense, the Montessori Method is informal, and not dominated by a lot of teacher talk and direction.

Should you be interested in sending your child to a Montessori school, be careful. The school may be selling one part of the method without the other. Keep in mind that Montessori herself understood well, and constantly asserted, that liberty and discipline are two sides of a single coin. You don't have a Montessori school without both.

NEIGHBORHOOD SCHOOL

In one of Molière's plays, a character is startled to learn that he has been speaking prose all his life. Up until then, he had thought of prose as some esoteric form of language quite beyond his capacity. Something a little like that has happened with the concept of the neighborhood school. Many Americans didn't know they had a neighborhood school until various court decisions resulted in their children being bused into black neighborhoods. The operative word here is not "bused" but "black." For about forty years, a majority of American schoolchildren have been bused out of their neighborhoods, without too much objection. In fact, the concept of a centralized school which serves many neighborhoods and even towns has been much favored by Americans, largely for financial reasons. What has brought the neighborhood school to the surface is the attempt to bus white children into black (or Hispanic) neighborhoods. With that attempt, the "neighborhood school" has become transformed into a revered tradition, on a par with Sunday doubleheaders and firecrackers on the Fourth of July. We have dealt with the issues surrounding all this under the heading "busing." Here we want only to point out that while it may or may not be a good idea to have neighborhood schools (we think it is), no strong argument can be made for them on the grounds of tradition. If anything, the thrust has been in the other direction for almost half a century.

NONGRADED CLASSROOM

A nongraded classroom is one in which elementary school children are brought together without being classified according to grades, as in "first grade," "second grade," "third grade," etc. The basic idea is to permit the teacher to be aware of children as children so that he or she can help them to learn things they want and need to know.

Unfortunately, when students are assigned to grades, the teacher frequently becomes preoccupied with the grade and what is "supposed to be learned" in it, and tends to become annoyed with children who don't learn what they're "supposed to learn."

A nongraded classroom helps schools to remember what business they're in—the business of helping children to become good learners.

OPEN CLASSROOM

This implies that the activities of students will, to a large extent, be determined by *their* interests and needs, not the convenience or predisposition of the teacher. Since one obvious need of young children is for mobility, the open classroom tries to provide ample freedom of movement. But the "openness" of the open classroom is not mainly physical. Children also need to communicate with each other, to ask their own questions, to seek answers in their own ways, and to pursue individual interests. All of this, the open classroom tries to do. If this sounds to you like warmed-up progressive education, you're right. However, the most influential models of open classrooms are presently coming from 1970s England, not from 1930s America. For example, the British Infant Schools. These schools correspond roughly to our primary grades. Americans have been especially interested in the experiments in Leicestershire, England, where teachers have developed a type of open classroom in which children move with relative freedom from one activity to another, in which there is little distinction between work and play, in which there is much opportunity for children to learn from each other, and in which there is a minimum of didactic teaching. Reports from England suggest that children are learning to read, calculate, and perform a wide range of other skills in such an environment.

American adaptations of the British Infant Schools have been many and various. For example, the "open corridor," introduced here by Lillian Weber, is an attempt to break away from the constricting presence of four walls and a closed door by making the corridors and indeed all the space in a school part of the learning environment. Unfortunately, in many places classes are called open simply because the doors are kept that way, even though instruction of the usual kind takes place. Of course, this is a perversion of a good idea. Simply, a closed classroom becomes an open one when its purpose it to satisfy the intellectual curiosity of children, instead of the requirements of a syllabus. If a teacher is not trying to do that, you still have a closed classroom, even if instruction takes place on 42nd Street and Times Square.

OPEN ENROLLMENT

This term refers to a college admissions policy that permits entrance to just about anyone who wants to go. It is widely believed, particularly in eastern states, that open enrollment will destroy the high level of moral and intellectual achievement of American civilization, as embodied, for example, in the humanity of our foreign policy, the grace of our urban centers, and the decency and profundity of our political leaders. In fact, what open enrollment represents is the extension of a populist traditon of making educational resources available to all who want to use them. The great state universities of the Midwest have had, for all practical purposes, a policy of open enrollment from their beginnings. Eastern colleges have tended to be more elitist, both intellectually and financially. The important point is that open enrollment is a means of equalizing economic power among different classes of people. Which is essentially the reason we have a free and open public school system.

OPEN SCHOOL WEEK

This is a yearly ritual during which a school operates in a totally unnatural way. Administrators are abundantly available, teachers are compassionate to a fault, and students, who invariably get into the spirit of things, are inordinately attentive to whatever idiocy constitutes their lesson. By and large, it is a harmless charade, except in those rare cases when a parent assumes that he or she is witnessing a real, archetypical event.

OPERANT CONDITIONING

This term refers to the central technique used to achieve what psychologists call behavior modification. Briefly, operant conditioning is based on four major principles. The first should come as no surprise to anyone—least of all, parents. It is that any living organism will tend to keep doing what it is "rewarded" for doing, and will stop doing what it's not "rewarded" for. We put the word "reward" in quotes here because it does not necessarily refer to pleasurable experiences. For that reason, behaviorists prefer the term "positive reinforcement," which is operationally defined as *any* response from the environment that keeps the organism doing what it's doing. (An important corollary of the positive-reinforcement principle *may* come as quite a surprise: for reasons too complex to explain here, but experimentally verified beyond doubt, punishment is a *less* effective means of stopping a behavior than no response at all.) Where laboratory animals are concerned, it's fairly easy to arrange for positive reinforcement. You simply deprive the animal of food for a few days, then give it food to "reinforce" the behaviors you want it to perform. With human beings, it's a little more complicated than that—although M&Ms seem to work nearly as well with most children as hamburger does with hungry dogs. In fact, a pocketful of M&Ms is practically a dead giveaway of the teacher who is practicing behavior modification in his classroom. So is a pocketful of plastic poker chips. These are an essential part of what school behaviorists call a "token economy" —by which they mean a system in which desired behaviors are "rewarded" or "reinforced" with tokens (blue chips, for example) which the child can trade in for something he wants.

You may be wondering at this point if the principle of behavior modification through immediate, consistent, positive reinforcement doesn't have a rather obvious flaw: namely, that the learner becomes dependent on the reward. After all, an accountant who will literally do his work only for M&Ms or blue poker chips won't go very far. This brings us to the second and third principles of operant conditioning. One involves a process called "transfer" or "association"—also well known to parents. Perhaps the best way to explain it is with an example: When you give your newborn baby milk, you satisfy a basic need—her hunger. The milk evokes in her a complex of responses we might call "pleasure." Since *you* inevitably appear along with the milk, she associates her pleasure with both stimuli—you and the milk—and eventually transfers her pleasure response to you alone. This is essentially the same process Pavlov used in conditioning dogs to salivate at the sound of a bell. It is also one process by which learners are weaned from one form of reward (like M&Ms) to some more subtle form (like a word of praise from the teacher). Another such process involves the third major principle of operant conditioning, which goes something like this: It's true that the learner requires immediate and inevitable positive reinforcement in the *initial* stages of learning some behavior. But once the connection between behavior and reward is firmly established, the reinforcement can come less and less often and the behavior will persist. Behaviorists refer to the changing frequency and timing of rewards for behavior as a "schedule of reinforcement." Through the precise use of such schedules, along with the process of transfer, they claim they can eliminate the learner's dependence, not on rewards (which are always necessary), but on obvious and frequent rewards.

Schedules of reinforcement are also important in leading a learner from simple behaviors to highly complex ones. But even more important in this process is the fourth major principle of operant conditioning. This is that any behavior, no matter how complex, can be broken down into a sequence of steps small enough for any learner to perform successfully—and thereby receive positive reinforcement. The process of breaking down a complex behavior into its component parts is sometimes referred to as "task analysis," and the small, goal-directed units of behavior identified in the process and marked for reinforcement are called "operants." Hence the term *operant conditioning*.

There is no question that the process of operant conditioning works effectively and efficiently to change animal behavior in the highly controlled environment of the laboratory. Whether the same technology can be applied—or more important, *should* be—in the classrooms of a democratic society, is a subject of the most intense, controversial, and heated debate. Some of the arguments for and against the application of operant conditioning to human learning are discussed under behavior modification. In general, though, the debate seems to center around two fundamentally different perceptions of technology. From the behaviorists' point of view, their technology is neutral—open to use for the achievement of the highest human goals, as well as the lowest. From the humanists' point of view, there is no such thing as a neutral technology. Every medium is its own message. And the message of operant conditioning is vividly described in George Orwell's 1984.

PARAPROFESSIONALS

A paraprofessional is anyone working in the schools, ostensibly for the purpose of helping children to learn, who is not a professional. A professional is anyone who has met certification requirements.

Most paraprofessionals are mothers who are concerned about the kind of schooling their children are getting, and who want to help.

The use of paraprofessionals has developed largely out of the attempt to reduce the amount of time teachers have to spend on such nonteaching chores as filling out forms, collecting money from or for kids, helping kids get winter clothing on and off, and so on.

PARKWAY PROGRAM

In the latter part of 1967, largely as a result of demonstrations by black students disenchanted with the education they were receiving, a program began to emerge in Philadelphia that has become a landmark in American public education. Clifford Brenner, a former newspaperman serving as an administrative assistant to Richardson Dilworth, then president of the Philadelphia Board of Education, wrote a proposal outlining a new form of public high school that came to be called "The School Without Walls." This school, designed to meet student objections to conventional high schools, was to be without a building or buildings. Brenner proposed that the part of Philadelphia that ran along Benjamin Franklin Parkway from City Hall to the art museum be the "campus," and that the new high school should draw upon the resources of the many institutions on or near the parkway for such physical facilities as its program might require.

The philosophy of the Parkway program was based on the central idea that students should actively participate not only in the formulation of school policy and program, but in the process of learning. Their education was to be action based, rather than an exercise in the manipulation of symbols that had no necessary connection with the real world in which they lived.

As the organizing director of the program, John Bremer, put it: "The city is our only curriculum and there is nothing else we need to learn about. The city is our campus. And our students and we ourselves have to re-create that curriculum and that campus."

The story of the Parkway program is long and complicated, but here are a few of the highlights. First, it was regarded with hostility by the Philadelphia school establishment, especially the superintendent. Second, it was funded for the first year by a $100,000 grant from the Ford Foundation, and without the grant it could not have gotten started. Third, since there were many more applicants than openings, the students were selected by lot from among volunteers who wished to participate in the program. Fourth, the curriculum emerged from joint planning by students and teachers. Fifth, the community was an integral part of the school. Sixth, with all the internal problems that any new venture experiences, the dropout rate was much lower than at any other Philadelphia public school and, obviously, student involvement was much higher. Finally, and in sum, Parkway—which continues to this day—was the most imaginative and productive response to the problems of public secondary education ever to occur in the cities.

We feel that it is necessary to emphasize that it began as a result of student dissatisfaction and the imagination of a newspaperman, and came to life under the direction of a man who was continually harassed by the central administration of the public school system. It did not come out of the system itself, and that is an ominous point to remember.

PROGRAMMED INSTRUCTION

Any subject matter designed in such a way as to permit a learner to get at it on his own through a machine, a "scrambled book," or some form of electronic information handling system, can be called programmed instruction. The material is in bits small enough to permit mastery by a learner not dependent on a human teacher. The design is intended to be incremental, or cumulative, the assumption being that mastery of preceding material is necessary to mastery of subsequent material.

Mastery is determined at the end of each segment of the program through questions that require the learner to recognize or recall the salient points in material immediately preceding the test. At any point where mastery is not achieved, the learner simply repeats that portion of the program until he can pass the test. What this means, given the assumptions of the programmed instruction approach, is that anyone who completes a program has achieved an A. Whether subsequent retesting on any given program sustains this judgment is another matter entirely. Most studies of retention (i.e., the duration of what is remembered from any kind of instruction) reveal that forgetting occurs at a much more rapid pace than learning. Moreover, it is worth noting that in this case, learning is equated with remembering, or even only with recognizing, a correct answer on a standardized test.

The nature of programmed instruction, to date at least, limits its use to subject matter that lends itself to linear, cumulative packaging. While almost any subject can be reduced to this form, mathematics, science, and other "closed system" material is generally more suitable than subjects that include some attempt to affect attitudes and beliefs.

Given the present school task of covering material, programmed instruction would seem to be more efficient and effective than conventional teacher-dominated classroom instruction. The learner can, nominally, proceed at his own pace, free of criticism by the teacher, and free of the penalty imposed by an inflexible judgment of failure at any given point. In addition, the learner is not increasingly penalized by being forced to proceed into material he cannot understand because he has not yet mastered an earlier concept upon which understanding is contingent.

To date, programmed instruction in the schools has not seemed to fulfill its early promise. The reasons are many and complex. The most common ones are the large capital outlay needed for the initial acquisition of the system—generally called "hardware" (even if it is only scrambled textbooks)—and the feeling that the material carried in the program (the "software") has not been good enough to warrant the expense of the hardware, no matter how good the hardware is.

READING GRADE LEVEL

In schools all over the country, children are continuously and soberly given standardized reading tests. Like an intelligence test, a standardized reading test is one that has been given to a fairly large population to determine how well the "average" child performs on the test. If, for example, 50 percent of all eighth graders taking the test get X correct answers, then that number becomes, by definition, an "eighth grade reading level." (Actually, reading levels are usually computed more meticulously, so that you can get a score for "eighth grade, third month.") Any eighth grader who takes the test subsequently is then measured by that standard. If a child scores below his grade level, he is generally considered a problem and is a candidate for remedial reading instruction or a slow-track class.

One of the many questions surrounding these tests, as well as the concept of a reading grade level, is, What exactly is the test measuring? For example, it can be demonstrated that students who score high on reading tests (i.e., above their grade level) can also have extreme difficulty in giving a coherent interpretation of a fairly simple poem. In fact, it can be shown that teachers themselves, even teachers of remedial reading classes, are not especially good readers when they are asked to interpret a wide range of expository material. (If you have any doubt about the last statement, see *Practical Criticism* and *Interpretation in Teaching* by I. A. Richards.) Most reading specialists will say that the most important thing reading tests measure is comprehension. But what is reading comprehension? This is a much more difficult question than is generally supposed. Comprehension goes far beyond being able to recognize which black scribbles correlate with which words. In fact, once you get beyond the matter of "cracking the code" (i.e., understanding how writing corresponds to speech), there really is no such thing as a *reading* comprehension problem. Any problems in reading at that level are problems in coping with language itself. Do most reading tests reveal what such language comprehension problems are? They do not. Standardized reading tests will indicate how well a student can deal with the type of material and the type of questions that appear on reading tests. And that's just about it. This means that even if a child scores well on a reading test, he may still have important comprehension problems. It also means that a child who does poorly on a reading test may nonetheless have above-average language abilities in several significant areas. And most important, it means that reading tests are not very useful for diagnostic purposes, which is why they are supposed to be given in the first place.

And yet, schools still rely heavily on such tests as a basis for screening children. In many places (New York City, for example), a child's performance on a standardized reading test can affect his entire school career, and, because of that, the course of his life. The most charitable explanation for such a state of affairs is that it is a temporary aberration caused by overcrowded classrooms and too few teachers. That is, there just isn't time to find out much about a child's language problems, and so the schools have settled for a gross, abstract, and oversimplified means of measuring one aspect of the complex process of meaning making. A more realistic explanation is that school people simply do not at the present time have an informed definition of literacy, nor a competent method of teaching it.

SCHOOL MOTTO

Any saying that is conspicuously displayed in the school building or chiseled onto the building's exterior is probably a school motto. Its purpose is to inspire students to work hard. Its chief characteristic is that (1) no one ever reads it, or (2) if read, it is not understood by anyone in the school. One of the most common school mottoes is A Sound Mind in a Sound Body. This motto is the basis for including in the curriculum such things as business arithmetic and gym, which have helped us to produce all the sound minds and bodies for which we are justly famous.

SCHOOL WITHIN A SCHOOL (MINI-SCHOOL)

Another form of alternative school produced largely by the search for relevance that characterized the schools in the 1960s is the "school within a school." What distinguishes SWAS from most other forms of alternative school is the fact that it has occurred mostly within the public school system.

Where it exists, SWAS is generally the result of the imagination and effort of teachers who succeeded in persuading their administrations to try the experiment of setting up a different form of schooling within their institutions.

So, various forms of open classrooms were started as "mini-schools" within elementary schools, while such alternatives as the Parkway program were started within existing secondary school systems. Many of these ventures persist and even expand today, despite the fact that they were started as emergency enterprises. It may even be that a new pattern has begun to emerge in American education, with students and teachers having the option of participating in the conventional program or some form of school within a school on a continuing basis. At the very least, SWAS constitutes one specific attempt to act as if students really do differ from each other, and that one monolithic school pattern just might not be adequate to meet the realities of a changing world. The most promising development along these lines will occur in Minneapolis, which is planning to offer early elementary school students a choice among four different types of schools.

STORE-FRONT SCHOOLS

During the tumult of the 1960s, various forms of alternative schools were started. One of these forms appeared in places that had been stores at one time, and the fronts still looked like stores. Generally, these former stores were in downtown areas of cities, which had been abandoned, as stores moved to shopping centers. Correspondingly, the rent, if any, was low. So, schools were started in stores simply because space was easily available at little expense.

What happened in store-front schools varied greatly, depending, of course, on who started them. Some were just as bad as the public schools they were intended as alternatives to, and some were excellent, using student and teacher judgment as the basic criterion for that estimate. Most were very short lived, but a very few, such as Harlem Prep, not only survived, but did a miraculous job in providing an opportunity for continuing their education to students who simply could not or would not have survived in conventional public high schools.

STRUCTURED CLASSROOM/UNSTRUCTURED CLASSROOM

All human encounters are structured—by the goals we set, the words we use, the environment we are in. Thus, the first of these phrases is redundant; the second, impossible. The argument about structured classrooms vs. unstructured classrooms is mostly phony. The real questions are: What kinds of structures? For what purposes? Who will do the structuring? The trouble with most classrooms is not that they are structured, but that their structure usually does not help to achieve desirable educational goals. For example, students are unlikely to learn how to be good question-askers if the teachers ask all the questions. Those who advocate "unstructured" classrooms usually mean that they want to experiment with unconventional structures, such as an open classroom.

STUDENT RIGHTS

Although it may be hard to remember, there was a time when people who were able to go to school were considered privileged. Now, in many circles, they are considered oppressed. In any case, the most unusual education discovery of this decade is that students are not merely people who attend school, but people who are required *by law* to attend school. And to obey their teachers. And to have their minds "modified," whether they like it or not. This discovery has started, inevitably, a movement to protect the rights of students. On pages 252–256, 262–273, we have discussed some of the most important court cases of recent years concerning those rights. Here it need only be said that the growth of the idea that students are citizens and, therefore, entitled to rights usually granted to other people, should be regarded as a healthy development by anyone who still believes in the U.S. Constitution. You should not find it hard to acknowledge that there are teachers and administrators who regard students at best as necessary nuisances, and who are sometimes guilty of obvious assaults on the bodies (see corporal punishment p. 145) and minds of the young. Of course, as many teachers are quick to point out, there are also many cases of students' assaulting teachers in various ways. But the protection of teachers' rights is fairly well taken care of through union and professional organizations. Students have no such pressure groups behind them, and as a consequence, are exceedingly vulnerable.

TEAM TEACHING

Team teaching is the name given to teaching done by more than one teacher. The original idea behind it was that students would benefit from the supposed synergistic effect produced by a team of teachers working (i.e., planning and presenting something) together. The dialogue in which the team engaged during planning and presenting was intended to engage student interest and enrich the teaching performance. In many cases, team teaching was also intended to produce an interdisciplinary approach, thus enabling students to see relationships between and among subjects that would otherwise be dealt with in isolation.

While it is still regarded as an innovation in some places, team teaching by and large has turned out to be the same as nonteam teaching since teachers seem not to be any better at working in teams than anybody else. The most common form of team teaching simply produces larger numbers of students in a class with the teachers appearing one after the other, each doing what he or she would do anyway.

UNITED STATES OFFICE OF EDUCATION (USOE)

Several federal agencies are under the direction of the executive branch of the government. That is, they are headed by secretaries appointed by the President, who comprise his cabinet. The secretaries are expected to support the President's policies in general, and those affecting their agencies in particular. The idea that the President might support secretaries and their agencies who did not agree with him has never caught on.

One of the subagencies under the Department of Health, Education, and Welfare is the U.S. Office of Education. It is headed by a Commissioner of Education. Commissioners are also expected to support presidential policies, even if they can't tell what those policies are, and they are never to take positions that reveal any possible difference with the President who appointed them, *about anything.*

As you can see, this does not make for very strong leadership among secretaries and commissioners.

One of the best secretaries of Health, Education, and Welfare that the United States has ever had was John Gardner. He resigned. One of the best Commissioners of Education that the United States has ever had was the late James Allen. He was *asked* to resign.

VOUCHER SYSTEM

Have we reached the end of public education in the form we have known it? We haven't, of course, but some people think we ought to. What would replace it? The most common answer is, the voucher system. There are in fact several different proposals concerning the use of vouchers (see Christopher Jencks, p. 225). In general, however, the voucher system is a proposed method for financing schooling whereby public funds for education would go directly to the consumer (i.e., parents) instead of to a school system. The funds would be distributed in the form of vouchers, each worth $1,200 or $1,400 or whatever the community and state normally spend on education for each child. Parents could then use the vouchers to buy whatever kind of education they wish from any reputable educational institution.

What are the advantages of a voucher system? Its advocates claim, in the first place, that it is more democratic in that it would give people greater freedom of choice than they presently have. In the second place, it introduces to public education the cherished(?) American concept of free enterprise. Under a voucher system, private schools would probably sprout all over the place, and a lively competition would ensue not only among them, but between them and the existing, old-fashioned school system. At the very least, vouchers would break the monopoly of the present school system and, in particular, the stranglehold it has on the poor. The poor and middle class would begin to enjoy options not unlike those presently available to the rich.

Roughly, that's the theory. The proposal is serious and the prospect, to many people, attractive. The U.S. Office of Education has even supported a few pilot ventures in the use of vouchers. What does the opposition say?

Surprisingly, some of the opposition comes from the poor. What would happen, they say, is this: the rich and the middle class would take the voucher, add some money of their own, and thereby develop an elite system of schools from which the poor would largely be excluded, simply because they would not have the extra money to gain entry. Advocates of some voucher proposals have designed their systems to protect against this (e.g., by prohibiting schools from charging more than the worth of the voucher), but many people still remain skeptical. Much of the opposition to vouchers comes from teachers' unions, which fear that the inevitable fragmentation of their organization would weaken teacher security. And opposition also comes from those who believe that, for all its faults, the public school is still the cornerstone of the American version of democracy.

We will all hear much about various voucher proposals in the years ahead, but it is our best guess that the pressures against the voucher system, including the force of institutional inertia, will prevail.

WORK-STUDY PROGRAMS

While work-study programs are not new, they gained impetus in the face of increasing charges of irrelevance from students.

As the name states, these programs provide an opportunity for students to work—for pay—while they study in school. In some programs, work and study occur together, with students working part-time and attending school part-time. In other programs, students work full-time for a term and then attend school full-time for a term. In most such programs, an attempt is made to correlate the study in school with the work the students do outside school. In some programs, however, the work bears no necessary relationship to the study, the feeling being that working in the "real world" has a salutary effect on students irrespective of whether or not it is directly related to school study. There is much reason to agree with this feeling, since students gain a much wider range of experience as well as an increase in self-esteem when they are doing something that they get paid real money for.

Work-study programs do have the effect of diminishing student tolerance for anything too abstract or "academic" or for learning anything they feel is not directly related to the possibility of increasing the pay they can earn. Depending on what one thinks the purposes of American education are, this effect can be a mixed blessing.

PEOPLE

INCLUDED here are descriptions of some seventy people who have made contributions to current thinking about schools. We wish to apologize in advance to those few (we hope) whose work would have merited their inclusion had we known enough about it. Nonetheless, we feel confident that we have included at least representatives of varying points of view that characterize the great school debate.

♯   ♯   ♯

DWIGHT ALLEN

Allen, who is presently dean of the School of Education at the University of Massachusetts, is perhaps the most ubiquitous American school critic. He goes everywhere, consults on everything, and knows everybody. He has vast energy and wide-ranging interests, and is generally credited with having introduced the concepts of modular scheduling and differentiated staffing to American schools. His most well known achievement to date has been to transform a small, moribund, unknown school of education (at the University of Massachusetts) into the most frenetic, creative, and controversial center for the study of education in the country. Whether or not it and he can last is an open question. For all his flamboyance, Allen is a practical reformer, who believes that schools can be vastly improved by inventing new conventions and procedures.

In a letter to Adelbert Ames, dated November 17, 1950, John Dewey wrote, "I think your work is by far the most important work done in the psychological-philosophical field during this century—I am tempted to say the *only* really important work."

The work Dewey was referring to consisted of a series of demonstrations (as Ames called them) "on the nature of perceptions and the nature of environmental phenomena."

Abandoning the practice of law, Ames studied art and became a painter. This led him to an interest in physiological optics, and he became first a research professor in physiological optics at Dartmouth and then, until his death in 1955, director of the Hanover Eye Institute, where he conducted his demonstrations on perception.

Ames is still virtually unknown to most academics, including educational philosophers and psychologists, largely because he never published anything about his work. He does, however, enjoy an almost religious reputation among a relatively small group of educators, primarily as a result of the writings of the late Earl Kelley.

Kelley presented his impressions of the educational implications of Ames' research on perception in a small but potent book titled *Education for What Is Real* (1947). The basic point revealed by Ames' research sounds deceptively simple, but its educational implications are most profound. The point is that the only reality each of us has available as the basis for our behavior is our personal perception, which is itself a combined product of our experience, assumptions, and purposes. Ames' work also revealed that "cognitive knowledge" has little effect on changing our perceptions as long as the behavior based on them is "satisfying." Only when our perceptions produce behavior that is frustrating is perception susceptible to change. This is crucial because the ability to learn consists essentially of the ability to relinquish inadequate or inappropriate perceptions. The ability to learn, then, derives from a consciousness of the role that one's experience, assumptions, and purposes play in shaping one's perception. Or, to restate this point in current educational terminology: activity in the "cognitive domain" is inseparable from and contingent upon the state of the "affective domain."

Thus, Ames' work provides an empirical base for humanistic psychology and at the same time raises serious questions about the efficacy of behavioristic psychology for anything other than the simplest kinds of training in physical activity. The distinction between *education* and training is, therefore, a critical one when decisions are being made about the functions and purposes of schooling.

While Dewey's predictions about the educational significance of Ames' work have yet to be realized, increasing frustration with failure-ridden school conventions may finally provide the opportunity to verify Dewey's sanguine judgment.

SYLVIA ASHTON-WARNER

"Organic reading is not new. The Egyptian hieroglyphics were one-word sentences. Helen Keller's first word, 'water,' was a one-word book." So begins Ashton-Warner's great book, *Teacher* (1963). In it, she describes her Creative Teaching Scheme, which she developed while teaching Maori children in New Zealand. Organic reading is a philosophical concept that rejects a mechanistic approach to skill learning; that is, it rejects the idea that reading (or anything else) can be effectively (i.e., humanely) taught without a deep regard for the emotional and cultural experience of the learner. In an area beset by famine, she says, it would make no sense to begin teaching reading with any words other than "crop," "soil," "hunger," "manure," and the like. First words, she believes, must be part of a child's being. As a result, she developed what she calls a Key Vocabulary.

It varies from group to group, but its essential characteristic is that each of its words is a "book," filled with emotional meaning. To some extent, Ashton-Warner's ideas have been appropriated by Paulo Freire in his work on overcoming the problem of illiteracy in Latin America. Her work, unfortunately, has not had great influence in the United States, where school people are apt to view the learning of skills as a technical, not an emotional, matter.

In recent years, Ashton-Warner has been in the United States, associated with an experimental school in Aspen, Colorado. She recorded her impressions of that experience in her book *Spearpoint* (1972).

CARL BEREITER AND SIEGFRIED ENGELMANN

These two controversial psychologists at the University of Illinois have translated B. F. Skinner's ideas about conditioning into a procedure for preparing underprivileged children to be successful in school. The procedure is designed to force children to work hard, mostly through drill, shouting, punishment, and isolation. However, if and when the children begin to do what the teacher wants them to do, Bereiter and Engelmann recommend rewards in the form of hugs, raisins, and cookies.

If this sounds strange to you, Bereiter and Engelmann reply that it works. In their book *Teaching Disadvantaged Children in the Preschool* (1966), they contend the following: traditional, well-rounded nursery schools are mostly designed for middle-class and upper-class children who already have mastered primary language skills; disadvantaged children, if they are to compete, must progress at a faster than average pace; and preschool programs for the disadvantaged should, therefore, have narrow educational objectives. In other words, in the Bereiter and Engelmann design there is little time for anything but the systematic development of basic language skills and arithmetic. Toward this end, they have devised a two-year reading program called DISTAR, which requires, among other things, two hours of drill each day with plenty of shouting. Bereiter and Engelmann declare that they have achieved startling results—at the end of a year one experimental group performed on achievement tests nearly as well as "gifted" children. Of course, even if such test scores are produced, critics wonder about the effects of such rigid and narrow procedures. Is this a method for helping disadvantaged children develop into fully functioning human beings? Bereiter and Engelmann say it will open the door. Some humanistic psychologists say it might keep the door closed permanently.

BRUNO BETTELHEIM

Bettelheim is a Freudian psychoanalyst, professor of psychology and psychiatry at the University of Chicago, and a world-famous authority on childhood psychosis. He is also principal of the University of Chicago's Sonia Shankman Orthogenic School, a residential institution for children suffering from severe forms of schizophrenia. In his book *Love Is Not Enough* (1950), he described his work at the Orthogenic School. Some psychiatrists have attacked his approach there as ultrapermissive (restraints are totally absent) although they acknowledge that he has been impressively successful in treating children whom no one else had been able to help.

His permissiveness at the Orthogenic School stands in sharp contrast to his reputation with his students at the university and among liberals, who are offended by his strongly conservative views on the subject of dissenting youth, especially on the college campus. Although he is a survivor of Buchenwald and Dachau (having been released in 1939 through the intervention of Herbert Lehman and Eleanor Roosevelt), Bettelheim believes in limiting the right to question figures of authority—the President, the teacher, the police. He wants us to instill in the young the feeling that things are essentially all right "though sometimes difficult and in need of improvement." In Bettelheim's view, the main causes of campus unrest in the 1960s were that too many students were attending universities who would have fared better with high-level vocational educations, and that permissive child-rearing practices had denied children the external controls they desperately need. He believes that many leaders of the student rebellions are sick emotionally.

One ambivalent critic of Bettelheim has described him as having a "molten core of humanity." His sensitivity to the human condition and concern for the well-being of children are very much in evidence in his writings on infancy and school-age children. He criticizes the schools for not taking into account the developmental stage of children—for example, for expecting them to work hard at learning before they've acquired sufficient ego strength to accept hard work for the sake of future rewards. In calling for a psychoanalytic theory of learning, Bettelheim suggests that instead of accepting the child's scribblings (id expressions) as creative, the teacher, by the use of criticism and appropriate standards, should slowly educate the child to be able to express himself to others (ego achievement).

Bettelheim is opposed to the grouping of children by ability or even by age in the public schools. He thinks preschool academic instruction is wrong—that four- and five-year-old children have more important things to learn than reading. Though some progressive educators might applaud many of his criticisms of the schools, they would probably withdraw their approval on hearing Bettelheim expound his Freudian-based belief that education can proceed only if children have learned to fear something before they come to school—at least to fear the loss of parental love. This theoretically leads to fear of the teacher's disapproval, and, in the correctly developing child, eventually to the fear of losing self-respect.

Bettelheim studied the communal child-rearing practices of an Israeli kibbutz in an attempt to learn why these children were not beset by many of the problems plaguing American youngsters, and in his greatly admired book *The Children of the Dream* (1969), he advises us to set up day-care centers for children of working mothers and for all children whose home enviroments do not prepare them for successful participation in society.

BENJAMIN S. BLOOM

A professor of education at the University of Chicago, Bloom has had a strong influence on the articulation of educational objectives. His *Taxonomy of Educational Objectives, Handbook I: Cognitive Domain* (1956) was a powerful factor in the attempt to reshape educational aims in the 1950s and 1960s. (It is also one of the most unreadable books of all time.) It sets forth a hierarchical classification system for minutely defined sets of objectives for teachers, and incorporates detailed descriptions of such goals, as well as tests to measure whether or not the desired learning has taken place at each level. Intellectual tasks are classified at six different levels—knowledge, comprehension, application, analysis, synthesis, and evaluation.

Bloom considers educational goals to fall into three different categories. The first, cognitive, was tackled in *Handbook I. Handbook II: Affective Domain* (written in 1964 with David Krathwohl and Bertram Masia) systematically classifies types of human reactions—feelings, attitudes, and emotions—and reduces them to what the authors believe are the behavioral equivalents of such feelings. The writers are planning a third handbook on the psychomotor domain. The idea behind all this classification is that if teachers understand precisely what it is they are trying to teach, they may be able to do a better job of it, and that if they can then measure in minute detail what each student has learned, they will know how well they have succeeded with their objectives. Supposedly the teachers will then adjust their methods to accommodate the fast and slow learners. In other words, Bloom is trying to make teaching a "science." And to those who feel this is desirable, Bloom's *Taxonomy* (as his work is popularly called) is considered a first and necessary step.

JOHN BREMER

Bremer was the first director of the famous Parkway program, the "school without walls" in Philadelphia. An Englishman, Bremer believes that the American high school, as it presently exists, has reached the end of its development. What we need now, he says, is a new kind of educational institution. By using the resources of an entire community as a school, Bremer hoped to build one. He is no longer with the Parkway program, however, and the future of the program itself is shaky. Nonetheless, the idea which he helped to develop in Philadelphia has stirred great interest around the country and has been copied to some extent in Chicago, Los Angeles, and several other places. Bremer has given a full description of his ideas in *Open Education: A Beginning* (with Anne Bremer, 1972) and *The School Without Walls* (with Michael von Moschzisker, 1971).

B. FRANK BROWN

B. Frank Brown left New York University and became principal of a brand new high school in a virtually nonexistent place named Melbourne, Florida. They were building a new high school there because the population was growing rapidly, not to say wildly. Melbourne was near a place called Cape Canaveral.

Brown turned out to be one of the few high school principals in the history of American education who actually had a new idea about how to run a high school, and even more unusual, he put it into practice. The school he developed came to be known as a nongraded high school. Brown noted that age makes no more sense as a basis for arranging children for educational purposes than does hair color or weight. He also decided that the 45-minute period so common in high school, the 5-days-a-week class, and the 15-week semester made no particular sense either. So he arranged for Melbourne High School to group students on the basis of what they *knew* or could get to know, and then (most other high school principals would still deny that you can do *this*) he arranged for the students to go ahead and learn other things once they showed they knew enough to do so. They weren't locked in by a calendar or by the grade levels that go with it. They learned in phases that replaced both the calendar and the grade levels, and they loved it.

JEROME BRUNER

A Harvard psychologist, Bruner established himself as an important school critic with the publication of his book *The Process of Education* (1960). The book, a report on the Woods Hole Conference of 1959, introduced into school vocabulary the phrase "structure of a discipline," by which Bruner appeared to mean that every discipline has a unique mode of question-asking and answer-finding. However, almost every educator seems to have his own interpretation of the phrase—to Bruner's everlasting chagrin. Bruner has urged that students be allowed to learn how practitioners of any discipline actually do their work, and that students should learn this by trying to replicate the processes by which scholarly work is done. Naturally, he is a leading spokesman for the inductive teaching method. His most widely quoted opinion is to the effect that any intellectual concept can be taught, in an academically respectable way, to children of any age, provided suitable methods are used. In this belief, Bruner is at sharp issue with Swiss psychologist Jean Piaget.

Bruner has published two other important school books: *Toward a Theory of Instruction* (1966) and *The Relevance of Education* (1971). He is an uncommonly open person and is not afraid to repudiate his own beliefs when he changes his mind. This he has done several times, and he is now inclined to believe that school reform must go far beyond improving methods of instruction.

EDWARD CARPENTER

A former college professor, Carpenter founded what is perhaps the most important alternative school in the country, Harlem Prep. With considerable help from his wife, Anne, and with funding from such sources as the Ford Foundation, Mobil, and the Mosler family, Carpenter has transformed the name Harlem Prep into a common noun in the lexicon of schools—for example, "Can we start a Harlem Prep in our community?" The school is located on 135th Street and 8th Avenue in New York City, in what was formerly a supermarket, which students helped to refurbish. It is designed to give dropouts (mostly blacks) a second chance. Its curriculum is conventional, and its goal is to help students get into college, where they will have an opportunity, if they wish, to become middle-class materialists like everyone else. To date, well over three hundred students have entered college via Harlem Prep. The Carpenters are hardly romantics, but they do believe that schools can be utilized to build the confidence and develop the potential of the poor and disaffected.

KENNETH CLARK

A psychology professor at City College in New York, Clark played an important role in marshaling evidence to show that segregated school systems had serious psychological effects on black children. The U.S. Supreme Court judged this evidence to be persuasive, and leaned heavily on it in rendering its historic 1954 ruling. In recent years, Clark has been concerned with the "reading problem," believing that reading retardation is the decisive factor in preventing black children from achieving success in school. In the early 1970s, Clark designed a curriculum for the Washington, D.C., schools, (from first grade through junior high school,) which concerned itself exclusively with reading. His plan has been something of a failure, although Clark believes that it was sabotaged. He believes that another cause of his—decentralization of schools—has also been sabotaged. Nonetheless, Clark remains undaunted in advancing causes. He is outspoken, for example, in opposing black studies programs or any other devices that would separate black students from the main stream of learning and life in America.

JAMES COLEMAN

A professor at Johns Hopkins University, Coleman was the principal author of a massive study of the effectiveness of schools. Sponsored by the U.S. Office of Education, the study was published under the name *Equality of Educational Opportunity* (1966), but is widely known as the Coleman Report. The Report stands as a powerful rebuff to all critics who devoutly believe that improved schools will make a substantial difference in the lives of children. The basic finding of the Coleman Report is that the great differences in achievement between middle-class and "minority"-class students *cannot* be attributed to differences in the quality of schools. Coleman discovered, for example, that black schools do not spend much less money per pupil than white schools; they do not have fewer textbooks, or larger classes, or older and more crowded buildings. Coleman concluded that students' upbringing and background are dominating influences on how they perform in school, and that variations in school programs, expenditures, and the like, do not have much effect. The Coleman Report has been attacked many times, partly because of Coleman's definition of a "better" school, and also because it calls into question a basic assumption of schooling, namely, that people are improved by the process.

ARTHUR COMBS

In 1967, Arthur Combs was president of the Association of Supervision and Curriculum Development, a department of the National Educational Association, to which virtually every school administrator concerned with curriculum belongs. He is presently the director of the Center of Humanistic Education at the University of Florida. He is also one of the very few professors of education included here.

In 1948, Combs, with Donald Snygg, published a book describing "phenomenological psychology." Its thesis was that, to put it too simply, each of us behaves in response to the way things seem to us (our phenomenological field), and if we want to understand or communicate with someone else, we must try to see how they see things, i.e., we must try to get into their phenomenological field.

Combs has been elucidating the dynamics of the relationship between perception and behavior for at least twenty-five years, in twelve books and hundreds of articles, as well as in countless lectures, and in various professional capacities.

While "phenomenological psychology" has not become a household phrase, the sense of it (especially in its implications for teaching) has been verified by research in human perception. It is also an integral part of most attempts at humanistic education, even when it is not called by name. Why many people still consider the idea that our attitudes, beliefs, assumptions, and purposes determine our perceptions exotic or useless or both is an interesting phenomenon in itself. Behavioral psychologists, for example, reject the educational implications of perceptual psychology, and in the process seem unaware of the fact that they are illustrating its basic principle when they do so.

LAWRENCE CREMIN

Cremin is probably the most respected historian of American education now living. He has performed his work serenely, as most historians are wont to do, rarely descending to discuss the present turmoil over the schools. When he does, it is usually to compare the vigor and substance of the Progressive Education movement with the present movement for school reform, almost always to the disadvantage of the latter. In this he is undoubtedly correct, since by almost any standard the present crop of school critics, radical or otherwise, is no match for the likes of John Dewey, George Counts, William Kilpatrick, Harold Rugg, and other progressives. Cremin will probably continue to hover above the battle and produce rigorous, carefully constructed histories of American education, such as his works *The Transformation of the Schools* (1961) and *The Genius of American Education* (1965). In general, he believes, along with most historians, that the American public school has been a major force in the promotion of democratic ideas.

JOHN CULKIN

If you can imagine a Friar Tuck-like ex-Jesuit with a Brooklyn accent who says Marshall McLuhan-like things, you have a general idea of how Culkin looks and sounds.

Culkin is one of the few academics (he was a professor at Fordham University) who have taken McLuhan's ideas seriously, and as a consequence, he spends much of his time exhorting people in the school business to try these ideas out with students. Culkin's long suit is provoking teachers to act as if movies and television play a more important role than print in the lives of children. One of McLuhan's lines that Culkin takes most seriously (and tries to get school people to take seriously) is that "nothing is inevitable if we understand the dynamics of the process that produces it." Culkin is one of the few, but growing, number of educators who believe that the media are worth serious study in the schools because they have a more potent effect on our society and the individuals that comprise it than any other institution.

GEORGE DENNISON

Through curious circumstances, Dennison found himself and his wife running a small free school in New York City. Although it was located on Sixth Street, it was called the First Street School, which was not the only unusual thing about it. Its distinguishing characteristic was the fact that its teachers used Tolstoi, A. S. Neill, and John Dewey as their spiritual and intellectual guides. A writer by trade, Dennison made the most of the experience by writing a remarkable, inspiring book, called *The Lives of Children* (1969). It is mostly a daily account of what happened in the school, written without jargon or other nonsense. Dennison does not regard himself as a professional educator and has steadfastly refused to exploit the success of his book by giving speeches, consulting, or making pontifical statements. His school, incidentally, no longer exists, but the influence of his book is still quite pervasive.

JOHN DEWEY

There is no telling how many times poor Dewey has turned over in his grave in the last ten years. He has probably dug a hole halfway to China, but he has no one to blame but himself. His ideas are so powerful that it is inevitable that everyone—the wise and the foolish—who speaks on the subject of schools is influenced by them. In intellectual terms, the present school reform movement is simply a replay of what Dewey started seventy-five years ago. No restatement of any of his ideas will be attempted here. It is sufficient to say that his spirit hovers over all school criticism and will probably not be allowed to rest for another century—if then. Coincidentally, the two most significant figures in education of this century—Dewey and Maria Montessori—died within less than a month of each other, she on May 6, 1952, he on June 1, 1952.

ERIK H. ERIKSON

Erik Erikson is one of the foremost living psychoanalysts in America. He has extended Freudian thought to deal with the questions posed by our changing society. Whereas Freud believed that the personality was decisively formed in early childhood, with development proceeding in psychosexual stages, Erikson views the developmental process as continuing throughout life in a series of crucial psychosocial stages. His main preoccupation has been to show how society affects ego development.

In *Childhood and Society* (1950) Erikson identified eight stages of life, each of which had its own crisis to be overcome. His is a more optimistic interpretation of psychoanalytic theory: each of his stages has positive as well as negative outcomes, and the failure to resolve one crisis successfully can be rectified at a later period of life. The first three stages cover infancy and early childhood, when the child is dependent on his home. The fourth stage deals with the elementary school years, from which period will emerge a sense of industry as the positive outcome or a sense of inferiority as the negative one. In this stage, according to Erikson, the child's developmental goal is very much at odds with the school's. The child is intent on improving the skills of living, on doing things with his hands, and on gaining the approval of his peers, but he is forced to spend his time and energy on academic tasks. The things he wants to learn how to do well don't seem to carry much weight with his parents and teachers. Erikson believes it is crucial for the schools to recognize the child's concern for competence and to see that his need to master *something* is met. He notes the danger to the child and to society when the child begins to feel that his background or the color of his skin, and not his wish to learn, will determine his identity. In fact, Erikson coined the term "identity crisis." He was professor of human development and lecturer in psychiatry at Harvard University from 1960 to 1970, when he retired. In addition to *Childhood and Society* (2nd ed. published 1963) he has written *Insight and Responsibility* and *Identity: Youth and Crisis* (1968).

MARIO FANTINI

Fantini is dean of the School of Education at the State University of New York at New Paltz. He was a key figure at the Ford Foundation when the foundation became deeply involved in an attempt to achieve meaningful decentralization in the New York City schools. Fantini has written, with Gerald Weinstein, an important book on how to deal with the affective domain of a child's school life. It is called *Toward Humanistic Education: A Curriculum of Affect* (1971). Presently, Fantini is an advocate of the idea that the best way to improve schools is to increase the number of alternative programs *within* a school. He estimates that a majority of parents in the country have no serious complaint against the schools, and believes that it is foolhardy to force them to accept changes. Nevertheless a substantial minority (he figures about 35 percent) distrusts (and even despises) the present arrangements, and he feels these people must be accommodated. The way to do it? By giving parents and students the right to petition for a particular school style. In other words, whenever a certain percentage of parents and students desire a certain kind of change, school authorities would be required by law to implement it.

JOSEPH FEATHERSTONE

Featherstone earned a place for himself in contemporary school criticism as perhaps the earliest publicist of the British Infant Schools. In a series of three articles published in 1967 in *The New Republic*, Featherstone described what was happening in British classrooms, and made the word "Leicestershire" part of the vocabulary of school people throughout the

United States. Since then, many people—among them Charles Silberman, Lillian Weber, and Alvin Hertzberg and Edward Stone (in *Schools Are for Children*, 1971)—have gotten into the act.

PAULO FREIRE

Born in Recife, Brazil, in 1921, Freire is probably the most controversial educator in Latin America. His work has exerted influence all over the world, however, especially among radical critics. He is best known for the development of a methodology for teaching reading to illiterate peasants. But "methodology" is not quite the word for it, since Freire's approach involves awakening the political consciousness of people to the ways in which they are oppressed. The "culture of silence" (Freire's phrase) in which the oppressed live is a product, Freire believes, of their acceptance of *someone else's* definition of the world. But each man has a right to "say his own word" and "to name the world" in his own way. Through the written word, one may develop a radical new consciousness of political and economic contradictions, and the will to do something about them. Thus, learning to read, for Freire, is not a mere technical problem but a process of learning how to redefine one's position in the world and to take action against one's oppressors.

Naturally, Freire's methodology has hardly been appreciated by establishmentarians, and Freire was thrown into jail by the military junta that took control of Brazil in 1964. He was released seventy days later and encouraged, in the strongest terms, to leave the country. He did, spending five years in Chile working on the development of adult education programs. He presently works out of the Office of Education of the World Council of Churches in Geneva, but travels all over the world lecturing on the "pedagogy of the oppressed," which is the name of his best-known book (published in English in 1972).

EDGAR FRIEDENBERG

A sociologist, Friedenberg attracted attention through his studies of adolescents, most notably in his book *The Vanishing Adolescent* (1959). His thought is far too complex to yield to summary, but it was he, more than anyone else, who articulated some of the "hidden" functions of school, such as its role in preparing students to fit the needs of American corporations. He also described how schools helped to promote passivity and to stifle real creativity. Eventually, Friedenberg came to the conclusion that a major function of school—perhaps *the* major function—is to define (i.e., categorize) young people as "adolescents" so that they may "legitimately" be deprived of certain rights and privileges. He became so depressed over this idea that he decided to absent himself from further involvement in school criticism. He has been absent for a couple of years now, and is likely to remain so.

CALEB GATTEGNO

Born in Egypt in 1911, Gattegno has spent a lifetime studying the learning process and trying to convince teachers that he is the definitive genius of world education. He may well be, although it is difficult to tell from his books (*What We Owe Children: The Subordination of Teaching to Learning*, 1970, and *Towards a Visual Culture*, 1969), which are written in a style that makes Marshall McLuhan seem well organized. His main effort is toward trying to discover the fundamental structure of the operations of the mind (in the manner of Piaget, two of whose books he has translated) *and* the structure of particular academic tasks, such as reading. For example, Gattegno (who considers himself the founder of the New Math) contends that algebra is a fundamental operation of the mind, not simply of mathematics, and he uses such algebraic concepts as substitution, addition, insertion, and reversals to teach reading.

He further believes that he has solved the problem of reading by identifying the ways in which it is isomorphic to speech (that is, similar in structure). But Gattegno is more than a theorist. He has put his theories on the line by producing a continuous flow of concrete teaching materials based on them. His well-known reading series is called *Words in Color*, and it is widely used throughout the United States, although not always with the degree of success that Gattegno assures everyone is possible. Gattegno is also responsible for a bowdlerized version of *Words in Color* that has appeared on NBC television as the *Pop-Up* series. In recent years, Gattegno has directed an organization in the United States known as Schools for the Future, whose main purpose seems to be to publicize his work.

ARNOLD GESELL

To Gesell, who died in 1961 at the age of eighty-one, we are indebted not only for pioneering and systematic research on normal child development, but also for numerous, clearly written books which have guided generations of parents in rearing their children. A mother who comments about her child's behavior, "I'm not worried, it's only a stage he's passing through," owes that insight to Gesell, whether she's aware of it or not.

According to Gesell, development proceeds in universal stages determined principally by biological maturation. The time schedule of development is relatively fixed: maturation determines the growth from one stage to another and practice or learning will do little to speed up the various processes, such as the age when a child first crawls, or stands, or walks.

While he was studying for his medical degree at Yale, Gesell persuaded that institution to set up the Yale Clinic for Child Development, of which he was director from 1911 until 1948. The purpose of the clinic was to determine the characteristics and range of normality for each successive stage of early child behavior. He and his associates there, notably Frances L.

Ilg and Louise B. Ames, built up an extensive library of motion pictures and stills of the natural behavior of children by photographing them through a one-way screen.

In 1950 Gesell's former associates at the clinic established the Gesell Institute of Child Development, where he served as consultant until 1958. Among the books which grew out of his work are *The First Five Years of Life* (1940), *Infant and Child in the Culture of Today* (with Ilg, Learned, and Ames, 1943), *The Child from Five to Ten* (with Ilg, 1940), and *Youth: The Years from 10 to 16* (1956). In them he described the typical traits of each age in connection with the problems of everyday living. His belief in the individuality of each child led him to caution parents to guide their children through the rapid growth of their formative years and to avoid either extreme rigidity or overpermissiveness.

HAIM GINOTT

Ginott is a psychotherapist who is trying to educate the adult world (particularly parents) in how to communicate with children. His books *Between Parent and Child* (1965) and *Teacher and Child* (1972) have been enormously popular, and he is much in demand on the lecture circuit and television.

Ginott is not a school critic. He is more an education theorist, in the sense that he wants to change the quality of interpersonal communication between adults and children. Since children spend a lot of their time in school with people called teachers, Ginott has recently become especially interested in how that interaction can be improved in a school setting. He recognizes that, in school, the teacher controls the tone of the interaction. Therefore, he urges that the teacher's primary goal should be the development in students of an accurate and positive self-image. Ginott believes that most "learning problems" stem from low self-esteem, and in this respect his work is in the same vein as that of Carl Rogers and other humanistic psychologists.

MARILYN GITTELL

Gittell is a professor of political economy at Queens College, director of the Institute for Community Studies, and an editor of *Social Policy*. She is largely associated with the fight for community control of the schools. Through her books (*Participants and Participation*, 1967), her solid research, and her active participation in political battles, she has established herself as an implacable enemy of bureaucracy and, like Boston Blackie, a friend to those who have no friends. She has been particularly interested in trying to abolish the Board of Examiners in New York City, and, like David Rogers (*110 Livingston Street*, 1968), has done much to show how large, centralized agencies ultimately defeat the quest for competence and involvement.

WILLIAM GLASSER

Glasser is director of the Educator Training Center in Los Angeles, president of the Institute for Reality Therapy, and a consulting psychiatrist to the Los Angeles City and Palo Alto schools.

After several years of working with delinquent girls at a reform school in California, he was urged to bring his "technique" into public schools. This technique, Reality Therapy, is designed to help people move toward successful behavior. Instead of worrying about "mental illness" the patient, through an intense personal involvement with his therapist, learns to face responsibility and not excuse himself for his behavior. By so doing he builds a successful self-image.

In *Schools Without Failure* (1969) Glasser describes how Reality Therapy can be applied to the schools to correct the practices that lead to school failure, dropouts, and delinquency.

Instead of expending so much energy identifying (grading) children who are succeeding or failing, schools, he says, must direct their efforts toward helping all children develop successful self-images. Since we all need an identity, a child labeled a failure will continue his antisocial behavior beyond school.

Some of his specific recommendations to teachers are: (1) forget the child's background—take him as he is and get involved with him; (2) get rid of failing grades, report cards, and objective tests. If a child needs more time to learn a subject, give it to him: (3) have heterogeneous grouping and make use of regular class meetings to give the children a voice in determining school rules; (4) rules are to be obeyed—excuses for bad behavior are not acceptable. The goal is involvement and personal responsibility.

Glasser has introduced his ideas in model elementary schools in Watts and in the suburbs, working with teachers and demonstrating the use of class meetings. He says that he found his clue as to why these schools succeed in a comment by Marshall McLuhan: "the students are searching for a role, not a goal." He believes that you can get children to work only if you first recognize them as individuals.

PAUL GOODMAN

If it is possible to give a specific date on which contemporary school criticism began, it would be the day the late Paul Goodman's *Growing Up Absurd* (1956) was published. Although hundreds of books have been written since, and thousands of speeches given, no one has really improved much on what Goodman had to say about the cultural context in which the young are presently required to grow. Goodman's main point was that it is extremely difficult for a young person to develop into a mature, responsible adult and, at the same time, function effectively within our existing social institutions. Such institutions, he tried to demonstrate, reward passivity and dependence, and induce a sense of alienation. Naturally, he included the schools. A city planner, a literary critic, a sociologist, an anarchist, and several other things to boot, Goodman was only partly interested in school reform. Nonetheless, in *Compulsory Mis-Education* (1964), he offered several proposals for improving the operation and, indeed, changing the function of the schools. One of these, the creation of store-front schools, was considered utopian at the time, but has since been adopted in various forms in several places, and is considered by some to be a practical idea.

ESTHER GREENBERG

She hasn't written a book on school reform. She doesn't give speeches or conduct workshops. Her name is never mentioned as an "influential." All she does is make children feel good about themselves and help them learn important things. In a sentence, she is a good teacher. She is included here as a symbol of thousands of good teachers who work under difficult conditions, do very little complaining, and who, somehow, make a positive difference in the lives of children. If every child had a teacher like Esther Greenberg, there would be no need for school reform movements. For the record, she teaches at PS 20 in Queens, New York, where a couple of children we know very well have benefited enormously from her talents, as they also have from the talents of many of her colleagues.

COLIN GREER

Greer is director of the University Without Walls of the City University of New York. He is also a "radical" and "revisionist" historian, whose book *The Great School Legend* (1972) was intended to explode the myth that the American public school has been a beneficent and egalitarian institution of particular usefulness to the poor. Greer has tried to show that the schools have perpetuated social and economic class differences, have (for the most part) kept the poor in their place, and as a consequence, have always had far more failing students than successful ones. Moreover, he believes that our present faith that schools can deliver the downtrodden from their unhappy condition is pure fantasy. Greer holds that there is nothing wrong with the schools, *given their real function,* which is, he claims, to perpetuate an indecent social order. If the schools are to serve a more humanistic purpose, he believes, their basic structure would have to be replaced. But like Illich, Friedenberg, Reimer, and other radical critics, Greer is strong on analysis, weak on suggesting practical alternatives.

BEA AND RON GROSS

A wife-and-husband team, they are perhaps best characterized as the Sol Huroks of the school reform movement. Through their anthologies (*High School,* 1971; *Radical School Reform,* 1970), their popular courses at NYU, and their nationwide consulting work, they have provided forums through which many school critics have reached a wide audience—for some of them, wider than they deserve. Ron Gross, on one occasion, even chaperoned Ivan Illich when the latter appeared on the Dick Cavett Show. And Illich needed him. In other words, the Grosses are, in the best sense of the word, "popularizers." Within the past year or so, Ron Gross has become particularly interested in what he calls Free Learning—new noninstitutionalized ways to empower individuals to take command of their lifelong education (as exemplified in auto-didactics),—and if he is not careful, he will soon need to have his own popularizer.

MARTIN HAMBURGER

A professor at New York University, Hamburger is especially interested in the relationship between economic factors in a society and schools. He believes that the relevance or irrelevance of school (from the students' point of view) rests on the extent to which the society can guarantee a meaningful outcome to schooling. By "meaningful outcome," Hamburger means a job—preferably one that offers security and dignity.

Hamburger is probably correct in his view. We are now experiencing large-scale defections from school, not only by the children of the lower class but by the children of the middle class as well. As the availability of jobs decreases, there is a corresponding growth of alienation from school, at all levels. That's Hamburger's Law. Hamburger's solution is rather complicated, but it runs along the lines of the fable in Chapter 4: have the schools develop new social roles and occupations for youth. The Peace Corps would be an example of how this might be done.

NAT HENTOFF

One of the outstanding journalists of this decade, Hentoff moved onto the school scene by writing a series of articles for the *New Yorker* about a sensitive, child-oriented New York City principal, Elliot Shapiro. The articles, which were made into a successful book, *Our Children Are Dying* (1966), made Shapiro famous, and to some extent, he became a metaphor for all the good-willed teachers and administrators fighting gallantly against "Them." Since then, Hentoff has pursued his interest in schools by doing a serious study, for the American Civil Liberties Union, of the legal aspects of students' rights—particularly the issue of corporal punishment. Hentoff is a strong advocate of enlarging students' rights, and he opposes, of course, all forms of corporal punishment. He has also engaged in continuous criticism of the UFT and Albert Shanker. To Hentoff's chagrin, Shanker's career has not in the least been impeded by such criticism.

JAMES HERNDON

James Herndon is a rare kind of teacher, no matter how you look at him. He's smart, funny, literate, and not only takes his teaching very seriously but writes books about it.

Writing books is not easy to do under the best of circumstances, and the fact that Herndon does so while he continues to teach English in junior high school in California provides another example of his rarity.

Herndon's first book, *The Way It Spozed to Be* (1968) tells the dismaying story of a teacher who discovers that "good intentions" really are not enough. It is also the autobiographical account of a teacher capable of learning from his mistakes. In his second book, *How to Survive in Your Native Land* (1971), he describes how he improved his teaching (and his strategies for dealing with forces that would impede him in his attempts) on the basis of what he learned during the experiences recounted in the first book.

JOHN HOLT

When anyone makes a list of critics of the schools, John Holt is always included, usually placed first or second. In his tender and angry little book, *How Children Fail* (1964), Holt laid bare much of what was destructive or silly in the classroom, and set the tone for a great deal of the school criticism that followed. His major point was that we have become so habituated to "teaching" that we no longer comprehend how learning takes place. A former elementary school teacher, Holt is a courageous and generous man, at his best when dealing with concrete examples of nonsense and how to correct them. However, the more rigorously he has pursued the logic of his own critical assumptions, the farther he has drifted from a concern for schools. Within the past two years, he has come heavily under the influence of Ivan Illich, which has meant that he has lost most of his interest in reforming the bad practices of schools. Instead, he has turned his attention to larger, vaguer, and generally more intractable issues, such as, What is the real meaning of freedom?

IVAN ILLICH

Illich is a Catholic priest, who was born in Vienna, worked in an Irish–Puerto Rican parish in New York, lives in Mexico, addresses himself to the world, and has gained a wide, worshipful following in the United States. For the past two years, his theory of education has influenced school critics immensely, especially those who are not directly engaged in school work. In essence, Illich believes that a good educational system should provide anyone who wants to learn anything with an opportunity to do so, by making resources and people easily available. Such a system would not exclude anyone, for example, by demanding diplomas, certificates, records, or anything else. Nor would it force anyone to submit to an obligatory curriculum. Naturally, Illich believes that a school system such as we have in the United States, and which most countries in the world have copied, does not qualify as a decent educational system. He contends that our schooling process is elitist, certification-oriented, authoritarian, and generally unresponsive to the needs of people. It is not so much that schools are bad, he says, but that schooling is bad, especially because all schools impose a "hidden" curriculum—that is, a set of restrictive assumptions built into the structure of schooling. As an alternative, Illich proposes a network of resources that would bring together things, people with special skills, other learners, and even educators. Some critics of Illich have remarked that his "network" sounds an awful lot like a "school." But Illich denies this and promises something close to paradise if his ideas were seriously and carefully implemented. Many of these ideas are expressed in detail in his book *De-Schooling Society* (1970).

With his close associate, Everett Reimer (*School Is Dead,*

1971), Illich operates out of the Center for Intercultural Documentation (CIDOC) in Cuernavaca, Mexico, where he runs a school.

CHRISTOPHER JENCKS

Jencks is located at the Harvard Center for the Study of Public Policy, from which there issued an extremely controversial report on the feasibility of the voucher system. The report was made possible through a grant from the Office of Economic Opportunity and is entitled *Education Vouchers* (1970). It was principally authored by Jencks, and he is widely associated with the idea. Jencks does not go as far as Milton Friedman, who in his book *Capitalism and Freedom* (1962), and in subsequent expressions, advocates that schools be treated as private enterprise, and that parents be free to buy whatever kind of education the marketplace can provide. Nonetheless, Jencks's idea—that people be permitted to purchase, with public funds, a private education—strikes at the foundations of the public school structure and is vehemently opposed by many groups.

Sometimes, the term voucher system is used as a synonym for "Jencks's system." This is not quite correct, since there are several different "voucher" proposals—for example, a proposal made by John Coons, William Clune, and Stephen Sugarman in their book *Private Wealth and Public Education* (1970).

Recently, Jencks has caused even more trouble with the publication of his *Inequality: A Reassessment of the Effect of Family and Schooling in America* (1972). The book is the result of a three-year study funded by the Carnegie Corporation. Its major conclusion contradicts one of the most pervasive American beliefs, to wit, that good schooling brings good prospects for economic success. Jencks and his Harvard researchers say no. Their data suggest that the schools, no matter how good, cannot do much to eliminate or even reduce the gap between rich and poor. Like the Coleman Report, with which it is often compared,

Inequality casts a long shadow over our faith in the schools' capacity to improve the social, economic, and intellectual status of students. But Jencks is far from gloomy about his own conclusions. He feels that school can be a significant experience for young people, if not in terms of money and social status, then possibly in terms of increased creativity, knowledge, enjoyment, and self-esteem. In other words, if schools were liberated from their obligation to do what they cannot do, they might turn out to be interesting places.

ARTHUR JENSEN

A professor at the University of California in Berkeley, Jensen has accomplished what few people have in any field: he has made his name into a common noun, as in "Jensenism." It all began in 1969, when his article, "How Much Can We Boost I.Q. and Scholastic Achievement?" appeared in the *Harvard Educational Review*. The article tried to show, first of all, that people with low IQs tend to differ *genetically* from people with high IQs. Nothing astonishing in that, especially since Jensen admitted that environment is also a factor in anyone's IQ. How much of a factor was his next question. He concluded from his study and reinterpretation of existing data that environment counts for about 20 percent of a person's IQ, and that genes account for the rest. He went further to say that what is true for individuals within a group is also true for differences *between* groups, especially between white and black Americans, who differ by about 15 points on IQ scores. The argument gets pretty technical, and one would have to know an awful lot about statistics, IQ tests, and other relevant studies to build an informed opinion. But it all added up to the proposition that American blacks have lower average IQ scores (and perform worse in school) than American whites because of their genes, not so much because of their environment. That proposition, naturally, fit nicely into any and all racist philosophies, and Jensen was lambasted. His critics challenged his interpretation of the data, his statistics, and to some extent, his motives. Jensen was defended by some, notably H. J. Eysenck, a renowned British psychologist. In his book *The I.Q. Argument* (1971), Eysenck asserted that Jensen was being attacked because, like any good scientist, he was simply telling the truth, as opposed to saying what people wished to hear.

Jensen also drew support from others, such as Harvard psychologist Richard Herrnstein who, in an article, "I.Q." (*Atlantic*, September 1971), contended that American society is becoming what he called a "stable hereditary meritocracy." The argument is based on the hypothesis that differences in mental abilities are inherited and that people close in mental ability tend to marry and reproduce. In short, the smart beget smart; the dumb beget dumb. In this way, he explains why changes in the environment (e.g., social reforms) fail to produce any substantial shift in the distribution of wealth: the smart stay rich, the dumb stay poor.

There are, of course, many arguments against the Jensen-Eysenck-Herrnstein point of view. Some of these are treated in Chapter 5, "Present and Future Issues." Here, it needs only to be said that in current usage, "Jensenism" refers to the belief that blacks have lower IQs than whites because of genetic factors. For a full explication of Jensen's views see his *Genetics and Education* (1972).

EARL KELLEY

The late Earl Kelley began his teaching career in a one-room schoolhouse in the Midwest and ended it as a professor of psychology at Wayne State University in Detroit. His personal career almost spanned the history of American public education as we know it.

Kelley was a humanist throughout his career, and not only advocated but practiced progressive education. He consistently pursued humanistic education even in the face of strident criticism for being too soft. He also never stopped learning, a characteristic which distinguished him from most people. His inquiring mind led him, for example, to Hanover, New Hampshire, where a largely unknown man, Adelbert Ames, was conducting demonstrations in perception. In his most important book, *Education for What Is Real* (1947) Kelley described some of the Ames' demonstrations and discussed their implications for schooling.

HERBERT KOHL

A former schoolteacher, Kohl attracted national attention with three sensitively written books, *36 Children* (1967), *Teaching the Unteachable* (1967), and *The Open Classroom* (1970). The books constituted an unusually vivid indictment of a bureaucratized, regimented school system, and also suggested sensible strategies by which teachers might move toward a humane competence, even within an "inhumane" system. Eventually, Kohl started his own private school, called Other Ways, in Berkeley, California. The school has become quite well known, not only because it is experimental and "open," but also because it was assimilated into the progressive public school system of Berkeley—whose present superintendent, Dick Foster, is an ardent supporter of alternative schools. Kohl has since separated himself from Other Ways, and has become increasingly interested in politics. For what it might mean, which is probably nothing, he and Jonathan Kozol were roommates at Harvard.

JOHNATHAN KOZOL

Kozol's first and most memorable contribution to school criticism was his shivering account of what it is like to be a student (and a teacher) in a ghetto school. The book, *Death at an Early Age* (1967), won a National Book Award, and although it has since been surpassed by other, more intense accounts of ghetto schools, also won for its author a large following of young radical school critics. Many of these people have founded or work in free schools, because they believe the public schools to be too regimented and bureaucratic to function humanely. Kozol certainly believes this to be true. Over the years however he has maintained and strengthened his commitment to the welfare of poor people, particularly blacks, and in his latest book, *Free Schools* (1972), he denounced those to whom free schools have become a means of promoting an exotic and elitist life style. No doubt, some of his old followers now view him as a traitor to the counterculture, but Kozol is too busy trying to develop workable alternative urban schools to care.

R. D. LAING

While he is not an educator in the usual sense, and while he has not written about schools specifically, R. D. Laing requires at least a brief mention here because he addresses himself to the kinds of human questions that schools profess to be concerned with, and because he is widely read by high school and college students.

Laing is a Scottish physician and psychiatrist who has written several books, including *The Divided Self* (1960) and *The Politics of Experience* (1967) which challenge the most basic assumptions not only of conventional psychiatry but of society itself. He has especially questioned psychiatric diagnostic and classification procedures, incurring the extreme displeasure of his psychiatric colleagues in the process. But, on this score, he is in good company, sharing the same kinds of doubts and concerns expressed by Karl Menninger in *The Vital Balance* (1963).

In particular, Laing attacks the arbitrary and technocratic language used to label, and then to treat, patients. Schizophrenia is the most common formal classification (i.e., diagnosis) of mental illness. Laing's observation about schizophrenia is that it is always "a special strategy that a person invents in order to live in an unlivable situation."

His analysis turns conventional modes of thought inside out by revealing the shocking possibility that a person judged to be mad as a result of not conforming to social and political norms (which may be mad in themselves) may not only *not* be mad, but may be the only sane person around. He shifts the onus from the judged to the judges, and the judges deeply resent this.

Laing's appeal to the young is possibly a consequence of the fact that he looks at therapy (teaching) from the patient's (student's) point of view, rather than only from the therapist's (teacher's). The way things look from the student's point of view is almost never considered in school talk—just as the patient's point of view is rarely considered in psychiatric talk.

Indeed, any student who fails to conform to some of the obvious destructive conventions of school is judged to be a problem. The only possible solution is for the student to "adjust" to the school. The idea that the school and its conventions might be the problem is anathema to conventional school thought, of course.

ROBERT F. MAGER

In 1962, when programmed instruction seemed on the verge of introduction into the schools, Robert F. Mager published a book titled *Preparing Objectives for Programmed Instruction*. As the emphasis shifted from programmed instruction to behavioral objectives, the *title* of the book (*not* the content) changed to *Preparing Instructional Objectives*. The fact that such a change in title could occur without any change in content reveals a good deal about the basic assumptions of behavioral objectives.

The book, however, is perceptive and witty, and is still probably the best single book of its kind for helping teachers and others to write statements of objectives in a way that permits an observation to be made about a behavioral change in students.

Because of his writing, Mager, who is a member of the American Psychological Association and the National Society for Programmed Instruction, is one of the better known experts and consultants on behavioral objectives.

In 1968 he published *Developing Attitudes Toward Learning*, a brief and gentle book, recapitulating the basic principles of learning psychology, and urging readers to use them humanely.

ABRAHAM H. MASLOW

A Brooklyn-born psychologist and chairman of the department of psychology at Brandeis University, the late Abraham Maslow was the founder of what is known as humanistic psychology or psychology's "Third Force" (behaviorism and Freudian psychoanalysis being the First and Second). He believed that human life could never be adequately understood unless man's highest aspirations are taken into account, and that values, such as altruism and integrity, are an essential part of human nature. He was horrified at the thought that human beings should be measured, classified, or statistically analyzed for the sake of prediction and control.

Maslow developed many terms and concepts now widely used: *need hierarchy* (there are levels of human needs, ranging from the physiological on upward, and only when the needs of one level are met can the person advance to the higher level), *self-actualization* (there is, in each individual, a hereditary inner nature which, if unhampered, will allow each person to become the best that he can become), and *peak experiences* (moments of experienced perfection). Self-actualization did not imply the complete absence of controls—Maslow believed that desirable controls could enhance gratification. He also believed that the concept of self-actualization required absolute equality of opportunity for every child.

Maslow felt that educators often deprive children of having peak experiences by taking the wonder out of life—a child who has just seen a rainbow for the first time doesn't benefit by being told about prisms and the scattering of white light. He further noted that peak experiences can only be transient and that major improvements in society and education could come about if we could give up dreams of finding perfection in human beings and in society.

Maslow died in June 1970 at the age of sixty-two.

ROLLO MAY

May is a New York City psychoanalyst and writer, and one of the leading spokesmen for humanistic psychology. Born in 1909 in Ada, Ohio, into a family of strong Methodist and somewhat Victorian beliefs, May insists that psychology must stress ethics and human values, qualities which man does not share with rats or machines. Naturally he is opposed to Skinnerians and behaviorists who believe that everyone can be made to fit into society. May's goal as a therapist is to help his patient understand himself, *not* to help him adjust to society. He believes that only crazy people would not have anxiety living in today's world. In this respect, May's beliefs parallel those of R. D. Laing. He attributes the sickness of our times to the loss of the symbols and beliefs that used to give meaning to life and looks forward to a new society built on such concepts as caring, human uniqueness, free choice, and cooperation.

May's critics accuse him of moralizing and of popularizing a simplistic view of man. However, although he is to some extent responsible for the new human-potential movement, he has himself protested against some of the more simplistic techniques (e.g., encounter therapy and body therapy) used by some humanistic psychologists.

Among his books are *Man's Search for Himself* (1953), *Love and Will* (1969), and *Power and Innocence* (1972).

RHODY MCCOY

McCoy was catapulted into national prominence in 1968 when, as unit administrator of the Ocean-Hill–Brownsville district, he squared off against the UFT, the New York City Board of Education, the Council of Supervisory Associations, the New York State Commissioner of Education, and, it seemed at times, the rest of the free world. A year earlier, Ocean Hill–Brownsville had been one of three ghetto areas in New York City selected as demonstration districts to determine whether or not community control was a viable political possibility. A battle was touched off in May 1968, when the governing board of Ocean Hill–Brownsville decided to transfer out of the district thirteen teachers, five assistant principals, and one principal, under the assumption that community control meant that a board elected by the district had such authority. All hell broke loose, mostly because the UFT felt that such authority would break the back of the union—i.e., rob teachers of their job security. The argument quickly descended to the worst kind of racist and anti-Semitic rhetoric, although not by McCoy, who is a serene and competent administrator. Inevitably, the community control forces lost. Through legislation, the experimental districts were abolished, and McCoy was sent packing. However, his name remains as a symbol of black control of schools in black neighborhoods. In recent years, McCoy has found a home at the School of Education of the University of Massachusetts, where he frequently lectures on the politics of schools.

MARSHALL MCLUHAN

McLuhan began his career as a proper English professor, delivering lectures and writing scholarly literary aritcles. Then, at the University of Toronto, he came under the influence of two colleagues, Harold Innis, an economic historian, and Edmund Carpenter, an anthropologist. Both Innis and Carpenter had—independently—come to study the role of communication modes in human affairs, and Innis was the author of two books, *Empire and Communication* and *The Bias of Communication*, that examined in minute historical detail the effects on the course of human events of shifts or changes in media of communication.

McLuhan's thinking was crystallized by Innis's work, and, with Edmund Carpenter (and with the support of a Ford Foundation grant) he established the Center for the Study of Culture and Communication at the University of Toronto.

In 1951 McLuhan published his first book of media analysis, *The Mechanical Bride*. Stating that the purpose of the book was to assist us, the public, to observe consciously how advertisers affected us unconsciously, McLuhan used the sailor in Edgar Allan Poe's story "A Descent Into the Maelstrom" as a metaphor, pointing out that "Poe's sailor saved himself by studying the action of the whirlpool and by co-operating with it." This is still McLuhan's primary motivation for studying, and for advocating that students in school study, the processes and effects of the mass media. One of his lines, frequently quoted by himself, but curiously neglected by his critics, is: "There is absolutely no inevitability as long as there is a willingness to contemplate what is happening."

McLuhan must be counted among those men who have written little-read but widely criticized books presenting new ways of looking at and thinking about ubiquitous and obvious aspects of our daily experience. Staring into the rearview mirror, as he puts it, is not only a curious way to tell where you've been, it can be fatal if you do it in order to tell where you're going. It is this point that McLuhan uses as the basis for his explicit suggestions for improving schooling. In a piece titled "We Need a New Picture of Knowledge" (*New Insights and the Curriculum*, Associates for Supervision and Curriculum Development, National Education Association, Washington, D.C., 1963), McLuhan suggests that schools should shift from imposing a passive role on students to emphasizing active student participation in exploratory and speculative dialogue about the processes, uses, and effects of human knowledge. His primary purpose in this is to develop what he calls "media literacy." This has led to his being accused of being "anti-print," despite the fact that he explicitly denies being so, in print itself and otherwise. He is saying that, as a result of developments in electric and electronic media, print today plays a role substantially different from the role it played when it enjoyed a virtual monopoly. He is not against print; he simply points out that it is now in competition with other media to an unprecedented degree. In school, the lack of attention to this phenomenon results in increasing (and increasingly disappointing) emphasis on writing to the virtual exclusion of attention to the spoken language upon which it depends, and which it ostensibly represents. It is, for example, virtually impossible to teach a child to read words that he does not have in his normal speech.

Children who live in an aural environment (where writing of any kind is relatively exotic) in which both the form and substance of their speech is perfectly adequate for daily survival purposes, are at a cultural disadvantage in school, where their primary task consists of the visual ability to decode writing that mostly reflects assumptions and things they do not experience and which consists almost entirely of words that they never use.

McLuhan has been probing media meanings for about twenty-five years now. Despite the disparaging criticism his ideas have evoked, the probability is that he will come to be viewed as one of the most important educational philosophers of our times. Frontier thinkers are usually alone on the frontier until it and they are subsumed by the growth of the larger community.

MARIA MONTESSORI

The first book Montessori ever wrote on education was published in 1909 and called *The Method of Scientific Pedagogy as Applied to Infant Education and the Children's Houses: Auto-Education in Elementary Schools*. Not exactly a catchy title, but in some ways the most influential book written on education in this century. The book described both her discoveries about the workings of a child's mind and the methods by which teachers can help children realize their intellectual potential. These discoveries were made largely by observation of sixty slum children—ages three to six—who were attending a special school in a tenement house in one of the worst sections of Rome. It is difficult for anyone today (when almost any fool will write a book on education) to understand how little was known or even hypothesized about child development at the turn of the century. In effect, Montessori discovered that children possess much more profound and various intellectual qualities than had previously been supposed. She found, for example, that children exhibited an enormous capacity for concentration, a love of repetition, a love for order, a need to make free choices, and, astonishingly, a preference for work over play. These discoveries formed the basis of the Montessori Method, which has spread throughout the world and has had powerful expression in the United States, right to the present time.

Montessori was born in Italy in 1870, and died in 1952. She was an advocate of women's liberation and was the first woman ever to get a medical degree in Italy. In fact, the same year she received her medical degree (1896), she was selected to represent the women of Italy at a feminist conference held in Berlin.

ANITA MOSES

Moses is one of the founders and was the first director of the Children's Community Workshop, an unusual and well-known alternative school in New York City. One of its unusual characteristics is that it is free not only in the sense of its approach to education, but also in a financial sense, particularly to neighborhood children to whom it is largely restricted. Because it charges no tuition, and because it is a neighborhood school, an attempt has been made to have it classified as a legitimate public school (and, therefore, entitle it to public funds)— but the attempt has so far failed.

Moses is an articulate, down-to-earth spokeswoman for experimental schools, with a particular interest in the schooling of young children. She has left her position at the Children's Community Workshop over a dispute about the school's philosophy, and she now conducts seminars for teachers who want to learn new methods.

A. S. NEILL

If there were an All-Star team of great and influential school critics, A. S. Neill would certainly be on it. He is, of course, the founder of Summerhill, probably the best-known free school in the world. Summerhill was started in 1921 in the small, wool-producing village of Leiston, England. From the outset, Neill tried to make Summerhill a noncoercive, nonrepressive educational experience for children from ages five through fifteen.

Neill believes that children are basically both good and wise, and that a school, therefore, should fit the child, rather than bend him to fit the school. As a consequence, at Summerhill, courses are optional, tests and grades are not given, university preparation is disdained, teachers and students transact freely and equally, and the entire school—teachers and students alike—participates in self-government.

Although the school has been in operation for over fifty years, little was known about it until 1960, when Neill's *Summerhill: A Radical Experiment in Child Rearing* was published.

From that time on, thousands of people have journeyed to Leiston (for many it is a pilgrimage) to see the ultimate model of a progressive school. What they find is thrilling to some, horrifying to others. The latter believe they are seeing a sequel to *Lord of the Flies*; the former, a viable experiment in educating for creativity and autonomy.

Among those who have received Neill's ideas enthusiastically are many Americans, some of whom have tried to start Summerhill-type schools here. For example, actor Orson Bean opened a "Summerhill" day school in New York City, amid much publicity. (The real Summerhill is a boarding school.) Most of these schools have failed, and the Summerhill Society, founded to encourage the growth of Neill's ideas, is presently broke. But there can be no doubt that Neill's influence remains powerful among the many advocates of free schools.

Unlike Dewey, Neill is not much of a theoretician. His written works are sparse and filled with rather obvious observations. His strength is in the fact that he has been *doing* radical education for a half century and, as a result, knows more about how to do it than anyone else in the world.

HENRY PERKINSON

A historian and philosopher of education, Perkinson has made an impact on the school scene with two books, *The Imperfect Panacea* (1968) and *The Possibilities of Error* (1971). The first is an attempt to show the ways in which Americans have historically and hysterically used their schools. Perkinson's main point is that we have always looked to our schools (even as we do today) as an instrument for solving our most serious social problems—whether they be racial, sexual, or pharmacological. Naturally, the schools can never quite manage to handle the burden, and as a consequence, they are always a disappointment. The thought is a humbling one, and it would be a great help if some of our more grandiose reformers read the book.

The Possibilities of Error is based on the philosophy of Karl Popper, and attempts, among other things, to make a case for prudence and rigor in the matter of social change. The book speaks against utopianism and for gradualism. It is not against change, but in favor of controlled change.

VITO PERRONE

Perrone is dean of the New School for Behavioral Studies in Education at the University of North Dakota. His school and he were made more or less famous by the thorough description of both given by Charles Silberman in *Crisis in the Classroom*. As Silberman says, the New School "was created specifically to be the principal instrument for reorganizing the elementary schools of North Dakota along individualized and informal lines." A major feature of the school's program is an exchange program whereby public school districts send teachers to study at the New School, and the New School replaces them, in return, with master's degree candidates. Another unusual feature is that the New School tries to teach its students in a way that is congruent with the way it is hoped the students will teach *their* students. That is *very* unusual. At the moment, Perrone's New School at North Dakota and Dwight Allen's school at the University of Massachusetts are the two best-known schools of education in the country.

JEAN PIAGET

Piaget was born in 1896 in Switzerland. He began his career as a zoologist, but during the past fifty years he has established himself as the foremost child psychologist in the world. His main interest has been in the cognitive development of children—that is, how they develop powers of perceiving, remembering, recognizing, generalizing—in a word, thinking. He insists that all children go through certain stages of intellectual development *in the same order,* the difference between a bright child and a dull one being that the former passes through these stages more quickly than the latter. Most of Piaget's work has involved rigorous observation of children, from which he believes he has discovered some of the basic operations and concepts included in learning to think. His most famous discovery concerns the development in children of the concept he calls "conservation" —the idea that a short, fat eight-ounce glass holds as much liquid as a tall, skinny eight-ounce glass. Piaget acknowledges that a child's environment can play a role in delaying or facilitating the movement from one stage of development to another, but he insists that the basic factor in determining the pace of learning is the child's internal equilibrium. He is both skeptical about and amused at educators' attempts, especially in America, to speed up cognitive development. (He calls that problem "the American question.") He has been sending out warnings for years that parents and teachers should not trifle with nature by trying to force children to learn things they are not ready to learn. For example, Piaget believes that reading instruction should probably not begin until the age of eight or nine for most children. Although he disagrees with Jerome Bruner in important respects, Piaget, like Bruner, is opposed to didactic teaching, and his theories have given support to school people who advocate inductive teaching.

NEIL POSTMAN AND CHARLES WEINGARTNER

Of course, modesty forbids our indicating the true place in the school reform movement of these aging professors. However, our respect for accuracy does permit us to recall what a leading educator said when informed that Postman and Weingartner were preparing a new book about schools. He said, "Who?" Other eminent educators having expressed themselves in a similar vein, we have no choice but to leave it to the reader to decide if our reputations have been advanced by the present volume.

MAX RAFFERTY

Rafferty is no longer an active or significant figure on the school scene. He was both when he served as superintendent of public instruction for the State of California from 1963 to 1971. Nonetheless, he is worth mentioning because his name has become a symbol of school conservatism. Rafferty believed—and probably still does—that John Dewey was a blight upon the earth, that patriotism is the highest virtue, and that the schools should concentrate on teaching the "basics"—reading, writing, arithmetic, and a proper love of country. His election to office was, in part, a result of the backlash against progressivism that was precipitated by *Sputnik I*. The main thrust of his administration was to prevent, wherever possible, any rays of reality from seeping into the schools.

FRANK RIESSMAN

Riessman is the editor of *Social Policy* and a professor of educational sociology at New York University. His book *The Culturally Deprived Child* (1962) made him nationally known and gave wide currency to the phrase "culturally deprived." He probably regrets that now, but in any case is not brooding about it. In fact, his most recent book, *Children Teach Children* (1971), with Alan Gartner and Mary Kohler, is one of the significant education books of recent times. It reviews most of the important research done on what happens when children teach each other. What happens is that both teacher and student get smarter, especially teacher. Riessman concludes that by not using students as teachers, we are wasting one of our most important resources.

But alas, as Caleb Gattegno has pointed out, teachers are impressed by research, but rarely influenced by it.

CARL ROGERS

Whereas B. F. Skinner is considered by many to be the enemy of "autonomous man" (Skinner says there's no such thing), Rogers is considered his undisputed champion. Rogers is one of the leading exponents of humanistic psychology, which holds that man is capable of directing himself toward positive goals. Rogers, the late Abraham Maslow, and other humanists believe that man has an inner need to "actualize" himself, and that in an environment of acceptance, understanding, and consistency, each person tends to make productive and rewarding choices of behavior—for himself. This implies, of course, that each person will develop differently from every other person. Thus, in Skinner's psychology an accepting environment would tend to make people behave in similar ways. In Rogers' psychology an accepting environment would produce different behaviors.

Rogers' most important school book is *Freedom to Learn* (1969). He is among a growing number of psychologists who believe that the classroom needs less, not more, control, and that it should be an environment which encourages each individual to determine his own direction. One of Rogers' most controversial remarks is to the effect that anything you can teach to another (in the traditional sense of "teach") is probably either trivial or harmful. Skinner thinks all such talk is pretty much nonsense. Rogers thinks Skinner has a very limited understanding of the human mind.

ROBERT ROSENTHAL

A professor of social relations at Harvard University, Rosenthal carried out, during the 1960s, a series of experiments on learning with humans, rats, and worms, designed to show that the outcome of experiments are strongly affected by the experimenter's expectations—that in some unintentional way the person performing the experiment communicates his wishes to the subject, who gets the message and complies. Rosenthal reasoned that if this is the case in psychological experimentation, would it not also apply to learning situations outside the laboratory? In 1964 he went into a public elementary school in San Francisco and tested his hypothesis that teachers' expectations may unintentionally determine their students' performance. All the children at the school were given a standard intelligence test. The teachers were not informed of the actual results but were led to believe that the test had measured a potential for intellectual "blooming." About 20 percent of the children, who had in fact been picked at random, were represented to the teachers as potential "bloomers." When the children were retested one semester, one year, and two years later, the "bloomers" had clearly advanced more than the other children.

Pygmalion in the Classroom, Teacher Expectation and Pupils' Intellectual Development (1968), coauthored by Rosenthal and Lenore Jacobson, principal of the elementary school, describes this study. It speculates that the teachers, perhaps by being more involved and encouraging, may unintentionally have motivated these children by expecting more from them than from their classmates.

Critics have noted weaknesses in Rosenthal's experimental studies, particularly accusing him of not being rigorous enough in his methodology. Yet, in real classrooms everywhere, teachers treat different children differently, and it is easy to join Rosenthal in wondering whether teachers' expectations may also be very damaging to children.

MATTHEW SCHWARTZ AND SEYMOUR FLIEGEL

The next time you hear a school administrator say, "I know things are bad, but what can I do?", tell him about Schwartz and Fliegel. Until recently, they were, respectively, principal and assistant principal of an elementary school (PS 146) in East

Harlem, in New York City. About 50 percent of their students were Puerto Rican, 45 percent black. The surrounding neighborhood is what most people call a slum. Aided by federal funds which permitted them to double their staff, Schwartz and Fliegel went to work. They individualized instruction, abolished homogeneous grouping, humanized methods of evaluation, opened the school to parents, made wide use of community resources, and in general created an atmosphere of respect for the rights of students. Within a relatively short period, their school was transformed from a typical inner-city disaster to one of the finest elementary schools in the country. Student attendance, performance, and interest ran high, surpassed only by teacher morale and competence. Schwartz, Fliegel, and their teachers proved that money, commitment, and enlightened theory can make a difference even in the most unpromising circumstances.

The story of PS 146 is instructive in many ways. For example, eventually the federal funds were withheld, the staff was decimated, and the school fell apart. Moreover, the local community school board—which had replaced the big, bad bureaucracy (the New York City Board of Education)—played an important role in destroying the program. How all this came about is a long story, having much to do with local politics, reverse racism, and a pinched budget. But the plain fact is that Coleman, Jencks, Jensen, and other gloomy statisticians are wrong: when school reform is done with intelligence, compassion, and money, the minds and hearts of children can be affected in the most positive terms.

ALBERT SHANKER

A former mathematics teacher, Shanker is a tough, no-nonsense labor leader who has done more than anyone else to transform a docile teaching profession into a sturdy, sometimes implacable union, at least in New York. As head of the UFT (United Federation of Teachers) and of the New York Congress of Teachers, Shanker has helped to provide teachers with increased economic security and, some say, increased self-respect. For some curious reason, many people have expected Shanker to exhibit statesmanlike qualities, or at least a driving interest in improving schools. They have been disappointed. Shanker operates the way any good labor leader does. Actually, Shanker is not *against* improving schools; but he is mainly interested in protecting the position of teachers—which is why they keep electing him to represent them. In the long run, Shanker and men like him may have more to do with deciding the future of the schools than a peck of philosophers, since his decisions always powerfully affect the conventions of the schooling process.

CHARLES SILBERMAN

An editor at *Fortune* magazine, Silberman was selected to do a comprehensive study of American schools for the Carnegie Foundation. His report, called *Crisis in the Classroom* (1970), added considerable respectability to the criticisms that had previously been made by radicals and dissidents. In other words, it said the same thing, only in a more boring fashion. It is practically impossible to find anyone who has read the book "personally," although almost everybody claims to know what it's about. Its most widely quoted phrase is that school is a "grim and joyless place," characterized by "mindlessness." However, Silberman went far beyond denunciation. For example, he described many different school experiments, including the "open classroom." What gave the book its importance was the fact that Silberman was an acknowledged objective observer when he began his inquiry, and, of course, that he had the prestige of the Carnegie Foundation behind him. Thus, *Crisis in the Classroom* made it official: schools need improvement.

SID SIMON

When Simon was a teacher at Temple University, he got into trouble because he did not believe in grades. Same thing when he was at Queens College. He's finally found a sanctuary, as have so many others, at the School of Education of the University of Massachusetts. Nonetheless, Simon continues to think about the grading system, and is probably the best-informed person in the country on what it does to students. His book *Wad-Ja-Get?* (1971), written with Howard Kirshenbaum and Rodney Napier, is both peculiar and delightful. Half fiction, half fact, it lays out the case against grading and includes a most informative review of the research on the subject. Simon and Kirshenbaum have also earned a growing reputation for their work in "value clarification," which is an attempt to help students (and teachers) gain insight into what they believe and why.

B. F. SKINNER

A colleague of Jerome Bruner at Harvard, Skinner is the preeminent behavioral psychologist in the world. This means that he takes little interest in the question, "What is going on inside the mind when we think?" In fact, he regards this as mostly an unanswerable question—at least at the present time. Instead, Skinner and other behaviorists are concerned to study the outward, observable signs of thinking: in a phrase, how we act. Skinner is particularly interested in how behavior can be changed—which is why his work has been of so much interest to school people. His principal instrument for changing behavior is what he calls "operant conditioning." This is somewhat similar to the procedures used by the great Russian psychologist Pavlov. Skinner believes that by reinforcing (through praise and other rewards) the behaviors you want, you will get repetitions of those behaviors. He takes it as axiomatic that we all learn just about everything by receiving positive reinforcement from our environment (i.e., from our parents, friends, and others). Skinner and other behaviorists claim to have helped everyone from stutterers to poor spellers through precise schedules of operant conditioning, and Skinner has even taught pigeons to play Ping-Pong (for reasons that best remain obscure). In his most recent work, *Beyond Freedom and Dignity* (1971), Skinner proposes that we reform our whole society by using the technology of operant conditioning. His critics accuse him of being a fascist and of leading us to Orwell's version of 1984. Skinner replies that he is merely describing how people learn, and that if well-meaning educators do not use sound principles, then ill-meaning politicians and other hucksters will. At the moment, the only practical application of Skinner's work that has had any impact on the school scene is the development of the ideas of programmed learning and behavioral objectives.

HAROLD TAYLOR

Taylor is easily the most durable of school critics. During the late 1940s and throughout the 50s, he singlehandedly kept alive the progressive tradition, and, in fact, was almost alone in producing any kind of critique of the schools. As president of Sarah Lawrence College from 1945 to 1959, he turned it into a repository of progressive and experimental ideas, from which, to this day, it still draws much of its vitality. But Taylor is no elder statesman. Although much of his attention is now directed to higher education (*Students Without Teachers*, 1969, and *How to Change Colleges*, 1971), his current criticisms of school conventions are, as always, sharp, witty, and thoughtful. He is particularly concerned with the shoddy treatment the schools give to the arts. He is also interested in international education and the development of "free learning" systems. He is one of the few school critics who, by education and experience, can bring to bear on present problems an historical and generally mature perspective of the role of schools in society.

THEY/THEM

All school criticism is dependent, at least to some extent, on the continuous existence of either "They" or "Them." As everyone knows, things would be much better if only They would allow it. The trouble is that They are unfeeling, evil, and fierce. They never allow anything, and always out of base motives. The most productive critics are those who have not been intimidated by Them. The most unproductive are those who are mainly interested in affirming their sense of moral superiority by contrasting their own pure motives with the motives of Them. But it is important to remember that They/Them *do* exist—not, of course, as implacable enemies, but as a system of interconnecting functions and conventions. They is an "it," which will accommodate quite easily to some kinds of changes, and not at all to others.

LILLIAN WEBER

A professor of education at City College in New York, Weber is perhaps the most knowledgeable proponent of open education in the country. After making an intensive 18-month study of informal British schools, she supervised the transformation of a conventional Harlem elementary school into an open classroom school. Weber is considered the inventor of the open corridor and is widely used as a consultant to those who want to move toward the British system. She believes, however, that Americans must invent their own style of openness, and in her book, *The English Infant School and Informal Education* (1971), she explains how this can be done.

FREDERICK WISEMAN

Wiseman is a professional film maker who is inclined toward doing *cinéma vérité* documentaries. One such film, *High*

School (1969), made an indelible impression on the school reform movement. Wiseman took his cameras into a middle-class Philadelphia high school and, seemingly, merely recorded what took place there. Of course, the film is carefully and brilliantly edited and is by no means a direct representation of what the school is like. Nevertheless, the film undoubtedly reflects accurately the oppressive extent of the regimentation, fatuousness, and just plain bullying that exists in so many schools. The film is a favorite at teachers' conferences and always generates controversy along the lines of either "That's the way it is" or "It just ain't so."

LEGAL
DECISIONS

THE COURTS VIEW
THE SCHOOLS

THE PURPOSE of this section is to give you some idea of the variety and complexity of legal decisions affecting the schools. We have made no attempt to supply a representative example of each type of case. That would require several volumes all by itself. Instead, we have chosen ten cases (especially of recent years), each of which has raised some significant (or curious) educational issue. From your reading of our summaries of these cases, you probably will get the following impressions, which we believe to be correct, as generalizations about the law and schools: (1) that the courts accept and repeatedly validate the basic *function* of American schools; (2) that the courts are willing (or would be) to overthrow school *conventions* if these conventions can be shown to be unreasonable; (3) that lower courts tend to be more conservative in their rulings than higher courts.

The first case presented led to the historic desegregation ruling of 1954. We include it here simply because of its importance, and on the off-chance that you are not familiar with its details.

The second case is the famous *Tinker* decision, which has to do with students' rights, and which, among civil libertarians, is as well known as any Supreme Court case of recent years. We hope you will take the time to read carefully the excerpts we have included from Justice Fortas's opinion. After reading them, perhaps you will agree with us that his forced resignation from the Supreme Court was one of the more depressing events of recent times.

The third and fourth cases have to do with the continuing problem of how to achieve racially balanced schools. Both these cases form the basis of Court-ordered busing and the present turmoil about the legality and wisdom of busing.

The fifth case is *Serrano* v. *Priest*, a landmark decision which may have the effect of revolutionizing school financing.

The sixth case is one that is commonly thought to challenge the basis of all certification criteria not based strictly on performance. The case is known as *Griggs* v. *Duke Power Company*, and it is a favorite of Ivan Illich and other deschoolers.

The remaining four cases, like *Tinker*, concern students' rights—everything from the right to wear buttons, to the right to wear long hair, to the right to be represented by counsel in certain kinds of hearings.

We trust you will find our accounts of these cases objective and informative. We trust, also, that some of you may be encouraged to use the courts as an instrument of relief and change should you or your child be the victims of an unreasonable school convention.

✠   ✠   ✠

BROWN ET AL. V. BOARD OF EDUCATION OF TOPEKA ET AL. (1954)

The plaintiffs in this case were black children who were attending segregated elementary schools in Topeka, Kansas. They brought an action before the U.S. District Court for the District of Kansas, contending that they had been denied admission to white schools and that this had deprived them of their rights under the Fourteenth Amendment.* The district court, while agreeing that segregation in the public schools had a detrimental effect upon black children, denied their right to attend the white schools on the grounds that the facilities (and teachers) in the black and white schools were essentially equal. The ruling was based on the Supreme Court's 1896 *Plessy* v. *Ferguson* decision, which established the "separate but equal" doctrine, specifically in relation to transportation facilities.

The plaintiffs then appealed to the U.S. Supreme Court, contending that segregated public schools can never be equal. The Court decided to look at the issue of equality not merely in terms of school buildings and teachers' salaries, but in terms of less tangible issues, posing the question, "Does segregation of children in public schools solely on the basis of race, even though the physical facilities and other tangible factors may be equal, deprive the children of the minority group of equal educational opportunities?" Citing psychological experts, the Court answered that it does, that it "generates a feeling of inferiority as to their status in the community that may affect their hearts and minds in a way unlikely ever to be undone" and that the doctrine of "separate but equal" has no place in public education. Segregation in public schools was thus declared unconstitutional, in an opinion written by Chief Justice Earl Warren in May 1954.

TINKER V. DES MOINES COMMUNITY SCHOOL DISTRICT (1969)

This is one of the most famous decisions in the history of students' rights, and it is often cited in other cases. The plaintiffs were John F. Tinker and Christopher Eckhardt, both high school students, and junior high school student Mary Beth Tinker. At a meeting of students and adults held in December

* The Fourteenth Amendment, adopted three years after the end of the Civil War, gave citizenship and equal protection of the laws to Negroes.

1965, these three young people had resolved to wear black arm-bands to protest the Vietnam war, and to show their support of a truce. The principals of the Des Moines public schools learned of the plan and, out of a fear of possible disruptions in the school, adopted a policy that any student wearing an armband to school would be asked to remove it and, if he refused, would be suspended until he returned without an armband. The three students involved defied the ruling and were suspended from school; they remained at home until after New Year's Day.

Thereafter, they brought the school district to court, stating that their Constitutional right to freedom of expression had been violated. First Amendment rights are probably the major issue in most cases involving students' rights. However, it is not always clear what constitutes pure speech, what is disruption, or what is a justifiable regulation.

Tinker v. *Des Moines* was heard first in the U.S. District Court in Iowa, where the students lost. The court pointed out that at the time "debate over the Viet Nam war had become vehement" and that "officials of the defendant school district have the responsibility for maintaining a scholarly, disciplined atmosphere within the classroom. These officials not only have a right, they have an obligation to prevent anything which might be disruptive of such an atmosphere." The court held that the school officials were within reason to assume that the act of wearing armbands, though peaceful in itself, could lead to violent responses by other students.

While the court upheld the right to controversy in the classroom, it also upheld the school officials' right to "regulate the introduction and discussion of such subjects in the classroom." Chief Judge Stephenson explained that the students' rights were only partially impaired, as they were "free to wear armbands off school premises." They were also free to take part in "orderly discussions" regarding Vietnam. So, in viewing the "rights" of both parties, the court held that "in this instance . . . it is the disciplined atmosphere of the classroom, not the plaintiffs' right to wear armbands on school premises, which is entitled to the protection of the law."

The case was next brought to the U.S. Court of Appeals for the Eighth Circuit and was "affirmed without opinion." Finally, the plaintiffs appealed to the U.S. Supreme Court. Because of the historic importance of the decision, several excerpts from Justice Fortas's majority opinion appear below:

[2, 3] First Amendment rights, applied in light of the special characteristics of the school environment, are available to teachers and students. It can hardly be argued that either students or teachers shed their constitutional rights to freedom of speech or expression at the schoolhouse gate. This has been the unmistakable holding of this Court for almost 50 years. . . .

[5] The District Court concluded that the action of the school authorities was reasonable because it was based upon their fear of a disturbance from the wearing of the armbands. But, in our system, undifferentiated fear or apprehension of disturbance is not enough to overcome the right to freedom of expression. Any departure from absolute regimentation may cause trouble. Any variation from the majority's opinion may inspire fear. Any word spoken, in class, in the lunchroom, or on the campus, that deviates from the views of another person may start an argument or cause a disturbance. But our Constitution says we must take this risk. . . .

The action of the school authorities appears to have been based upon an urgent wish to avoid the controversy which might result from the expression, even by the silent symbol of armbands, of opposition to this Nation's part in the conflagration in Vietnam. It is revealing, in this respect, that the meeting at which the school principals decided to issue the contested regulation was called in response to a student's statement to the journalism teacher in one of the schools that he wanted to write an article on Vietnam and have it published in the school paper. (The student was dissuaded.)

It is also relevant that the school authorities did not purport to prohibit the wearing of all symbols of political or controversial significance. The record shows that students in some of the schools wore buttons relating to national political campaigns, and some even wore the Iron Cross, traditionally a symbol of Nazism. The order prohibiting the wearing of armbands did not extend to these. Instead, a particular symbol—black armbands worn to exhibit opposition to this Nation's involvement in Vietnam—was prohibited.

[15–17] The principle of these cases is not confined to the supervised and ordained discussion which takes place in the classroom. The principal use to which the schools are dedicated is to accommodate students during prescribed hours for the purpose of certain types of activities. Among those activities is personal intercommunication among the students. This is not only an inevitable part of the process of attending school; it is also an important part of the educational process. A student's rights, therefore, do not embrace merely the classroom hours. When he is in the cafeteria, or on the playing field, or on the campus during the authorized hours, he may express his opinions, even on controversial subjects like the conflict in Vietnam, if he does so without "materially and substantially interfer[ing] with the requirements of appropriate discipline in the operation of the school" and without colliding with the rights of others. . . .

[18–21] Under our Constitution, free speech is not a right that is given only to be so circumscribed that it exists in principle but not in fact. Freedom of expression would not truly exist if the right could be exercised only in an area that a benevolent government has provided as a safe haven for crackpots. The Constitution says that Congress (and the States) may not abridge the right to free speech. This provision means what it says. We properly read it to permit reasonable regulation of speech-connected activities in carefully restricted circumstances. But we do not confine the permissible exercise of First Amendment rights to a telephone booth or the four corners of a pamphlet, or to supervised and ordained discussion in a school classroom. . . .

As we have discussed, the record does not demonstrate any facts which might reasonably have led school authorities to forecast substantial disruption of or material interference with school activities, and no disturbances or disorders on the school premises in fact occurred. These petitioners merely went about their ordained rounds in school. Their deviation consisted only in wearing on their sleeve a band of black cloth, not more than two inches wide. They wore it to exhibit their disapproval of the Vietnam hostilities and their advocacy of a truce, to make their views known, and, by their example, to influence others to adopt them. They neither interrupted school activities nor sought to intrude in the school affairs or the lives of others. They caused discussion outside of the classrooms, but no interference with work and no disorder. In the circumstances, our Constitution does not permit officials of the State to deny their form of expression.

We express no opinion as to the form of relief which should be granted, this being a matter for the lower courts to determine. We reverse and remand for further proceedings consistent with this opinion.

Reversed and remanded.

DONALD DAVIS, JR., A MINOR BY HIS MOTHER, ET AL. V. SCHOOL DISTRICT OF THE CITY OF PONTIAC, INC. (1970)

Black schoolchildren living in Pontiac, Michican, brought this action against the Pontiac School District and the Pontiac Board of Education. They contended that *de facto* segregation existed as a result of the board's policies in selecting sites for new schools and in assigning black teachers and principals to schools. The board's position was that its policies were based on the "neighborhood school concept" and that it did in fact consider the goal of integration when selecting sites for new schools. Admitting *de facto* segregation in certain elementary schools, the board argued that it had no duty to undo this segregation since it was not a result of the board's policies but of Pontiac's segregated housing pattern.

In fact, starting in 1948, the Pontiac Board of Education had begun to issue a series of policy statements favorable to racial integration: hiring within the school system was to be without regard to race or color; new schools were to be constructed to serve children regardless of race, color, or creed; pupils were to attend schools in the district in which they lived, irrespective of race; emphasis was to be placed on achieving a racially integrated school system; it was desirable to achieve an equitable distribution of black and white teachers in the various schools; etc.

The court found for the plaintiff, stating that the board had failed to use its power to select sites for new schools or to arrange boundaries in such a way as to make integration possible; that it had a great deal to do with creating the segregated pattern and could not claim that it had no duty to undo it while another generation of black children remained in an unbearable situation; and that the fact that one or two black teachers had been assigned to white schools was insufficient evidence that the board was trying to integrate the faculties of the schools.

The court concluded that the Pontiac School Board "cannot use the neighborhood school concept as a disguise for the furtherance or perpetuation of racial discrimination;" and that the "present day officials have an immediate obligation to overcome the effects of past discriminatory acts." The court ordered that the Pontiac School District integrate its school system at all levels—students, teachers, and administrators—before the beginning of the 1970 school year and further ordered that the district submit by March 1970 a plan to integrate the school system by revising the boundary lines within the district and by busing children.

The Pontiac School District appealed the ruling, but in May 1971 the U.S. Court of Appeals, Sixth Circuit, upheld the findings of the district court.

SWANN ET AL. V. CHARLOTTE-MECKLENBURG BOARD OF EDUCATION (U.S. SUPREME COURT, APRIL 1971)

Although the U.S. Supreme Court decided in 1954 in *Brown* v. *Board of Education* that segregation in the public schools was unconstitutional, the matter did not end there. A year later the Court held, in a case referred to as *Brown II*, that school authorities have the primary responsibility for working out policies necessary to achieve school desegregation and that the courts would have to consider whether they were acting in good faith toward that goal. By 1968, many states with a long history of maintaining a dual school system had still made little progress, and in that year, in *Green* v. *County School Board*, the Supreme Court stated: "The burden on a school board today is to come forward with a plan that promises realistically to work . . . *now* . . . until it is clear that state-imposed segregation has been completely removed." In *Swann* v. *Charlotte-Mecklenburg Board of Education*, the Court formulated certain guidelines for the lower federal courts which "had to grapple with the flinty, intractable realities of day-to-day implementation" of the large constitutional principles.

As of June 1969, two-thirds of the 21,000 black children in Charlotte, North Carolina, were going to schools either totally or more than 99 percent black. The district court ordered the school board to devise a plan to desegregate both the faculty and the students of these schools. The board formulated a plan which the court found unacceptable, especially with regard to the elementary schools, and the district court thereupon appointed Dr. John Finger, an expert in education, to prepare an alternate plan. Dr. Finger proposed pairing elementary schools in the inner city with schools in outlying areas so that every school in the system would have 9 percent to 38 percent black children. Black students from first to fourth grades would be bused to the outlying white schools, and white fifth and sixth graders would be bused to the inner-city black schools. The district court accepted the Finger plan, but subsequently the court of appeals reversed the district court's ruling on the basis that although the board's plan was inadequate, the pairing and grouping of elementary schools "would place an unreasonable burden on the board and the system's pupils."

In its review of this case, the Supreme Court reaffirmed that when school authorities fail in their obligation to convert to a unitary school system, the district courts have broad powers to remedy the situation. The Court noted that the selection of sites for new schools and the closing of old ones are often used as weapons in the fight against desegregation, and that the district courts are responsible for seeing that such anti-desegration plans do not succeed. With regard to assigning students to schools, the Court set down four guidelines:

1. Desegregation does not require that every school in every district have a certain quota of blacks, although a limited

use of ratios can be a starting point and is within the discretion of the district court.

2. The existence of a few black inner-city schools does not by itself prove that segregation is still practiced, but the burden is on the school system to prove to the courts that the pupil imbalance is not the result of discrimination. Free busing should be made available to any white student who would voluntarily attend a black school.

3. A district court can order the busing of children—"desegregation plans cannot be limited to the walk-in school"—although objections to busing may be valid when the distance is so great that the child's health or the educational process is in jeopardy.

4. Generally speaking, the Court said, the district courts have the power to insist on plans that are "reasonable, feasible and workable." However, "substance, not semantics, must govern, and we have sought to suggest the nature of limitations without frustrating the appropriate scope of equity."

SERRANO V. PRIEST (AUGUST 1971)

The plaintiffs in this case were Los Angeles County public elementary and secondary school children and their parents; the defendants were the county school superintendent, treasurer, and tax collector; and the case was heard in the California Supreme Court.

The plaintiffs alleged that the California public school system was primarily financed by local property taxes, that as a result there were substantial disparities among school districts in the amount of money available per pupil, and that therefore children living in the "poorer" districts were denied equal protection under the Fourteenth Amendment to the Constitution. They asked the court to declare the California school financing system unconstitutional and to reallocate school funds to remedy the inequities.

The court noted that although the state did subsidize poor school districts, vast inequalities remained because of the enormous variations in assessed property values. The court agreed with the plaintiffs that the financing system discriminated on the basis of wealth and that residents of poorer districts would have to impose impossible tax rates on themselves to obtain the same, or even less, funds for education as more affluent districts. The affluent districts, the court said, "can have their cake and eat it too: they can provide a high quality education for their children while paying lower taxes." The court ruled that since education is of fundamental importance to our society, and since in this case a child's education depends ultimately on his parents' pocketbook, the California financing system denied the plaintiffs equal protection under the Fourteenth Amendment and must be found unconstitutional.

GRIGGS ET AL. V. DUKE POWER COMPANY
(U.S. SUPREME COURT, MARCH 1971)

The plaintiffs, Negro employees of the Duke Power Company plant at Draper, North Carolina, pursued this case through the district court, the Court of Appeals for the Fourth District, and finally the U.S. Supreme Court, contending that the company's hiring and promotion policies violated Title VII of the Civil Rights Act of 1964, since these policies, which demanded possession of a high school diploma or passing of intelligence tests, did not measure a person's ability to learn or to perform a particular job.

The district court found that prior to the Civil Rights Act of 1964 the company's hiring practices had openly discriminated against Negroes. In 1965 the company began to require a high school diploma and satisfactory performance on two aptitude tests for any job not in the two lowest categories. Both the district court and the court of appeals concluded that since the company applied its standards to both whites and Negroes, it intended no discrimination, even though a disproportionate number of Negroes were excluded from promotion.

The U.S. Supreme Court, however, reversed the rulings on the grounds that the Civil Rights Act prohibits employment practices that discriminate against Negroes, even if not overtly, unless these practices can be shown to be directly related to job performance. An investigation disclosed that white personnel without high school diplomas who had been hired and promoted prior to the institution of the testing procedure were performing satisfactorily in their jobs. "The facts of this case demonstrate the inadequacy of broad and general testing devices as well as the infirmity of using diplomas or degrees as fixed measures of capability." The Court noted that Title VII of the Civil Rights Act protected the employer's right to insist that job applicants be qualified to perform the job, but that any tests used "must measure the person for the job and not the person in the abstract."

BLACKWELL V. ESSAQUENA COUNTY BOARD OF EDUCATION (1966); BURNSIDE V. BYARS (1966)

These two cases, both of which were cited in *Tinker*, were decided in the same courts. The facts of each case are almost identical and the lower court's ruling was the same in both. But when they were appealed, the lower court's ruling was upheld in one case and reversed in the other.

In both cases, the issue was whether the school authorities were reasonable in regulating student expression—specifically, the wearing of "freedom buttons." The controversy in Blackwell began at all-black Henry Weathers High School, where a group of about thirty students appeared one day wearing buttons about one inch in diameter, depicting a black hand and a white hand joined together with "SNCC" inscribed in the margin. The principal, Mr. Jordan, was informed that some of the students were "creating a disturbance by noisily talking in the hall when they were scheduled to be in class," and he spoke to three of them, telling them that because of the "disturbance," they would have to remove the buttons.

During the next two school days, the number of students wearing buttons increased and, according to affidavits signed by school personnel, so did the disturbances. According to the principal's report, students were traveling through the halls handing out buttons and forcing them on students who did not want them. The students were told that if they came to school again wearing the buttons, they would be suspended, and that this course was necessary to "maintain decorum and to keep from disturbing classrooms and other students."

The next day, about two hundred students appeared wearing buttons, and they were suspended. According to affidavits, the suspended students continued to disrupt school routines by distributing buttons, entering classes in session, and tossing buttons through school windows. More students were suspended as the week went on. Their parents met with school officials and eventually brought the case to district court in a "Civil Rights action to enjoin school officials from enforcing regulation forbidding the wearing of buttons."

The district court held that the school officials were reasonable in their actions because school routines had been disrupted and the rights of other students infringed, and the U.S. Court of Appeals for the Fifth Circuit upheld the decision. As Judge Gewin wrote: "Their [the students'] actions in the school building are indeed reprehensible and the school officials certainly have the authority to mete out punishment as they deem appropriate for their discourteous behavior toward school authorities, their disregard for the orderly progression of classroom instruction, and their complete disregard for the rights of their fellow students."

Acknowledging the importance of freedom of expression, the court nevertheless stated that "the law recognizes that there can be an abuse of such freedom." In the opinion of the court, the school authorities were reasonable in ordering the removal of the buttons in order to restore discipline in the school. "It is always within the province of school authorities to provide by regulation the prohibition and punishment of acts calculated to undermine the school routine. This is not only proper in our opinion but is necessary."

In the case of *Burnside* v. *Byars*, the confrontation began at Booker T. Washington High School in Philadelphia, Mississippi, when the principal of the school learned that some students were planning to wear freedom buttons to school and informed them that they would not be allowed to. Wearing the buttons, he said, would disrupt the school routine. Time would be wasted by handing out and discussing the buttons; moreover, the buttons "didn't have any bearing on their education."

Nevertheless, on September 21, 1964, three or four children appeared at school wearing the buttons, and upon being told they could either remove the buttons or go home, went home. On September 24, thirty or forty students came in with buttons; the offer of "no buttons, no trouble," was repeated, and the great majority elected to return home. Thereupon, they were suspended for a week, and the principal sent the following letter to their parents: "Dear Parent: This is to inform you that your child has been suspended from school until you can come and have a talk with me. It is against the school policy for anything to be brought into school that is not educational."

Three of the parents—Mrs. Burnside, Mrs. English, and Mrs. Morris—refused to comply, and took the matter to district court, where they lost. But the court of appeals overturned the decision.

The court agreed that school officials have the right to abridge freedom of expression if the circumstances call for it. Although the student, as a citizen, is protected against the state, he is not unlimited in his actions. "The interest of the State in maintaining an educational system is a compelling one, giving rise to a balancing of First Amendment rights with the duty of the State to further and protect the public school system. The establishment of an educational program requires the formulation of rules and regulations necessary for the maintenance of an orderly program of classroom learning."

Thus, certain limitations on students—as, for example, not permitting them to speak in class—are, according to the court, reasonable. But, by the same reasoning, the court ruled that in this case there was no disruption of school routine serious enough to warrant the regulation against the freedom buttons. The court pointed out that even the principal admitted that the students were punished for disobeying a rule, not for causing a disturbance.

In light of the Blackwell decision, the following excerpt from the Court's opinion is particularly interesting: "Thus it appears that the presence of freedom buttons did not hamper the school in carrying on its regular schedule of activities nor would it seem likely that the simple wearing of buttons unaccompanied by improper conduct would ever do so."

The court distinguished wearing buttons as a form of expression from others such as leafleting, "speechmaking," and "carrying banners," which are assumed to be potentially disruptive by their nature. In this case, because of the absence of any disorder, the court concluded that "the regulation forbidding the wearing of 'freedom buttons' on school grounds is arbitrary and unreasonable, and an unnecessary infringement on the students' protected right of free expression in the circumstances revealed by the record."

EISNER V. STAMFORD BOARD OF EDUCATION (1971)

This case, which was decided in the U.S. Court of Appeals, Second Circuit, on March 5, 1971, concerns the "distribution of printed or written matter on school grounds" and was considered by the court to concern freedom of expression as it pertains to a public school system.

The Stamford, Conn., Board of Education had established the following policy concerning the distribution of printed or written matter:

> The Board of Education desires to encourage freedom of expression and creativity by its students subject to the following limitations:
>
> No person shall distribute any printed or written matter on the grounds of any school or in any school building unless the distribution of such material shall have prior approval by the school administration.
>
> In granting or denying approval, the following guidelines shall apply:
>
> No material shall be distributed which, either by its content or by the manner of distribution itself, will interfere with the proper and orderly operation and discipline of the school, will cause violence or disorder, or will constitute an invasion of the rights of others.

The plaintiffs, students at Rippowam High School in Stamford, contended that this policy violated their right to freedom of expression. The U.S. District Court of Connecticut agreed with the students, because of certain faults it found in the statement of policy: that it did "not specify the manner of submission, the exact party to whom the material must be submitted, the time within which a decision must be rendered; nor . . . provide for an adversary proceeding at any time or for a right of appeal."

The court of appeals upheld the decision of the lower court, but with some reservations. The students had challenged the policy on its face, and not as it applied to their particular publication. In delivering the opinion, Judge Irving Kaufman cited several cases relating to the validity and constitutionality of prior restraint on materials, and provided a listing of situations in which prior restraint was permissible. The opinion cites

Tinker, pointing out that "many cases, following in the choppy waters left by *Tinker*, have applied the quoted language either to validate or to restrain a school's attempt to prevent students from engaging in constitutionally protected activity." According to Judge Kaufman, *Tinker* stressed that a school might regulate free speech *if* there was sufficient evidence that the speech might lead to the endangerment of school routine and the rights of others. "But we cannot deny that Connecticut has the authority to minimize or eliminate influences that would dilute or disrupt the effectiveness of the educational process as the state conceives it."

The court agreed with the plaintiffs that certain aspects of the policy were indeed too vague. But while agreeing with the board's right to formulate such a policy, it stated that if the policy had been more specific as to the review of the material, the period of review, and the word "distribution" itself, a court case might have been avoided. "It is to everyone's advantage that decisions with respect to the operation of local schools be made by local officials."

Judge Kaufman's opinion makes clear the point of disagreement between the court of appeals and the lower court: "Because we disagree with the district court's conclusion that under all circumstances, any system for prior submission and restraint would be unconstitutional, the district court must modify its grant of injunctive relief so as to restrain only the enforcement of this particular policy."

FERRELL V. DALLAS INDEPENDENT SCHOOL DISTRICT (1968)

This case was born when Phillip Ferrell, Stephen Webb, and Paul Jarvis were not allowed to enroll at W. W. Samuell High School in Dallas, Texas, "because of their 'Beatle' type haircuts."

The three boys were members of a musical group known as

Sounds Unlimited, and they contended that their hairstyle was important to them because it was a factor in their appeal as rock 'n' roll performers. Indeed, their contract referred to their hair lengths, and although, as the court pointed out, a contract cannot be enforced against minors, its mention of hairstyle proved the importance of hair to the young musicians. The plaintiffs also charged that denying them admission to school was a violation of the Texas State Constitution, of the Fourteenth Amendment, and of the Civil Rights Act.

The boys were fully aware that their hair length would be a problem when time came for enrollment on September 7. On September 6, their manager, Kent Alexander, "sometimes referred to as 'Alexander the Great,'" called Mr. Lanham, the school principal, and informed him that he (Mr. Alexander) had $4,000 invested in the group "and had planned to invest an additional $1,000." He told the principal that he was coming to school to discuss the problem, and that "he would bring the radio and television media to the school."

The following day the boys and two of their mothers met with the principal. "Alexander the Great" was excluded from the meeting, although it was later discovered that he represented one of the fathers. Mr. Lanham told the group that he had the authority to establish rules and regulations "concerning the appearance of students at the school" and "that the length and style of the boys' hair would cause commotion, trouble, and distraction and a disturbance in the school." The boys refused to cut their hair and were then denied admission. (Paul Jarvis had cut his hair to attend summer school and "was not refused admission until later"). Mr. Alexander, true to his word, brought the media to the high school, and following the meeting the boys held a press conference outside the school. They also wrote and recorded a "protest" song about hair, which was played on the radio.

In district court, the boys contended that long hair had become popular and was "accepted by the younger generation."

Mr. Lanham, however, cited incidents of violence in the school as the result of long hair. "Long hair boys" had been the target of "obscene language," they had been "challenged to fight" and "had been told by others that the girls' restroom was right down the hall." Several boys with long hair testified, some denying any incidents, others admitting to trouble as the result of their hair length. The district court concluded that the school authorities had not acted arbitrarily in refusing the boys admission to school.

The court of appeals affirmed the decision, denying that the school officials had violated the state constitution. Judge Gewin—who had delivered the court's opinion in both the *Blackwell* and *Burnside* cases—pointed out that the constitution grants authority to the state legislature "to establish and make suitable provision for the support and maintenance of an efficient system of public free schools." The legislature, in turn, granted authority to school officials "to adopt such rules and regulations as they deemed proper in order to effectively manage and govern the schools."

As to the violation of the Fourteenth Amendment, the court *assumed* for *this* case, based on the statements of the students, that "a hair style is a constitutionally protected mode of expression." But the court went on to say: "The Constitution does not establish an absolute right to free expression of ideas, though some might disagree." Judge Gewin cited *Blackwell* to reaffirm the right of school authorities to infringe on the freedom of expression of students if there is an obvious, serious threat to the operation of the school. In this case, the court ruled that the authorities were within their rights. "We conclude that there was no denial of substantive due process; and further, we find no evidence in the record to support appellants' contention that they were denied procedural due process."

The court further stated that the regulation did not interfere with the boys' musical career. "It is common knowledge that many performers are required to use special attire and make-up, including wigs and/or hairpieces, for their public appearances." Without further comment, Judge Gewin stated that the court found no violation of the Civil Rights Act.

The comments of the two other appeals court judges are interesting. In his concurring opinion, Judge Godbold stated that, right or wrong, "the American community calls upon its schools to, in substance, stand *in loco parentis* to its children for many hours of each school week." With this in mind, and with regard to safety, "the courts must give full credence to the role and purposes of the schools and of the tools with which it is expected that they deal with their problems, and careful recognition to the differences between what are reasonable restraints in the classroom and what are reasonable restraints on the street corner."

In dissenting, Judge Tuttle made the following statement: ". . . we find courts too prone to permit a curtailment of a constitutional right of a dissenter, because of the likelihood that it will bring disorder, resistance or improper and even violent action by those supporting the status quo.

"These boys were not barred from school because of any actions carried out by them which were of themselves a disturbance of the peace. They were barred because it was anticipated by reason of previous experiences, that their fellow students in some instances could do things that would disrupt the serenity or calm of the school. It is these acts that should be prohibited, not the expression of individuality by the suspended students."

MADERA V. BOARD OF EDUCATION
OF CITY OF NEW YORK (1967)

The question of due process is the essential ingredient in this case. Here, however, the issue is not the right to a hearing, but rather the right to have an attorney present at the hearing.

In February 1967, Victor Madera, a seventh grader at

Junior High School 22 in New York City, was suspended from school "after a period of more than a year of behavioral difficulties," and his parents were sent a letter asking them to a guidance conference.

The Maderas threw a curve into the standard procedure by seeking the aid of an attorney, who wrote to District Superintendent Theresa Rakow "asking to appear on behalf of Mr. and Mrs. Madera and their son at the conference." Miss Rakow informed him that he could not attend, in accordance with General Circular No. 16 (1965–1966): "Inasmuch as this is a guidance conference for the purpose of providing an opportunity for parents, teachers, counselors, supervisors, et al., to plan educationally for the benefit of the child, attorneys seeking to represent the parent or child may not participate."

The Maderas, not convinced, went to court. After hearing the case, the district court issued a permanent injunction against the board of education on the grounds that "the right to a hearing is a due process requirement of such constitutional significance as to void application of defendants' 'no attorneys' provision' to the District Superintendent's Guidance Conference."

The board then took the case to the court of appeals, where the decision was reversed, on the grounds that the guidance conference was not a criminal proceeding and therefore an attorney was not required: "There is no showing," the opinion stated, "that any attempt is ever made to use any statement at the Conference in any subsequent criminal proceeding." For this reason the court decided that Victor's Fifth Amendment privilege against self-incrimination was not in need of legal protection.

On the question of due process, raised in the lower court decision, the appeals court wrote: "[due process] must depend upon the nature of the proceeding involved and the rights that might possibly be affected by that proceeding." Since school attendance is a requirement by law, any attempt to deprive a student of attendance at school requires due process. But "the suspension of a pupil who is insubordinate or disorderly or who endangers the safety or morals of himself or other minors, is authorized by section of 3214 (6) of the Education Law."

The district court had been quite concerned about the consequences to Victor of a guidance conference, suggesting that thereafter he might be sent to Youth House, the psychiatric division of Kings County Hospital, or to Bellevue Hospital, or that he might be institutionalized. Judge Moore made it clear that before a child could be sent to a school for socially maladjusted children, the written consent of the parent or guardian was necessary. "However, if the parents refuse to give such consent they may be prosecuted for violation of the compulsory education laws."

Judge Moore was trying to show that the possible results of the district superintendent's conference were not of a "criminal" nature. Aside from the placement in a special school, the student might return to his class, or a different class in the same school, or a different school of the same type. The superintendent might *refer* the case to a social agency or to the attendance court. The important point according to the court, is that no punitive action is taken as a result of the guidance conference, and no testimony is used in court if the student ends up there.

The appeals court also took exception to the district court's implication that the right to counsel was an inherent right in any hearing. Judge Moore cited several cases to establish that "the right to representation by counsel is not an essential ingredient to a fair hearing in all types of proceedings." Regarding the type of hearing in this case, Judge Moore stated that "the conference is not a judicial or even a quasi-judicial hearing." The court argued also that the purpose of the conference was to aid the child, not harm him.

Finally, the question once again came down to jurisdiction. The court doubted its right in the first place to interfere in such matters as guidance conferences: "Law and order in the classroom should be the responsibility of our respective educational systems. The courts should not usurp this function and turn disciplinary problems involving suspensions, into criminal adversary proceedings—which they definitely are not." The court appeared convinced that the guidance conference proceedings showed a "high regard in the best interest and welfare of the child."

RESOURCES

SOME THINGS WORTH KNOWING
ABOUT FOR PEOPLE INTERESTED IN
IMPROVING WHAT HAPPENS TO KIDS
(AND TEACHERS) IN SCHOOL

YOU MIGHT find it useful to know about some resources—books, magazines, films, sources of information, and ideas—that provide specific examples of different ways of improving what goes on in school.

You can use these resources, if you wish, in a variety of ways in your attempts to initiate some change in school. For example, you can ask your child's teacher whether he or she knows about the things listed here. If the teacher doesn't, you can help to do something about changing *that*. Another possible use of this list, especially the films, is to develop PTA programs concerned with alternative ways of conducting school. At the very least, you can always request your local library to acquire items that are of interest to you, if it doesn't already have them, and you can encourage others—parents, students, teachers, administrators, or community organizations—to use these materials for the purpose of improving one or another aspect of the school environment.

This list is relatively short, since we limited ourselves to what we thought would be most useful and economical. Many of the books and periodicals mentioned include long lists of resources.

BOOKS, PERIODICALS, PAMPHLETS

Affective Education Bibliography

Plato said it more than two thousand years ago: "In order for education to accomplish its purpose, reason must have an adequate emotional base." "Affective education" is concerned with the development of educational experiences that build on the emotional involvement of students. Most of what we "know" (that is, what we *do*) is a result of its having deep emotional meaning for us. If it doesn't have this, it is itself meaningless.

Affective Curriculum Research Project
Division of Instructional Materials
Audio-Visual Office, Room 328
Board of Public Education
Parkway, South of 21st Street
Philadelphia, Penna. 19103

The Art of Asking Questions by Stanley L. Payne. Princeton University Press, 1951.

While the date of this book makes it "old," the material in it is totally new since most teachers have never heard of it. Despite the fact that knowing how to ask questions is one of the most important intellectual abilities anyone can develop, the art of questioning is not taught in school. This book deals with the *art* of question asking in practical, human terms. Anyone interested in human learning and inquiry should take a good look at it.

Big Rock Candy Mountain

This is "the son of *Whole Earth Catalog*," but it deals solely with education. While *BRCM* is a quarterly, there is a special edition, "Resources for Our Education" edited by Samuel Yanes and Cia Holdorf and published by Delta Books. This issue is just full of fascinating material, and could be an education in itself.

Portola Institute
1115 Merrill Street
Menlo Park, Calif. 94025

Changing Schools: An Occasional Newsletter on Alternate Public Schools

Published four times a year, this well-written newsletter is concerned with the development of alternate schools within a public school setting. It will keep you well informed of important ideas and information concerning the school within a school movement.

Indiana University
Bloomington, Ind. 47401

Children As Film Makers by John Lidstone and Don McIntosh. Van Nostrand-Reinhardt, 1970.

This is a book intended for children who want to make films. Despite the names on the book, it was written by children who were making films with the "help" of Lidstone and McIntosh. The kids were smart kids, and this is a smart book.

Clearinghouse

A unique source of information about new, and better, ways of helping children learn. Includes information you probably won't find in most other publications. Especially good for teachers.

Department of Education
University of Massachusetts
Amherst, Mass. 01002

Deschool Primer #4

In a tabloid format on newsprint, this is a collection of ideas, materials, and things to do that is all humanistically oriented. It is also reality oriented, which many people find disconcerting. *Deschool Primer* apparently derives from Illich's "deschooling society" notion, and is strongly political in its orientation. Issue #4 is the one full of goodies for teachers, mostly of young children. Zephyrus annual memberships include two boxes of learning materials twice a year, September and March.

Zephyrus Materials Exchange via
Ron Jones
1201 Stanyan Street
San Francisco, Calif. 94117

Education and Ecstasy by George B. Leonard. Delta Books, 1969.

An imaginative look at what schools—and education—can be in the future. The book emphasizes the affective side of life and learning.

Free Schools by Jonathan Kozol. Revised paperback edition, Bantam Books, 1972.

A practical handbook for parents and teachers who have the courage to start schools of their own. It is directed primarily at parents and teachers in ghettoes and poor rural areas, although it has also been used by the middle class and groups seeking to cut across class and racial lines in establishing alternative schools. It is nontechnical, practical and political, including such things as building codes, procedures for raising money, hiring teachers, etc.

A Guide for Film Teachers to Filmmaking by Teenagers by Roger Larson

Making films (and videotapes) can be an end in itself or a vehicle for getting children to *do* all kinds of learning that they otherwise would not. Having kids make films can be magic, especially if they are not particularly taken with the usual school subjects.

Department of Cultural Affairs
830 Fifth Avenue
New York, N.Y. 10009

How to Change the Schools: A Parent's Action Handbook on How to Fight the System by Ellen Lurie. Random House 1970.

A mother's description of her fifteen-year-long effort to make public schools the kind of place she felt would be good for her five children. This kind of information comes only from the actual experience of getting involved, being informed, and persevering in the face of infuriating inertia.

Learning to Feel—Feeling to Learn by Harold C. Lyon, Jr. Charles E. Merrill Publishing Co.

As the title suggests, this is for teachers who want to try making school more humanistic, for themselves as well as for children. While it may not turn any teachers around, it could be helpful to those who are already there but want some more ideas.

The Little Red Schoolbook by Søren Hansen and Jesper Jensen. Pocket Books, 1971.

This is an American version of a British translation of a Danish book that was written specifically to help students cope with bad teachers and bad schools. It is full of material kids need to know—which means that parents should know it too. The kids, however, won't be as shocked at some of the things in it as many parents will. Kids all over the country buy it and read it by the thousands, even though their teachers and parents don't.

Looking In On Your School

A checklist of questions to ask about your child's school. Includes sources of information for parents who are seriously interested in improving the school.

National Congress of Parents and Teachers
700 North Rush Street
Chicago, Ill. 60611

Making It Strange

A new approach to creative writing and thinking. Kids get smarter while they're enjoying themselves. Four-part series.

Harper & Row, Publishers
School Department
Keystone Industrial Park
Scranton, Penn. 18512

Media and Methods

This magazine is published monthly during the school year, and is full of up-to-the-minute information on how teachers can use TV, films, recordings (tape and disc), and books to help kids become smarter. This is different from using "audiovisual aids" to cover content faster. Most of the descriptions of "methods" are written by classroom teachers who are distinguished by having a philosophy and purpose. That is, they know *why* as well as how. *M&M* is particularly useful for high school English, social studies, and humanities teachers.

P.O. Box 8698
Philadelphia, Penn. 19101

Media Mix: Ideas and Resources for Educational Change

145 Brentwood Drive
Palatine, Ill. 60077

The Journal of Open Education

Institute of Open Education
Newton College of the Sacred Heart
885 Centre Street
Newton, Massachusetts 02159   One year subscription—$5.50

The Open Classroom by Herbert A. Kohl, Random House, 1970.

A description of "open education" by a teacher who has been involved in it—for teachers who haven't. Good for parents who'd like to know what one of the pioneers of the open classroom movement means by the term so that they can judge local versions of it.

New York Review of Books
250 West 57th Street
New York, N.Y. 10019

The Open Education Newsletter

All kinds of current and choice information about open education—mostly by and from teachers. While it is largely oriented toward New York City, the information in it can be used anywhere.

Professor Hal Sobel
Education Department
Queens College
Flushing, N.Y. 11367

Parents Can Be a Problem by G. Gilbert Wrenn and Shirley Schwarzrock.

One of a series intended to help teen-agers deal with the problems they face and are concerned about. Could be used in a variety of ways in any affective education effort, including one intended for parents. Could even be used at PTA meetings to help develop a sense of the way children look at things. Comes with teacher's manual!

American Guidance Service, Inc.
Circle Pines, Minnesota 55014

Reach, Touch, and Teach: Student Concerns and Process Education by Terry Borton. McGraw-Hill, 1970.

The title of this book, by one of the most sane and humane teachers around, could not be more apt. This is a powerful description—derived from the author's personal experience—of a way of teaching that really does have the personal development of kids as its central purpose. Moving and practical. Includes an excellent selection of films and resources.

Rules for Radicals: A Practical Primer for Realistic Radicals by Saul D. Alinsky. Vintage Books, 1972.

While not specifically intended for people who are concerned with schools, this last book by the late Saul Alinsky synthesizes the wisdom of one of America's true heroes. It is the sum of a lifetime devoted to effecting social and political change desperately needed by people who had no powerful advocates. Although it is probably the most incisively practical handbook for working toward institutional change, it is grounded in an informed humane philosophy. Do yourself a favor and study this book.

Schools Where Children Learn by Joseph Featherstone. Liveright, 1971.

A description of how some American schools are developing their own versions of open British Infant Schools. If there is any kind of a "movement" in American elementary education today, it derives from the models provided by the open British Infant Schools.

The Teacher Paper

Accounts by teachers who are really trying to do things that are good for children which describe what the teachers are trying and how children respond.

    280 North Pacific Avenue
    Monmouth, Ore. 97361

Teaching Human Beings: 101 Subversive Activities for the Classroom by Jeffrey Schrank. Beacon Press, 1972.

This book is loaded with excellent ideas, suggestions, and information about all kinds of materials for getting into important things for all of us to know—if we're interested in coping with reality. If you have kids in junior or senior high school, do them, yourself, and their teachers a big favor by getting this book to teachers who will use it. It is the best single resource book for secondary school around.

Tests and Measurements Kit

Since schools use tests extensively, this free kit should be known and used not only by teachers and guidance counselors, but also by parents and children. The technical information is as good as it can be, but it is advisable to consider the source when making an estimate of possible bias.

Educational Testing Service
Princeton, N.J. 08540

The Tyranny of Testing by Banesh Hoffman. Collier Books, 1964.

Even if you aren't familiar with the technical details of testing, you should know some of the peculiar assumptions on which tests, particularly "standardized tests," are based. All tests, and especially *test scores*, are dangerous in the hands of those who don't know the limitations—and there are many—of tests, standardized and otherwise. Hoffman is a distinguished mathematician who logically dissects some of the most sacred cows of tests and test makers. Knowing the kind of thing Hoffman explicates here can help you to protect your children against the capricious use of tests and test scores. There are few things that all teachers should be required to read—and know—and this is one of them.

What Do I Do Monday by John Holt. Delta, 1970.

In our judgment, the best book by one of the best critics of the schools. While obviously intended for teachers, the range of sources on which Holt draws in writing his answer to the title question comprises an education in itself—for anyone concerned about education. Just about every page has specific suggestions as to really smart things to do along with *why* they should be done. Includes a list of books, films, and sources of information about new developments in education that reflects Holt's incisive perception. If you were to buy just three books to read and share with your child's teacher, this should be one of them.

When Teachers Face Themselves by Arthur T. Jersild. Bureau of Publications, Teachers College, Columbia University, 1955.

This report of a study of teachers' fears, worries, feelings, and concerns sheds more light on why so much schooling is just wasted time and effort than all the studies of curriculum and methods put together. It helps to make the frequently ignored point that teachers are only people, just like you.

Will the Real Teacher Please Stand UP? A Primer in Humanistic Education by Mary Greer and Bonnie Rubinstein. Goodyear Publishing Co., 1972.

Here is a book that will make you feel good—even just to look at. From the Magritte on the cover to the epilogue, it is all sweet and smart—the point of view, the things to do, and the funny things, too. A beautiful book.

Yellow Pages of Learning Resources, ed. Richard Saul Wurman. MIT Press, 1972.

This is an interesting format: a kind of classified directory of all kinds of things to do, places to go, and people to see in any city. Teachers and kids might find it most useful as a takeoff from which to do their own version, since it is rather elementary.

FILMS

Charlie and the Golden Hamster. 30 minutes, color.

The philosophy and purpose of a nongraded elementary school done with charm and wit by I.D.E.A.

> Films, Educational Resources
> University of South Florida
> Tampa, Fla. 33620

Eye of the Storm. 25 minutes, color.

An ABC news special on a teacher who conducted a lesson on prejudice by dividing her class into "superior" and "inferior" on the basis of the color of their eyes. A dramatic illustration of the way an imaginative teacher translated an abstract concept into a real, personal experience for her students.

> Films, Educational Resources
> University of South Florida
> Tampa, Fla. 33620

High School.

A documentary shot in a high school in Philadelphia by Frederick Wiseman. Some people find it devastating, some find it encouraging, some find it distorted, and some find it nothing. It cannot be shown in Philadelphia, however. The best place to show it probably would be a large high school PTA meeting, at which a number of students and teachers are present.

> Zipporah Films
> 54 Lewis Wharf
> Boston, Mass. 02116

How Children Learn. 23 minutes, color.

An NBC news special reporting on new teaching techniques developed specifically on the basis of what is known about the way they learn.

Films, Educational Resources
University of South Florida
Tampa, Fla. 33620

Infant School. 30 minutes; black and white.

A thorough description of the open, nongraded British Infant School by Lillian Weber, an American teacher, who has made as complete a study of this kind of school as is possible.

Educational Development Center
55 Chapel Street
Newton, Mass. 02158

No Reason to Stay. 29 minutes, black and white.

Near-documentary study of why one boy—who gets good grades —drops out of high school. A rare portrayal of school from a student's point of view. Raises many crucial questions.

Films, Educational Resources
University of South Florida
Tampa, Fla. 33620

Odyssey of a Dropout. 19 minutes, black and white.

A study of Scott, a high school dropout, and the dilemma he faces, as he thinks about how he can make his life "mean something."

Films, Educational Resources
University of South Florida
Tampa, Fla. 33620

Primary Education in England. 12 minutes, color.

Documentary on the nongraded approach in a British Infant School. For those who cannot imagine a school not segregated into grades.

Films, Educational Resources
University of South Florida
Tampa, Fla. 33620

They Can Do It. 35 minutes, black and white.

A more detailed description of an Infant School, for those whose curiosity is whetted by the preceding film.

Educational Development Center
55 Chapel Street
Newton, Mass.

US. 28 minutes, color.

A cool look at us and our "cultural context." Good for developing a perspective on the society in which schools are supposed to function.

Films, Educational Resources
University of South Florida
Tampa, Fla. 33620

EDUCATIONAL GAMES

If you don't know what has been going on with games, especially educational games, in the last ten years or so, you are not in touch with an important way of learning. There is too much to say about them here, so we'll suggest where you can find out everything you need to know about them. See the October 1970 and the November 1971 issues of *Media and Methods* for the best concise description of games and simulations. The list of games we include here is from the October 1970 issue. In addition, if you really want to become expert about games, see *Serious Games* by Clark Abt (Viking Press, 1970) and the comments about educational games in *The Adolescent Society* by James Coleman (Free Press of Glencoe, 1962).

One more thing: If you have children in elementary school, you might take a look at the games listed here. Your children might learn something that will help them in school, and you might learn something about your children.

The Folkways Omnibus of Children's Games by Iris Vinton. Stackpole Books.

Children's games, 1,001 of them from various countries, that reflect national culture in general and the culture of childhood in particular. Fascinating and lots of fun.

Games to Improve Your Child's English by Abraham Hurwitz and Arthur Goddard. Simon & Schuster.

More than 300 pages of games that involve language abilities. Even if you think half of them are somewhat foolish, you still have 150 pages of games that are a lot more engaging and useful than any grammar workbook.

Mathematical Games by Clara Lukacs and Emma Tarjan. Walker & Co.

The basic idea here is that "mathematics can be fun." The games focus on developing an understanding of mathematical functions, rather than on memorizing formulas and rules.

If you can't see yourself playing these games with your children, check to find out whether their teacher knows about this kind of approach to helping them learn some of the basic things they need to know without the usual drudgery.

SELECTED "SIMULATION" GAMES

Community Disaster (Michael Inbar), New York: Western.

A board game for 6–16 players at senior high level that teaches players how to adapt to a major disaster for the best benefit of all in the community. Directly useful for civics classes, but practical for all students. Takes 2–6 hours, best played in one sitting.

Consumer (Gerald Zaltman), New York: Western.

Simulates the problems and economics of installment buying for junior high and up. Predates the truth-in-lending law, yet remains of use for providing an appreciation of financial institutions. Takes about 2 hours; easily breaks into several sessions, 13–30 players.

Dangerous Parallel (Foreign Policy Association), Glenview, Ill.: Scott-Foresman.

A disguised version of conditions leading to the outbreak of the Korean war. A popular game for high school classes in history and international relations. Takes several 40-minute periods involving the entire class.

Democracy (James S. Coleman), New York: Western.

A set of eight games for junior high and older that simulates such activities as participatory democracy, legislative sessions, and legislative committee sessions. Length of play varies—all games fit into a two-week period.

Destiny, Lakeside, Calif.: Interact.

One of a series of historical simulations produced by this group. Focus is upon the American political situation during the period leading to the Spanish-American War. Contains both two-week curriculum materials and the simulation itself.

Diplomacy, Boston, Mass.: Games Research.

Although designed for entertainment, this is one of the most enticing games to interest students in the intrigue of diplomatic relations. Modeled on the outbreak of World War I. Takes up to 7 players; play can be protracted over time. Not practical for entire class to play, but useful as extra-course work.

Disunia, Lakeside, Calif.: Interact.

Two-week unit for high school level on the politics of the Articles of Confederation.

Division, Lakeside, Calif.: Interact.

Two-week unit for high school on internal U.S. politics of the 1850s.

Down With the King (Thomas E. Linehan and David G. Roach), New York: Herder & Herder.

A simulation of medieval politics, unique for its integration of art and social science. For junior high. Needs one class session and floor space to build "castles."

Dynasty (Paul Huang), New York: Dynasty International.

A simulation of the problem of development in a mythical Oriental country, in which players deal with problems of population growth, law and order, taxation. Though designed for the adult entertainment market, the game has potential for high school students and will be especially useful when the proposed *Teacher's Guide* to accompany the game is published.

Economic Decision Games (Erwin Rausch), Chicago: Science Research Associates.

Eight games for high school economics, including aspects of the market, the firm, the community, banking, scarcity, international trade, collective bargaining. Each game takes about 45 minutes; entire class is involved.

Economic System (James S. Coleman and T. Robert Harris), New York: Western.

A basic economy of 7–13 players who take roles of worker, farmer, or manufacturer. Advanced levels of the game introduce investment, the creation of capital, taxation. For junior high and up. Many parts to the game.

Generation Gap (E. O. Schild and Sarane S. Boocock), New York: Western.

This misnamed board game—once entitled "Parent-Child"—is really a model of power, negotiation, and compromise in the context of family life. Hence it is useful for any discussion of power and bargaining. For four players up to entire class. Takes about one hour. Junior high level.

Gettysburg (Charles S. Roberts), Baltimore, Md.: Avalon-Hill.

One of a series of popular entertainment military games. Others include *Waterloo, 1914, Stalingrad, Midway*. Exceptional design qualities make them all candidates for stirring the interest of students. Not practical for use in the classroom, except for small, select groups.

Ghetto (Dove Toll), New York: Western.

A board game that teaches 7–10 players about the frustrations of inner-city life, neighborhood organization, illegal activities, and economic deprivation. A game for middle-class kids, not inner-city ones (who already know the score). For junior high and up. Takes up to 4 hours, but play can be interrupted.

High School Geography Project, New York: Macmillan.

Six classroom units that incorporate simulations with other activities. The games include *Portsville, Section, Point Roberts, Flood Hazards*. Each unit fills 4–8 weeks of daily classes.

Life Career (Sarane S. Boocock), New York: Western.

Presents the U.S. marriage, education, and labor markets as they affect social mobility. Useful for guidance counseling as well as social science courses. Takes up to 4 hours in 40-minute sessions.

Marketplace, Security Pacific National Bank, 1307 South Alverado Street, Los Angeles, Calif.

Teaches principles of economics (factors of production, supply and demand, circular flow of money, etc.) for high school students. Requires 2–12 hour-long periods. One of the most expensive games (over $100), yet also one of the most elegantly designed.

NAPOLI (NAtional POLItics), La Jolla, Calif.: Simile II.

The legislative process as influenced by party and regional affiliation. For junior high and older. Takes 3–6 hours.

Panic, Lakeside, Calif.: Interact.

A two-week unit on the economic crisis of 1929. For high school history classes.

Plans, La Jolla, Calif.: Simile II.

A simulation of the conflicts among powerful interest groups in American society. For junior high and older.

The Road Game (Thomas E. Linehan and Barbara Ellis Long), New York: Herder & Herder.

A game that deals with problems of competition and cooperation on an abstract level. For junior high and older.

SIMSOC (William Gamson) New York: Free Press.

Players create their own social order in a mock society. Requires 12 hours of play, the rounds played daily for several weeks. For senior high school sociology or political science classes.

SITTE, La Jolla, Calif.: Simile II.

Simulates the conflicts among interest groups within a typical American city. For junior high and older.

Smog, Cambridge: Urban Systems.

Players cope with pollution in terms of zoning, population growth, taxation, industrial growth. Though a popular game for up to 4 players, this may be useful as an extra assignment. (Also has one of the most poorly written rulebooks and scoring sheets, but they're worth deciphering.)

Starpower, La Jolla, Calif.: Simile II.

A mock society that provokes discussion of class structure, power and its use (or abuse). Very simple in design, yet unusually compelling. For junior high and up. Takes about 2 hours.

Trade and Develop (Samuel A. Livingston), Baltimore, Md.: Academic Games Associates.

International trade and developing countries. For junior high. Takes one class period. Advanced levels of the game are included.

The Value Game (William Irving and Thomas E. Linehan), New York: Herder & Herder.

A brief game to demonstrate the problems with an ethical system based upon absolute rights or wrongs. For junior high and older.

PUBLISHERS

Academic Games Associates, 430 East 33rd Street, Baltimore, Md. 21218.

Avalon-Hill, 4517 Hartford Road, Baltimore, Md. 21214.

Dynasty International, 815 Park Avenue, New York, N.Y. 10021.

Free Press, 866 Third Avenue, New York, N.Y. 10022.

Games Research, Inc., 48 Wareham Street, Boston, Mass. 02118.

Herder & Herder, 232 Madison Avenue, New York, N.Y. 10016
Interact, P.O. Box 262, Lakeside, Calif. 92040.
Macmillan, 866 Third Avenue, New York, N.Y. 10022.
Science Research Associates, 259 East Erie Street, Chicago, Ill. 60611
Scott, Foresman & Co., Glenview, Ill.
Security Pacific National Bank, Banker's Equipment Department, 1307 South Alverado Street, Los Angeles, Calf. 90006.
Simile II, P.O. Box 1023, 1150 Silverado, La Jolla, Calif. 92057.
Urban Systems, Inc., 1033 Massachusetts Avenue, Cambridge, Mass. 02138.
Western Publishing Co., 850 Third Avenue, New York, N.Y. 10022.

OTHER SOURCES OF INFORMATION ABOUT
NEW DEVELOPMENTS, LEGAL DECISIONS, MATERIALS,
RESEARCH, FILMS, AND IDEAS IN EDUCATION

Affective Education Development Program
Att: Norman Newberg
Board of Public Education
Parkway, South of 21st Street
Philadelphia, Penn. 19103

Center for Student Citizenship, Rights, and Responsibilities
1145 Germantown Street
Dayton, Ohio 45408

Educational Development Center
55 Chapel Street
Newton, Mass. 02160

Information and Services Division
Institute for Development of Educational Activities, Inc.
P.O. Box 446
Melbourne, Fla. 32901

Herb Kohl
178 Tamalpais Road
Berkeley, Calif. 94708

Jonathan Kozol
Education Action Fund
21 East Springfield Street
Boston, Mass. 02118

National Congress of Parents and Teachers
700 North Rush Street
Chicago, Ill. 60611

Synectics Educational Systems
121 Brattle Street
Cambridge, Mass. 02138

And don't forget the lists in the books mentioned earlier. You can write to these places and have your name put on their mailing list.

EPILOGUE

IN ORDER TO have an educational program, whether it is in your own home with your own children or in a school building with the children of others, you really need only two things: (1) a conception of what a "good" person is, and (2) some more or less consistent procedures by which you hope to produce the kind of person you want. The first is a matter of values—what we used to call religion, but which we now call philosophy. The second is a matter of technique—which was never called philosophy, but is now close to a religion. And therein lies a problem with which we would like to conclude our book. It is this: About 99.9 percent of all the hollering about schools and education seems to concern technique—*how* to do something. The articles and books one sees, the research cited in the press, the agenda of PTA meetings—wherever one looks for information and ideas about education, one finds mostly a discourse on method.

That this should be so cannot be surprising to anyone living in America at the present time. For close to a century now, America has been the focal point of an unrelenting assault by technique. In all of mankind's prior history there is nothing, even remotely, to compare with it. Not a year has gone by, in the past seventy, that has not brought with it a new or improved technique—hard or soft—for something: for traveling, for healing, for cleaning, for seeing, for hearing, for dying, for killing, for loving. The question never came up as to whether or not we wanted to be "improved" or whether such improvements would come at too high a cost. It all happened too fast, the promises were too glorious, and the psychological soil was too fertile. Morse, Edison, Ford, Goddard, Lindbergh, Disney—they are all home-grown American boys who knew a future when they saw one. Of course, we were not without a naysayer or two. Of the technological revolution, Steven Benet wrote, at the close of *John Brown's Body*: "Say neither it is cursed nor blessed/Say only, it is here." Not bad advice, but hardly the way it worked out. For we have come very close to blessing our technology, and, if not that, at least to giving it our most heartfelt expressions of devotion. Why, we cannot even use the word "progress" anymore, unless we mean by it a new technique.

Now, we are not about to launch into some romantic tirade against the movement of history. But we do intend to say that technique—new, improved, or anything else—makes for very bad religion and is, in any case, no substitute for human values. Nowhere is this more true than in the field of education and in the institution of school.

To begin with, by "technique" we do not simply mean something technological. A computer, a jet plane, a videotape—they are the products of an advanced technology, but, more than that, they represent a way of getting something done. And in that sense they are like modular scheduling or team teaching or behavioral psychology or IQ tests: they are all designs for minimizing human effort and maximizing human achievement. But if you ask of a technique, What achievements are worth having? you can receive only two possible replies. One is that technique has nothing to say on the question. The other is even worse. It is that what is worth achieving is what the technique can best serve to achieve. In other words, if a method can do something, then it is worth doing. Do we have a new technique for teaching spelling? a new technique for teaching arithmetic to two-year-olds? a new technique for keeping school halls quiet? a new technique for measuring intelligence? Then by all means let's use them. That's what education is all about.

But, of course, that is *not* what education is all about. It is all about helping the young to become people who will be satisfactory to themselves and helpful to others. But what kind of person is *that?* What does it mean to be "satisfactory" to oneself or "helpful" to others? What about love, and good manners, and respect for tradition? Where do they fit in? And who says anyone's intelligence should be measured? And where is it written that a two-year-old mathematician is worth having? Now, these are questions that are worth a serious person's attention. They are questions too long neglected, about where you stand, and what you would like to believe in, and what you think your children can reasonably become. They in no way concern technique, which may make them slightly un-American, but they are no less important for all that.

We hope our book has helped you to understand more clearly what the schools are doing. No book can tell you what they *should* be doing. That vision must come from a different source.

INDEX

For a full discussion of the people, terms and court cases referred to in this index, see the entries in Part II (that is, italic numbers from page 127 on).